Savoring America

WILLIAMS-SONOMA

Savoring America

Recipes and Reflections on American Cooking

Text
JANET FLETCHER

Recipes
KERRI CONAN, ABIGAIL JOHNSON DODGE,
JANET FLETCHER, MICHAEL McLAUGHLIN,
CYNTHIA NIMS, RAY OVERTON

General Editor
CHUCK WILLIAMS

Recipe Photography
NOEL BARNHURST

Illustrations
MARLENE McLOUGHLIN

BORDERS.

CANADA

NORTH DAKOTA

SOUTH DAKOTA

THE GREAT PLAINS

MONTANA

ROCKY MOUNTAINS

WYOMING

COLORADO

UNITED

NEBRASKA

KANSAS

KANSAS

OKLAHOMA

SANTA FE

NEW MEXICO

TEXAS

MEXICO

SALT LAKE CITY

UTAH

THE SOUTHWEST

ARIZONA

IDAHO

NEVADA

CALIFORNIA

SAN FRANCISCO

CALIFORNIA

LOS ANGELES

WASHINGTON

SEATTLE

OREGON

THE PACIFIC NORTHWEST

PACIFIC OCEAN

HAWAII

HONOLULU

HAWAII

ALASKA

ANCHORAGE

ALASKA

ALEUTIAN ISLANDS

BERING SEA

104°

104°

114°

114°

44°

34°

24°

STATES

GULF OF MEXICO

CUBA

BAHAMAS

ATLANTIC OCEAN

THE MIDWEST

NESOTA

LAKE SUPERIOR

WISCONSIN

LAKE MICHIGAN

LAKE HURON

IOWA

ILLINOIS

CHICAGO

MICHIGAN

LAKE ERIE

LAKE ONTARIO

NEW YORK

NEW ENGLAND

NEW HAMPSHIRE

VERMONT

MAINE

NEW YORK

MASSACHUSETTS

BOSTON

RHODE ISLAND

CONNECTICUT

MID-ATLANTIC

PENNSYLVANIA

NEW JERSEY

DELAWARE

MARYLAND

WASHINGTON D.C.

WEST VIRGINIA

OHIO

INDIANA

KENTUCKY

SOUTH VIRGINIA

NORTH CAROLINA

SOUTH CAROLINA

GEORGIA

FLORIDA

MIAMI

ALABAMA

MISSISSIPPI

TENNESSEE

LOUISIANA

NEW ORLEANS

ARKANSAS

MISSOURI

LAS

MILES
0
100
100
200
300
200
KM
0

Contents

INTRODUCTION

The American Table

MANY HAVE CALLED THIS COUNTRY a melting pot, but it's really more of a giant buffet that can satisfy almost any craving at almost any time. Shaped by natural abundance, by nonstop immigration, and by the sheer variety that the nation's geography allows, the exuberant, all-encompassing American way of eating almost defies defining.

What could be more typical than a pizza, after all, or a doughnut or a pot pie? But all those dishes had foreign passports once and were swept up in the American embrace. For more than five hundred years, cooks have eyed the unfamiliar, adapted it to their tastes, and then enthusiastically called it their own. Pizza with smoked salmon or duck sausage might be hard to find in Italy, but both are part of this country's repertoire.

Certainly, America's vision of itself as a land of almost unlimited resources has shaped how people think about food. They now know that their rivers, coastlines, forests, and fields are not inexhaustible, but still shop with an expectation that everyday ingredients will be plentiful and cheap. If a freeze hammers Florida citrus, surely Texas and California will fill the gap. Many are surprised, traveling abroad, at how costly food is and how limited the choice compared with the year-round cornucopia of their supermarket.

The immigrant contribution is profound and ongoing. Beginning with the English and Dutch colonists, the nation has provided a new

Left: In the waning days of summer, jam-packed corncribs are a common sight in the Midwest. The huge harvests are turned into cooking oil, cereals, flour, and sweeteners, among many other products. **Top:** A lone fly-fisher alongside a Rocky Mountain creek casts his line into the crystal-clear waters in hope of hooking a cutthroat trout. **Above:** Cotton pods in Mississippi split to reveal fluffy bolls, which are allowed to dry in the open air before picking. By the 1850s, the American South was providing 80 percent of all the cotton used in England's mills.

home to French Canadians in the eighteenth century; to waves of Irish, Germans, Italians, Scandinavians, Chinese, and eastern Europeans in the nineteenth century; and recently to Mexicans, Central Americans, Southeast Asians, Cubans, and Indians. Whether settling in urban centers or small towns, these immigrants introduced their native foods to their new communities. In the eyes of many people today, one quality-of-life measure for a city is the breadth of its ethnic restaurants.

The country's sheer size and geographic and climatic diversity mean that cooks enjoy unparalleled variety. Almost anything will thrive somewhere. Hawaii, Florida, and Southern California keep markets supplied with tropical and subtropical fruits. Arizona grows winter lettuces. North Dakota produces wheat. Iowa pork, Wisconsin cheese, Kentucky bourbon—every state contributes something to the national larder. Add to these riches the nation's twelve thousand miles (twenty thousand km) of coastline, and it becomes difficult to imagine a country more blessed with resources.

Many cooks' daily meals exhibit regional flavor—a southerner's fried catfish supper comes to mind—but holidays offer a chance to see Americans at their culinary best. Most

Top: The *Julia Belle Swain* carries passengers on a journey down the Mississippi River. Acquired by the United States from the French as part of the 1803 Louisiana Purchase, the mighty waterway welcomed its first steamboat in 1811.
Above: From April into October, fans across the country gather at baseball stadiums to cheer for their local teams.
Right: The hot dog's origins are debatable, but one thing is certain: New Yorkers love their world-famous street food, typically dressing it up with sauerkraut, relish, or mustard.

families have ritual foods that define a celebration, often dishes that reflect their heritage. In an Italian American household, cannelloni might accompany the Christmas roast. At a Chinese American Thanksgiving, the turkey might be stuffed with rice and shiitake mushrooms, and the leftover carcass made into *congee* (rice porridge) the next day.

Memorial Day and Labor Day bracket the barbecue season and present an excuse for neighborhood potlucks or picnics. Often the host will fire up the grill and cook spareribs, salmon, or sausages while the guests bring side dishes and desserts. The assembled buffet almost always exhibits an identifiable regional style. Pinto beans, coleslaw, and pecan pie? Must be Texas. Marinated asparagus and blueberry tart? Washington State. Pickled shrimp and angel food cake? The South, no doubt. Corn on the cob, rhubarb pie, and blackberry slump? Probably New England.

No holiday gets Americans cooking with more enthusiasm than Thanksgiving. In many homes, as many as three generations of cooks gather to bake pies and argue over how long to cook the turkey. By noon on Thanksgiving Day, kitchens across the country are filled with the mingling aromas of roasting poultry, browning pie crusts, and simmering stock, the prelude to giblet gravy. As the day progresses, the cooks scramble to put the finishing touches on family favorites made only once a year, such as corn bread stuffing, cranberry relish, and creamed onions.

Dining out gives many people their chief taste of immigrant food. In major cities, office workers lunch on Vietnamese *pho*, Chinese dim sum, or South Indian curry. Largely through restaurants, Americans have learned to appreciate the taste of fish sauce, chipotle chiles, cilantro, oyster sauce, and coconut milk, and have welcomed these formerly exotic ingredients into their own kitchens.

To generalize about a country as vast as the United States is to risk oversimplifying reality. A sharper, truer portrait emerges when you view the nation as a collection of regions, each with its own past, character, geography, climate,

and culture. Despite the impact of mass marketing and national advertising, regional tastes and sensibilities endure.

In New England and the Mid-Atlantic, the craggy coastline has long supported a prosperous fishing industry, although recent times have seen populations of several species plummet. Many nineteenth-century fortunes were built on cod—the so-called codfish aristocracy—and restaurants in Boston and Providence made their reputations on recipes for broiled cod, baked scallops, finnan haddie (smoked haddock), and lobster stew. Even for inlanders, the coast remains a powerful part of the New England experience. Stretching from Long Island Sound to Cape Cod and beyond to the Canadian border, it lures weekenders and vacationers in summer, who flock to the Cape or the Connecticut shore to feast on clams, oysters, lobsters, and crabs. Fortunately, efforts to restore stocks of cod, flounder, haddock, and swordfish are paying off, offering the hope that this ocean harvest will remain a vital part of the New England table.

Left: In late October, hundreds of field pumpkins of all sizes and shapes await transformation into candlelit jack-o'-lanterns for displaying on front porches and in living-room windows. Cooks rely on smaller, more fully flavored pumpkin varieties for making holiday pies, creamy soups, and crumbly cookies. **Below:** Gold and burnt orange leaves frame a picturesque Vermont church. From late September into November, New England towns, known for their showy fall foliage, welcome a steady stream of visitors in search of the season's changing colors.

The extreme and unpredictable weather of the Midwest and Great Plains has always made them difficult places to raise cash crops. Instead, the focus is on commodity crops like wheat, soybeans, and corn and, after the buffalo disappeared, on cattle ranching. Although Kansas City has no more stockyards and Chicago is no longer a meat-packing hub, the region still has a key role in the nation's beef production. Dairy cattle thrive in Wisconsin and support the state's considerable cheese production. Mirroring a nationwide trend, several small Wisconsin dairies have emerged with the mission of making top-quality specialty cheeses. Many of these cheeses can be found at the Dane County Farmers' Market in Madison, the largest such market in the country with, in the heart of summer, more than three hundred vendors.

Southern hospitality is famous across the country; even among those who have never experienced it firsthand. The reputation probably arose during plantation days, when estate

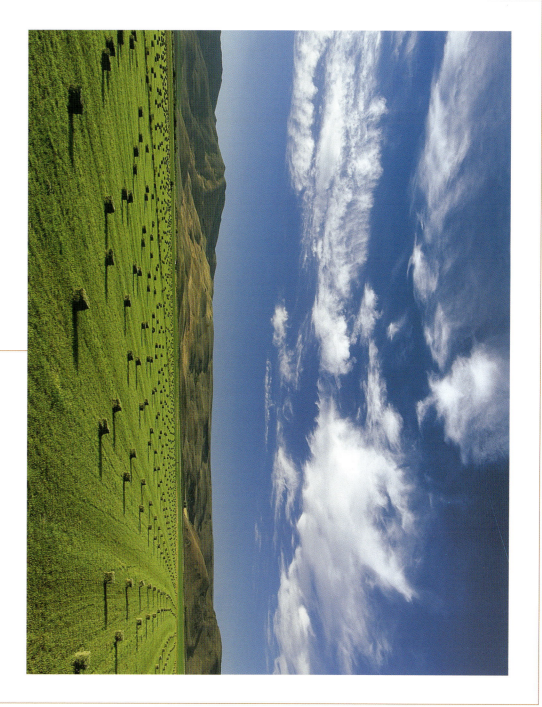

Left: America's first apple trees were planted in Massachusetts in the early 1600s. Today, apple lovers all over the country eagerly await the fall harvest, with its promise of pies, crisps, cobblers, and cider. **Top:** Widely known for its big potato harvests, Idaho, a rugged Rocky Mountain state, also boasts productive grain fields and imposing landscapes. **Above:** At farmers' markets around the country, shoppers seldom pass up the chance to buy plump, sun-ripened tomatoes from local growers.

their long interaction with the Pueblo Indians produced the New Mexican food of today. At its most authentic, the cooking is simple, even austere, an outgrowth of life in the high desert. Chiles are at its core, used mostly in their fresh green state in the south and dried in the north. Arizona food shows much less Hispanic influence because the Apaches were so skillful at keeping the Spaniards out. Like the state of Sonora, its Mexican neighbor, this is cattle country and well suited to wheat. Consequently, flour tortillas prevail in Arizona, and the Mexican-style dishes are mild, sometimes served with a tame red chile sauce along with a cooked or fresh salsa for heat.

California tends to view itself not as a border state, which it is, but as yet another Mediterranean country. Living in a climate that nurtures olive trees, vines, and citrus, Californians, particularly in the north, like to think of themselves as kindred spirits to residents of Tuscany or Provence. The farms that make the state the nation's leading producer of many fruits and vegetables also fill local markets with magnificent produce, inspiring chefs to cook in concert with the seasons, a practice that has put simple, seasonal California cuisine on the world culinary map.

owners entertained lavishly as a sign of status. Even today, many southern families maintain the tradition of hunt breakfasts, Kentucky Derby mint-julep parties, and Mardi Gras balls that underlies their image as stylish hosts.

Historically, African American cooks prepared most of the food in these grand homes and perfected the techniques for the South's legendary hot rolls, sweet potato biscuits, and corn bread. Making these breads well is still a point of pride in the South, and no longer only in the African American community. Other regions may start the day with toast or packaged cereal, but a respectable southern breakfast, even at a roadside truck stop, includes ham, grits, and hot biscuits.

The food of Texas, New Mexico, and Arizona often appears undifferentiated to outsiders, but those who live there recognize each state's distinctiveness. The Texas version of Mexican food, widely referred to as Tex-Mex cooking, is larger than life, highly seasoned, generously portioned, and rich. Restaurants serve combination plates crowded with tamales, enchiladas, and tacos, typically seasoned with cumin and chili powder instead of chiles.

The Spaniards arrived in Sante Fe before the Pilgrims sailed into Plymouth harbor, and

In the Pacific Northwest, where the forecast often calls for either rain or more rain, residents particularly relish the clear days. Sport fishing, hunting, crabbing, and mushrooming lure many residents outdoors in good weather and bring local bounty to the table. The cool, moist climate favors pears and apples, keeping Washington the nation's leading apple producer. Washington and Oregon provide a large percentage of the country's raspberries, blackberries, and blueberries, and Oregon grows almost all of America's hazelnuts. Like so many others across the country, Pacific Northwest cooks are renewing their sense of pride in regional foodstuffs. The top chefs have begun to celebrate the local, showcasing Pacific salmon, Oregon wine, and morels foraged in nearby forests, instead of filling their menus with air-freighted wares from afar.

This attitude shift is revolutionizing American cooking, as more chefs and shoppers show support for small, local farms and for artisans producing everything from bread to brandy. Quickly eaten meals and agribusiness will continue to influence the American table, but today's cooks and diners also have the choice to slow down, seek the best, and savor the enduring taste of their region.

Top: Buffalo lumber past the spray and mist of an erupting geyser in Yellowstone National Park in Wyoming. The nation's first national park, established in 1872, has nearly ten thousand geysers, mud pots, and other thermal features. **Above:** In southeast Alaska, a boldly carved and colored Tlingit totem pole depicts a traditional story.

Starters

Soups, salads, and finger food reflect both local traditions and contemporary influences.

LACKING CENTURIES OF SHARED table traditions, Americans remain open-minded about what constitutes the proper start to a meal. The occasion, the crowd, and the tastes of the host are more likely to dictate how a dinner gets under way than any sense of expectation or propriety. A weekday family meal may have no starter at all. A casual dinner party among friends might begin in the host's kitchen with a platter of crudités before moving into the dining room.

Many foods that are popular as starters come from the cocktail-hour tradition and the knowledge that a mixed drink requires a more substantial complement than a couple of olives. Consequently, Americans have become experts at finger food, the little nibbles that guests can eat standing up, with a highball or wineglass in one hand. Miniature quiches, tiny turnovers, two-bite crab cakes, cheese twists and puffs—any caterer or avid party giver stockpiles recipes for savory tidbits that require no plate, knife, or fork.

Few national occasions prompt more elaborate displays of appetizers than Super Bowl

Preceding pages: Bees build their intricate combs inside wooden boxes placed in blossom-filled fields. **Top:** Early settlers found the prairies and buttes of southwestern South Dakota nearly impossible to traverse, prompting them to nickname the area "the bad lands." In 1978, this landscape, now appreciated for its natural beauty, was designated the Badlands National Park. **Above:** The Dungeness crab, caught along the Pacific Coast, conceals sweet, firm meat. **Right:** A California baker uses a long-handled peel to remove hot breads from a traditional wood-burning oven.

replaced the cocktail hour and subtly influenced the before-dinner menu. With that first glass of Chardonnay or Sauvignon Blanc, more hosts are offering wine-friendly foods in the European tradition, such as marinated olives, focaccia, grilled *bruschetta*, or *crostini* topped with a savory spread.

Once seated at the table, Californians typically choose a salad or cooked-vegetable starter, as befits the residents of a state known as the nation's salad bowl. Many easterners, with stronger ties to Europe, shrug their shoulders at this behavior; like the French, they generally prefer their greens lightly dressed and served after the main course, to cleanse the palate and pave the way for dessert. But California's creative salad makers rarely stop at lightly dressed greens. They top baby leaf lettuces with a round of warm goat cheese, or add crunch with shaved fennel and walnuts. The following evening, they might toss California-grown radicchio, endive, and

Sunday, when hosts offer a buffet that keeps their guests satiated for at least three hours. In San Francisco, one might put out bowls of pistachio nuts and whole heads of soft, spreadable roasted garlic to accompany Sonoma goat cheese and crusty sourdough bread. At the other end of the state, San Diego's football fans might nibble on homemade guacamole and salsa, with chips from a local Mexican market. In Dallas, where football is close to a religion, a bubbling pot of *chili con queso*, a sort of southwestern cheese fondue, might provide a halftime diversion. While viewing the same game twelve hundred miles (two thousand km) away, residents of upstate New York might be savoring the region's famous Buffalo chicken wings, deep-fried and served with celery ribs, hot sauce, and a cooling blue cheese dip.

Although beer may dominate at such casual events, wine appreciation is on the rise in America. In many homes, the wine hour has arugula with farmers' market figs and blue cheese, or with avocado and oranges.

That crisp, mild wedge of iceberg lettuce that once symbolized the California lettuce industry now has flavorful competition from *mesclun*—the delicate mixed baby lettuces sold in bulk in many markets—and from frisée, escarole, baby spinach, leaf lettuces, cresses, and other salad-bowl choices. For time-pressed shoppers, California lettuce packers have developed precut salads—washed, dried, and especially bagged to extend their shelf life. Some of these salads are even packed with a dressing. In better supermarkets, beautifully trimmed romaine hearts tempt many shoppers to prepare their own Caesar salad, certainly one of the most popular restaurant starters in the state.

With gardens and farms that yield vegetables year-round, Californians naturally look to the harvest when planning a meal. Dinner might start with roasted peppers or marinated beets, with asparagus or leeks vinaigrette, or with a whole steamed artichoke for each diner. Not content to let their lovely vegetables hide in the shadow of fish or meat, they celebrate them in a course all their own.

Soup also launches meals and tells stories of America's immigrant past. The matzo ball soup in a Brooklyn deli, though it may appeal to New Yorkers of every stripe, derives directly from the German and eastern European Jewish experience. Waves of European Jews entered the United States in the second half of the nineteenth century, settling in urban areas and opening delicatessens to provide the growing Jewish community with a taste of home. New Orleans's beloved gumbo has its roots in the cooking of West Africans who worked in the sugarcane plantations. They brought with them seeds for okra, a valued vegetable known to them as *ngombo*, and exploited its gelatinous properties to thicken soup made with the local oysters, crayfish, and shrimp (prawns).

America's regional soups, like soups everywhere, reflect local resources and the efforts of cooks to transform or stretch what is readily available. Consider clam chowder, found on menus from coast to coast today but originally associated with New England fishing villages. Challenged to find ways to keep fish palatable

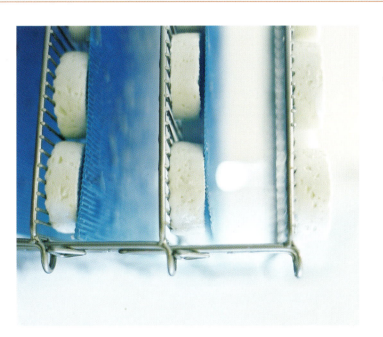

Left: Goats grazing at a Northern California farm stop to sun themselves outside one of the barns. Their milk is used for making artisanal cheeses. **Below:** As European-style goat cheeses have gained greater appreciation, the nation's cheese makers are producing more types to satisfy the growing clientele. **Bottom:** On the Fourth of July, red, white, and blue capture the spirit of the day as people celebrate the nation's independence with parades, barbecues, and fireworks.

to fishermen facing a steady diet of it, coastal cooks made soup, combining fish or shellfish with salt pork, onion, potatoes, milk, black pepper, and sometimes crackers for thickening—the predecessor of today's cream-and-butter-enriched New England clam chowder. The soup traveled to Washington and Oregon with migrating New Englanders, who adapted the recipe to the local razor clams.

In Rhode Island, home to an Italian immigrant community, cooks omitted the milk and added tomato and herbs, a variation that purists have never embraced. James Beard, who loved New England clam chowder, called the Manhattan type, as the tomato-based version came to be known, "that rather horrendous soup." In the coastal cities of Charleston and Savannah, fish soup featured the local blue crabs. She-crab soup, a creamy concoction made with the female crabs and their roe and a dash of sherry, survives on local restaurant

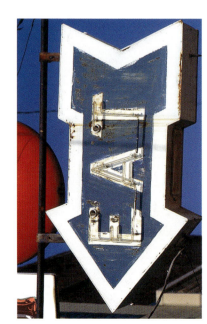

Below: A no-nonsense neon sign in Indiana points hungry diners in the correct direction. **Bottom:** Throughout the year, locals and tourists enjoy a varied calendar of music and art festivals in Santa Fe, New Mexico's four-hundred-year-old capital city. **Right:** Every day from November to March, Wollman Rink, in New York's Central Park, welcomes more than four thousand skaters from early morning into the evening.

and hotel menus and in many traditional homes. In the San Francisco Bay Area, fish soup means hearty cioppino, showcasing the local Dungeness crab. Made with tomato, bell pepper (capsicum), herbs, and red wine, it bears the stamp of the Italian immigrants who dominated the Northern California fishing industry in its early days.

In the Southwest border states of Texas, Arizona, and New Mexico, cooks make a tortilla soup in the Mexican tradition, a clear broth with shredded chicken and the stale tortillas that inevitably accumulate in local kitchens. Otherwise, soup rarely launches a meal, which is surprising given how often it does south of the border. In casual Texas restaurants, the opening role that soup plays elsewhere might go to a cup of thick, meaty chili topped with chopped onion and grated cheese.

Perhaps the soup with the most compelling origins is Philadelphia pepper pot, a rib-sticking mix of tripe and potatoes liberally dosed with black pepper. Legend has it that a desperate chef created it at Valley Forge, Pennsylvania, when General George Washington begged him to transform the camp's meager provisions into a nourishing meal for the starving troops. In the nineteenth century, Philadelphia street vendors served steaming bowls of pepper pot from milk cans, and it remains in the local repertory.

For people who live near a coast, local seafood is a favorite first course. No longer as abundant as it once was, it can be the priciest starter on a restaurant menu. Overfishing has drastically reduced populations of the wild oysters, shrimp (prawns), crab, and abalone that were once so plentiful. Lobsters were so common in seventeenth-century New England that fishermen used them as bait for cod and people complained of having to eat them too often. Old cookbooks commonly

include recipes that call for one hundred or two hundred oysters, a profligate amount today. Oyster bars once thrived in many cities, and still do in San Francisco, Seattle, New York, and New Orleans.

With farmed oysters filling in for the wild ones once teeming in its bayous and bays, New Orleans continues to induce oyster mania. Gulf oysters on the half shell, fried in po'boys and oyster loaves, or simmered in gumbo define the local style. In the town's fine dining establishments, customers start their meal with oysters Rockefeller (baked with herbed spinach or watercress with Pernod), oysters Bienville (with shrimp sauce), or a few of each.

In recent times, diners have discovered sushi bars and the pleasures of raw seafood Japanese style: thin slices of tuna or yellowtail sashimi served with a dipping sauce, or draped over pearly rice. Like sashimi, Hawaiian *poke*, marinated raw tuna, appeals to those with a taste for culinary adventure. Whether tuna tartare will ever rival the popularity of fried squid or crab cakes is anyone's guess, but it would have to be added to the list of potential contenders.

Top: Around the country, the appearance of apple blossoms signals the arrival of spring. **Above:** At an outdoor market in Southern California, farm-fresh, organic eggs are checked by a customer before purchasing. Eggs are the stars of the breakfast table, where they turn up scrambled, poached, or fried. **Right:** Travelers passing through the town of Good Thunder, Minnesota, usually stop to take a close look at the murals that cover the Thunder Feed and Grain Elevator. Created by Ta-Coumba Aiken, the impressive paintings commemorate the area's rich history.

South

Chilled Tomato Soup with Cucumber and Mint

This delicious soup, which draws on the South's bountiful summertime gardens, is an adaptation of gazpacho, introduced to the region by Spanish settlers.

1 red bell pepper (capsicum), seeded and finely diced

1 cucumber, peeled, halved lengthwise, seeded, and finely diced

1 yellow onion, cut into chunks

2 cloves garlic

1 lb (500 g) plum (Roma) tomatoes, peeled and seeded

4 cups (32 fl oz/1 l) tomato juice

¼ cup (2 fl oz/60 ml) red wine vinegar

⅓ cup (1½ oz/45 g) dried bread crumbs

1 cup (8 oz/250 g) sour cream

1 teaspoon celery seed

2 teaspoons sugar

1 tablespoon chopped fresh thyme

4 tablespoons (⅓ oz/10 g) chopped fresh mint

salt and freshly ground pepper to taste

2 green (spring) onions, thinly sliced

❦ Set aside ¼ cup (1½ oz/45 g) each of the bell pepper and the cucumber. In a food processor, combine the remaining bell pepper and cucumber, the yellow onion, and the garlic. Process until finely chopped. Add the tomatoes, tomato juice, vinegar, and bread crumbs. Process until smooth. Add ½ cup (4 oz/125 g) of the sour cream, the celery seed, the sugar, the thyme, and 2 tablespoons of the mint. Season with salt and pepper. Cover and refrigerate for at least 4 hours or for up to 12 hours to allow the flavors to meld.

❦ In a bowl, mix together the reserved bell pepper and cucumber, the remaining 2 tablespoons mint, and the green onions. Season with salt and pepper. Cover and refrigerate until ready to serve.

❦ Stir the soup, taste it, and adjust the seasoning. Ladle into chilled bowls. Top with the remaining ½ cup (4 oz/125 g) sour cream, floating a small dollop on each bowl. Garnish with the bell pepper–cucumber mixture and serve.

serves 6–8

South

Marinated Shrimp Salad

The waters off the Atlantic and Gulf Coasts deliver an abundance of shrimp for use in recipes like this marinated salad on a bed of lettuce.

2 cups (16 fl oz/500 ml) cider vinegar

1 cup (7 oz/220 g) firmly packed light brown sugar

2 teaspoons salt

bouquet garni of 1 tablespoon crushed coriander seed; 1 tablespoon each mustard seed, dill seed, and celery seed; 10 peppercorns; 6 whole allspice; and 1 teaspoon ground turmeric

1½ lb (750 g) large shrimp (prawns), peeled and deveined

1 Vidalia onion, thinly sliced

1 red bell pepper (capsicum), seeded and thinly sliced

1 small celery root, peeled and cut into 2-inch (5-cm) matchsticks

4 banana chiles, halved lengthwise, seeded, and thinly sliced

1 tablespoon capers, rinsed and drained

1 lemon, thinly sliced

2 cloves garlic, chopped

⅓ cup (3 fl oz/80 ml) extra-virgin olive oil

leaves from 2 heads Bibb lettuce

❦ In a large nonaluminum saucepan, combine the vinegar, brown sugar, and salt. Put the bouquet garni ingredients on a square of cheesecloth (muslin); bring the corners together, and tie with kitchen string. Add to the pan and bring the contents to a boil. Reduce the heat to low and simmer, uncovered, until the brine is a light curry color, about 15 minutes. Add the shrimp, onion, bell pepper, celery root, chiles, capers, lemon, and garlic. Return to a boil, remove from the heat, cover, and let cool.

❦ When the mixture is cool, remove the cheesecloth bag and discard. Stir in the olive oil and refrigerate for at least 8 hours or for up to 2 days, stirring the mixture occasionally.

❦ Line individual plates with the lettuce. Divide the shrimp and pickled vegetables among the plates and serve.

serves 6–8

Mid-Atlantic
Broiled Oysters

The relatively moderate ocean temperatures off the East Coast from Long Island to Virginia yield more subtly flavored oysters than New England's chillier waters. To savor every drop of the bivalves' luscious liquor, cooks anchor oysters on the half shell in a bed of rock salt.

2–4 cups (1–2 lb/500 g–1 kg) rock salt

20 medium oysters such as Long Island or Chincoteague

⅔ cup (5 oz/155 g) crème fraîche

1 large shallot, minced

4 tablespoons (⅓ oz/10 g) minced mixed fresh chives, chervil, tarragon, and basil

1 teaspoon finely grated lemon zest

1 or 2 dashes Tabasco sauce or other hot-pepper sauce

freshly ground pepper to taste

☙ On a rimmed baking sheet, spread a ½-inch (12-mm) layer of rock salt. Rinse the oysters, then shuck them: Using a folded, thick cloth to protect your hand, hold an oyster with the flat top shell facing up. Insert the tip of an oyster knife into the dark, rounded spot at the hinge of the oyster, and then twist the knife to sever the hinge. Run the knife along the inside of the top shell, severing the muscle that attaches the oyster to the shell. Discard the top shell. Run the knife along the bottom shell to loosen the oyster, being careful to keep the oyster and its liquor in the shell. Nestle the shells in the salt.

☙ Preheat a broiler (grill). In a bowl, combine the crème fraîche, the shallot, 2 tablespoons of the herbs, and the lemon zest. Season with hot-pepper sauce and ground pepper. Spoon a scant 2 teaspoons of the crème fraîche mixture on top of each oyster.

☙ Place the baking sheet under the broiler 4 inches (10 cm) from the heat source and broil (grill) the oysters until the tops are just beginning to brown, 3–5 minutes. Transfer the oysters to individual plates each sprinkled with a layer of rock salt. Garnish with the remaining 2 tablespoons herbs and serve.

serves 4

Southwest

Guacamole with Tostaditas

This traditional Mexican preparation has so thoroughly invaded not only the Southwest but all of America that few have ever tasted it at its best. Instead, the popularity of the deliciate and perishable guacamole has led to the development of frozen versions, convenient for restaurants where they are dolloped over hamburgers, omelets, and so on, but not at all representative of the fresh and simple thing guacamole ought to be. For that, guacamole needs to be made at home, with buttery-ripe, black-skinned Hass avocados and the fewest number of other ingredients, and eaten more or less immediately, scooped onto just-fried corn tortilla chips (tostaditas). This classic version dispenses with garlic, lime juice, sour cream, and chili powder—common additions that tend to mask the nutty, subtle flavor of the main ingredient.

GUACAMOLE

1 cup (1½ oz/45 g) coarsely chopped fresh cilantro (fresh coriander)

5 medium-large Hass avocados, halved, pitted, and peeled

¼ cup (1 oz/30 g) chopped yellow onion coarsely chopped

1 jalapeño chile or 2 or 3 serrano chiles, coarsely chopped

¾ teaspoon salt, plus salt to taste

1 tomato, seeded and chopped

¼ cup (1 oz/30 g) chopped red onion

TOSTADITAS

18 yellow or blue corn tortillas, or a combination, each 6 inches (15 cm) in diameter

corn oil for deep-frying

kosher salt

❧ To make the guacamole, in a food processor, combine the cilantro, half of 1 avocado, the yellow onion, the chile(s), and the ¾ teaspoon salt. Process, stopping to scrape down the sides of the work bowl as needed, until fairly smooth.

❧ In a bowl, coarsely mash the remaining avocados (a potato masher works well). Stir in the cilantro-avocado purée, tomato, and red onion. Adjust the seasoning (avocados require a lot of salt). Set the guacamole aside while preparing the tostaditas, but for no more than 30 minutes.

❧ To make the tostaditas, stack the tortillas. With a long, sharp knife, cut the stack into 6 equal wedges. Spread the wedges on a kitchen towel in a single layer to dry them slightly, about 20 minutes.

❧ Pour the corn oil to a depth of 4 inches (10 cm) into a deep, heavy frying pan and heat to 375°F (190°C). Working in 3 or 4 batches to avoid crowding the pan, add the tortilla wedges, stir with a spoon to separate, and fry until crisp, 1–1½ minutes. Using a slotted spoon, transfer the wedges to paper towels to drain. Immediately season with the kosher salt.

❧ Place the guacamole in a serving bowl, set the bowl on a plate, and surround it with the warm tostaditas. Serve at once.

serves 6

A shared border has put many Mexican dishes on the Southwest table.

Artichokes

Prickly on the outside but tender within, artichokes are one of nature's more peculiar vegetables. They are actually the flower bud of a large-leaved perennial in the sunflower family, and if left on the plant, the buds would gradually open to reveal glorious purple blossoms. Instead, harvesters cut them when they are tightly closed.

Many Californians consider artichokes a symbol of the Golden State. In fact, almost 100 percent of the nation's crop comes from California, with three-quarters of it grown in cool, foggy Monterey County, south of San Francisco. The tiny town of Castroville, surrounded by silvery artichoke fields and boasting the nation's only artichoke processing plant, proudly proclaims itself the Artichoke Center of the World. At harvesttime in spring, pickers move swiftly through the fields, wielding a short, sharp knife. Probing among the prickly plants, they cut the mature artichokes, leaving some of the stem attached.

Some markets carry egg-sized "baby" artichokes, perfect for pizza, pasta, and salads. These aren't immature; they are fully grown, but because they grow low on the plant, hidden from the sun, they stay small. After paring, they are completely edible, with no fibrous choke.

California

Artichokes with Aioli

Artichokes thrive in the mild coastal climate of California's Monterey County. The town of Gilroy is famous for garlic, so it is hardly surprising that aioli, or garlic mayonnaise, often accompanies steamed artichokes as a dip.

4 large artichokes

½ lemon, plus fresh lemon juice (optional)

1 tablespoon mixed pickling spice

1 egg yolk, at room temperature

½ teaspoon warm water

¾ cup (6 fl oz/180 ml) extra-virgin olive oil

1 large clove garlic, or more to taste

pinch of salt

To trim each artichoke, cut the stem flush with the bottom. Using a serrated knife, cut about 1½ inches (4 cm) off the top of the artichoke. Using scissors, snip off the pointed tips of each leaf. Rub the artichoke all over with the lemon half.

Pour water to a depth of 1 inch (2.5 cm) into a large pot and add the pickling spice. Bring to a boil over high heat. Place a steamer rack in the pot, making sure that the water does not touch the rack, and add the artichokes, stem end up. Cover and adjust the heat to maintain a gentle simmer. Steam until a knife pierces the bottoms easily, 40–45 minutes. Remove the artichokes and let stand, stem ends up, on several thicknesses of paper towels for a few minutes.

Meanwhile, make the aioli: In a small bowl, whisk the egg yolk with the warm water, then whisk in the olive oil drop by drop. Once an emulsion has formed, gradually add the oil a little faster until all of it has been incorporated and a mayonnaise-like sauce has formed. In a mortar, combine 1 garlic clove and the salt and pound to a paste. Whisk the paste into the egg-oil mixture. Whisk in a few drops of lemon juice, if desired. Add more pounded garlic, if desired.

Using your fingers, gently spread apart the center artichoke leaves. Pull out the prickly innermost leaves. With a spoon, scrape out the hairy choke. Serve the artichokes hot, warm, or chilled. Spoon the aioli into the center of each artichoke or alongside it.

serves 4

Pacific Northwest

Gravlax

This Scandinavian specialty of dill-cured salmon is perfectly at home in the Northwest, where salmon are abundant and Scandinavian heritage dates back to some of the area's earliest settlers. Traditionally, two whole fillets are cured at once, with the curing ingredients sandwiched between them, but this results in more cured salmon than most cooks today are prepared to serve. This recipe calls for two smaller fillet portions. Be sure to plan ahead, as the gravlax should cure for a minimum of two days before serving.

In Scandinavia, cooks might splash a little aquavit over the salmon as well. A more modern Northwest touch adds a drizzle of lemon vodka to the curing ingredients. The color and crunch of lightly pickled red onion make a great finish to this elegant appetizer.

2 center-cut salmon fillet pieces of equal size, about 2½ lb (1.25 kg) total weight, with skin intact

¼ cup (2 oz/60 g) kosher salt, plus pinch of salt

¼ cup (2 oz/60 g) plus 1 tablespoon sugar

1 tablespoon crushed or coarsely ground white peppercorns, plus pinch of ground white pepper

1 large bunch fresh dill, coarsely chopped

2 tablespoons lemon vodka

1 small red onion

boiling water as needed

½ cup (4 fl oz/125 ml) red wine vinegar

thinly sliced pumpernickel cocktail bread or toasted baguette slices

❧ Rub your fingers along the surfaces of the salmon fillets, and then use needle-nose pliers or tweezers to remove any fine pin bones. Lay a long piece of plastic wrap in a shallow dish, such as a baking dish, and set one of the fillet pieces, skin side down, on the plastic.

❧ In a small bowl, combine the ¼ cup (2 oz/60 g) kosher salt, ¼ cup (2 oz/60 g) sugar, and 1 tablespoon peppercorns and stir to mix. Scatter half of the salt mixture evenly over the salmon in the dish. Scatter the dill over the salt mixture and then drizzle with the vodka. Sprinkle the remaining salt mixture over the dill. Set the second piece of salmon, flesh side down, over the first, and draw up the plastic wrap to enclose the pieces fully. Lay a piece of aluminum foil on top, followed by another baking dish or small pan. Add a few cans of food to weight the salmon, and refrigerate for 2–3 days. Every 12 hours or so, remove the weights and turn over the wrapped package of curing salmon.

❧ An hour or so before you plan to serve the salmon, thinly slice the red onion and put it in a heatproof bowl. Add boiling water just to cover the onion and let stand for 5 minutes, then drain well. While the onion is still warm, return it to the bowl and add the vinegar and the 1 tablespoon sugar with a pinch of kosher salt and white pepper. Toss to mix until the sugar has dissolved. Let cool, then drain off the vinegar. Cover and refrigerate the onion until ready to serve.

❧ When the salmon is ready, discard the plastic wrap and scrape away the dill and other seasonings. Very briefly pass the salmon under running cold water and pat dry thoroughly with paper towels. Using a sharp, narrow-bladed knife, and working at a sharp angle, cut the salmon into paper-thin slices.

❧ Arrange the salmon on bread slices (halving the fish pieces first if quite large). Garnish the salmon with the pickled red onion slices and serve.

serves 20–24

California
Warm Goat Cheese Salad

Chez Panisse, the Berkeley, California, restaurant, popularized baked goat cheese salad, which has roots in France. Panfrying the cheese instead of baking it produces a nicely browned coating. Mesclun, delicate baby greens, make a refreshing counterpoint.

4 tablespoons (2 fl oz/60 ml) plus 5 teaspoons extra-virgin olive oil

1 tablespoon Champagne vinegar

1 shallot, finely minced

salt and freshly ground pepper to taste

¼ cup (1 oz/30 g) very fine dried bread crumbs

½ lb (250 g) fresh goat cheese with no rind

6 oz (185 g) mesclun

½ cup (2 oz/60 g) coarsely chopped toasted walnuts

freshly cracked pepper to taste

⚜ In a small bowl, whisk together 3 tablespoons of the olive oil with the vinegar, shallot, salt, and pepper to make a vinaigrette. Let stand for 30 minutes.

⚜ Spread the bread crumbs on a plate. Using a thin-bladed knife, cut the goat cheese into 4 rounds of uniform thickness. Coat each round with 1 teaspoon olive oil. Coat the rounds on all sides with the bread crumbs, patting the crumbs into place.

⚜ In a large bowl, combine the *mesclun* and the walnuts. Add as much of the vinaigrette as needed to coat lightly, then toss well. Adjust the seasoning and divide among individual plates.

⚜ Heat a nonstick frying pan over medium heat. Add the remaining 1 tablespoon plus 1 teaspoon olive oil. When the oil is hot, add the goat cheese rounds. Cook on the first side until nicely browned, 45–60 seconds. Turn and cook until the cheese is quivery to the touch, 45–60 seconds longer. Do not allow it to burn or melt. Transfer the goat cheese to the plates, placing 1 round atop each pile of greens. Sprinkle the cheese with cracked pepper and serve.

serves 4

Midwest

Onion Soup with Maytag Croutons

Iowa, famous for state-fair pies, corn-fed pork, and some of the best blue cheese in the world, sits right at the center of the Heartland. For decades, the Maytag family has been based in the small town of Newton, where they now run a multinational kitchen appliance empire based on the washing machine. But at Maytag Dairy Farms, Inc., cheese making has changed little since Fred Maytag II started the business in 1941. The company's cow's milk blue cheese is still aged for six months, twice as long as most other American blues, which deepens the flavor and results in a creamy texture. If Maytag is unavailable, look for another artisanal blue cheese, especially one local to your region.

SOUP

bouquet garni of 6 fresh flat-leaf (Italian) parsley sprigs, 2 fresh thyme sprigs, 1 teaspoon white peppercorns, and 6 juniper berries

8 green (spring) onions

3 tablespoons unsalted butter

1 tablespoon olive oil, or as needed

1 large shallot, thinly sliced

6–8 red, yellow, white, and sweet onions, in any combination, about 3 lb (1.5 kg) total weight

1 tablespoon all-purpose (plain) flour

2 teaspoons sugar

1 teaspoon kosher salt or coarse sea salt, plus salt to taste

¼ cup (2 fl oz/60 ml) Cognac

8 cups (64 fl oz/2 l) beef stock or vegetable stock

freshly ground white pepper to taste

CROUTONS

1 baguette

½ lb (250 g) Maytag Blue cheese, at room temperature

To make the soup, place the bouquet garni ingredients on a small square of cheesecloth (muslin), bring the corners together, and tie securely with kitchen string. (Alternatively, place the ingredients inside a large tea ball.) Set aside.

Cut the bulb onions in half through the stem end and slice crosswise paper-thin. Trim off the green tops from the green onions and reserve. Thinly slice the white portions.

In a large, heavy saucepan over medium-high heat, melt the butter with the 1 tablespoon olive oil. Add the sliced onions and shallot and cook, stirring constantly, until they start to wilt, 3–5 minutes. Continue to cook the onions until they begin to color, stirring frequently, to loosen any caramelized bits, about 10 minutes. If the onions start to stick, add a drizzle of olive oil.

Reduce the heat to medium-low, cover, and sweat the onions, stirring occasionally, until they begin to turn golden, about 30 minutes. Uncover, raise the heat to medium-high, and add the flour, sugar, and 1 teaspoon salt. Cook, stirring constantly, until the onions darken, about 5 minutes. Carefully pour in the Cognac and stir to scrape up any browned bits on the pan bottom. Add the stock and the bouquet garni and bring to a boil. Reduce the heat to low, cover partially, and cook, stirring occasionally, until the soup thickens and the onions break down, about 30 minutes. Season with salt and white pepper. (The soup can be made up to this point and refrigerated for up to 2 days before continuing.)

Meanwhile, make the croutons: Preheat an oven to 375°F (190°C). Slice the baguette on the diagonal into ½-inch (12-mm) slices. You should have about 32. Spread on a large baking sheet and toast in the oven for 10 minutes. Turn the slices over and toast until golden on both sides, about 5 minutes longer. Remove from the oven and let the slices cool on the baking sheet until they can be handled. Using about ¼ lb (125 g) of the blue cheese, smear a little on one side of each crouton. Trim away any tough portions of the reserved green onion tops, then thinly slice.

When ready to serve the soup, preheat a broiler (grill). Remove the bouquet garni from the soup and discard. Crumble the remaining cheese evenly over the croutons on the baking sheet. Slip the baking sheet under the broiler about 4 inches (10 cm) from the heat source and broil (grill) until the cheese starts to melt and the croutons turn brown around the edges, about 1 minute. Remove the sheet from the broiler, transfer the croutons to a serving plate, and sprinkle with the green onion tops.

Ladle the soup into warmed bowls. Top with the croutons and serve.

serves 8 as a first course, or 4 as a main course

SAVORING AMERICA

Corn and Black–Eyed Pea Salad

Native to Asia, black-eyed peas were likely introduced to the South from Africa. The field peas were initially grown for animal feed, but in the years after the Civil War, black-eyed peas became a relatively inexpensive source of protein for the devastated region.

Today, the beige beans, each with a distinctive black "eye," are a pantry staple, used in soups, main dishes, and salads like this starter. They are the centerpiece of such southern classics as hoppin' John, pairing the peas with rice, and Georgia caviar, an appetizer that combines the peas with bell peppers (capsicums) and chiles. The southerner's New Year's Day meal always includes black-eyed peas, as they are said to bring twelve months of good luck to anyone who eats them on the first day of the year. Black-eyed peas are readily available fresh, dried, frozen, or canned. If fresh peas are unavailable, use 2 cups (14 oz/440 g) frozen shelled peas in this salad.

2 lb (1 kg) fresh black-eyed peas, shelled

4 cups (32 fl oz/1 l) water

salt and freshly ground pepper to taste

6 slices bacon, coarsely chopped

1 small red onion, chopped

2 cloves garlic, chopped

kernels from 1 ear sweet yellow or white corn

⅔ cup (5 fl oz/150 ml) cider vinegar

1 tablespoon sugar

2 plum (Roma) tomatoes

1 cucumber

2 tablespoons fresh lime juice

⅓ cup (3 fl oz/80 ml) extra-virgin olive oil

¼ cup (⅓ oz/10 g) chopped fresh cilantro (fresh coriander)

2 teaspoons ground coriander

about 4 cups (4 oz/125 g) watercress sprigs, tough stems removed (2–3 bunches)

2 green (spring) onions, including tender green tops, finely chopped

In a saucepan over high heat, combine the black-eyed peas, water, salt, and pepper. Bring to a boil, then reduce the heat to medium. Cover and cook until the peas are fork-tender, 25–30 minutes. Drain and cool under running cold water. Drain again and set aside.

serves 6–8

In a frying pan over medium heat, fry the bacon, stirring often, until crispy and golden brown, about 10 minutes. Using a slotted spoon, transfer the bacon to paper towels to drain.

Add the red onion, garlic, and corn kernels to the hot drippings in the pan and cook over medium heat until tender, about 5 minutes. Stir in the vinegar and the sugar. Continue cooking until the liquid has reduced by one-third, 3–5 minutes. Using a slotted spoon, transfer the contents of the frying pan to a large bowl.

Seed and coarsely chop the tomatoes. Halve the cucumber lengthwise and then peel, seed, and finely dice. Add to the black-eyed peas and season with salt and pepper. Toss to mix well. Add the lime juice and the olive oil to the pan and swirl over medium heat until heated through, about 1 minute. Stir in the cilantro and coriander.

Divide the watercress among individual plates. Divide the black-eyed pea mixture evenly among the plates. Spoon the hot dressing over the salad, again dividing evenly. Garnish with the green onions and bacon and serve at once.

New Orleans, home to gumbo and jambalaya, beignets and po' boys, jazz and zydeco, was America's first great restaurant city.

Southern Ports

The South is home to a quartet of atmospheric ports, Charleston and Savannah on the Atlantic and Mobile and New Orleans on the Gulf of Mexico. From their earliest days, these lively cities pushed the region to flourish both economically and at the table.

Exotic foods and spices were often part of a ship's cargo, and once off-loaded, they were put on trains, steamboats, and horse-drawn wagons and carried to the farthest reaches of the region. Later, with the completion of the Panama Canal, foods from Asia regularly turned up on the same docks.

Sesame seeds, okra, black-eyed peas, sweet potatoes, collard greens, and rice, arriving from the west coast of Africa, influenced the distinctive Low Country cuisine of South Carolina; cinnamon sticks and curry powder from India and olive oil from the Mediterranean found their way into dishes from Louisiana to Georgia; and spices and fruits from the Caribbean expanded the southern cook's dessert pantry. Legend has it that Country Captain, a southern classic that combines chicken and vegetables in a curry sauce and said to have been a favorite of President Franklin Roosevelt's, was introduced to Charleston cooks in the early 1800s by a sea captain who had spent years in Indian ports.

New England
Clam Chowder

Northeasterners are opinionated when it comes to chowder. Defining the "authentic" bowl inevitably leads to heated discussions about what ingredients should or should not be included. In general, potatoes, corn, celery, milk or cream, and, of course, clams, are givens. The main point of friction is the tomato. While most New Englanders boast of tomatoes as an important local crop, residents of the upper region—Maine, Vermont, New Hampshire, Massachusetts—would never dream of putting them in their chowder kettles. But drifting south through Rhode Island and Connecticut, people are more forgiving of the occasional tomato addition, while next door in New York, tomato-based Manhattan clam chowder is a bona fide classic.

3½ lb (1.75 kg) hard-shelled clams such as littleneck, quahog, or mahogany, scrubbed

¾ cup (6 fl oz/180 ml) water

2 cups (16 fl oz/500 ml) fish stock or bottled clam juice, or as needed

3 oz (90 g) pancetta, sliced ¼ inch (6 mm) thick and diced

2 tablespoons unsalted butter

2 small leeks, including tender green tops, diced (about 1 cup/4 oz/125 g)

2 small celery stalks, thinly sliced

1 clove garlic, minced

1 teaspoon chopped fresh thyme

½ lb (250 g) red potatoes, unpeeled and diced

freshly ground pepper to taste

1½ cups (12 fl oz/375 ml) heavy (double) cream

1 cup (6 oz/185 g) fresh or frozen corn kernels

salt to taste

2 tablespoons minced fresh chives

❧ Discard any clams that fail to close to the touch. In a heavy soup pot over high heat, combine the clams and the water and bring to a boil. Cook, shaking the pot occasionally, until the clams just begin to open, about 3 minutes. Scoop the clams into a large bowl, discarding any that failed to open; set aside to cool. Pour the remaining liquid through a fine-mesh sieve set over a 4-cup (32-fl oz/1-l) measuring pitcher. Add fish stock or clam juice as needed to make 3 cups (24 fl oz/750 ml). Set aside.

❧ Wipe out the soup pot and add the diced pancetta. Place over medium heat and sauté until crisp but not dry, about 5 minutes. Using a slotted spoon, transfer the pancetta to a small bowl and set aside. Add the butter to the pot over medium-low heat and stir until melted and bubbling. Add the leeks and celery and cook, stirring frequently, until the vegetables are tender, about 10 minutes. Add the garlic and thyme and cook until fragrant, about 1 minute. Stir in the potatoes and season with pepper. Pour in the reserved clam liquid and the cream. Bring to a boil over high heat. Reduce the heat to low and simmer gently, uncovered, until the potatoes are just tender when pierced with the tip of a knife, about 10 minutes.

❧ Meanwhile, remove the cooled clams from their shells, saving their juices and discarding the shells. Roughly chop the clams and add to the soup. Pour any accumulated juices through a sieve lined with cheesecloth (muslin) and add to the soup. Stir in the reserved pancetta and corn. Simmer gently until just heated through. Taste the soup and adjust the seasoning with salt and pepper.

❧ Ladle into warmed bowls and sprinkle with the chives. Serve immediately.

serves 6

California
Fava Bean Bruschetta

The growing popularity of Italian cooking in America has helped make tender, sweet fava beans prominent on spring restaurant menus, especially in California. The beans grow particularly well in the cool coastal climate of Half Moon Bay, south of San Francisco. Seek out the best-quality extra-virgin olive oil for drizzling on the bruschetta before serving.

1½ lb (750 g) fresh fava (broad) beans, shelled

4 tablespoons (2 fl oz/60 ml) extra-virgin olive oil, plus oil for brushing and drizzling

1 large clove garlic, minced

salt and freshly ground pepper to taste

6 large fresh basil leaves, torn into small pieces

12 slices coarse country bread, each about 4 inches (10 cm) long, 2 inches (5 cm) wide, and ¼ inch (6 mm) thick

4-oz (125-g) piece ricotta salata cheese

🌱 Bring a saucepan of water to a boil. Add the fava beans and blanch for 1 minute, then drain and immerse in a bowl of ice water. When the beans are cool, drain again. Using a small knife or your finger-tips, slit the skin of each bean and gently squeeze to remove the bright green bean inside.

🌱 In a small frying pan over medium heat, warm 2 tablespoons of the olive oil. Add the garlic and sauté to release its fragrance. Add the peeled fava beans and season with salt and pepper. Add 2 tablespoons water, cover partially, reduce the heat to low, and simmer until the beans are tender, 8–10 minutes. Transfer the contents of the pan to a food processor. Add the basil and the remaining 2 tablespoons olive oil and purée until smooth. Taste and adjust the seasoning.

🌱 Preheat a broiler (grill). Arrange the bread slices on a baking sheet and brush both sides with olive oil. Place in the broiler and toast, turning once, until lightly browned. Divide the fava bean purée among the warm toasts, spreading it evenly. Shave a little ricotta salata over the purée; you may not need the entire piece. Drizzle with olive oil and serve.

serves 6

California

Beet, Orange, and Avocado Salad

In late winter, when California's navel oranges are at their sweetest, Hass avocados are also at their peak. Take advantage of nature's good timing to make a tricolored salad of navel oranges, avocados, and beets.

3 tablespoons extra-virgin olive oil

1 tablespoon sherry vinegar

1 large shallot, very finely minced

1 large clove garlic, very finely minced

salt and freshly ground pepper to taste

3 red beets, about ¾ lb (375 g) total weight

2 navel oranges or blood oranges

1 ripe, but firm avocado

chopped fresh cilantro (fresh coriander)

In a bowl, whisk together the olive oil, vinegar, shallot, garlic, salt, and pepper to make a vinaigrette.

Preheat an oven to 400°F (200°C). Remove the beet tops, if attached, leaving ½ inch (12 mm) of the stem. Put the beets in a baking dish and add water to a depth of ¼ inch (6 mm). Cover and bake until a knife pierces the beets easily, about 50 minutes. When they are cool enough to handle, peel and slice into thin wedges. Place in a bowl and add enough of the vinaigrette to coat. Toss gently, then adjust the seasoning. The beets may need additional vinegar.

Cut a slice off both ends of each orange so it will stand upright. Stand it on a cutting board and, using a large, sharp knife, cut away the peel and white pith by slicing from top to bottom, following the contour of the fruit. Using a small knife, cut along either side of each segment to free it from the membrane. Put the segments in a bowl and drain off any juice. Add enough vinaigrette to coat the oranges and toss gently. Halve and pit the avocado. Using a large spoon, scoop the flesh from each half in one piece. Put each half cut side down on the cutting board and slice thinly crosswise. Add the slices to the remaining vinaigrette and toss gently with your hands to coat.

Choose a rectangular platter. Arrange the avocado slices, orange segments, and beet wedges in separate rows. Garnish with cilantro and serve.

serves 4

New England
Apple-Butternut Soup

Hardy apples and winter squashes are common staples of New England larders. Apple varieties that stored well, like Baldwin and Northern Spy, date back to the 1750s and remain popular today. The large Hubbard squash, which usually rides the scales at a minimum of twelve pounds (6 kg), has long been appreciated for its fine taste and extended shelf life. Nowadays in the Northeast, the butternut is one of the most favored of the hard-shelled squashes available. It not only has the same rich, dense, string-free flesh as the much beloved Hubbard, but also is one of the easiest winter squashes to handle. Its smooth, thin skin peels with little effort.

6 tablespoons (3 oz/90 g) unsalted butter

1½ lb (750 g) apples (about 4 large), peeled, cored, and chopped

2 yellow onions, chopped

leaves from 10 fresh thyme sprigs

1 butternut squash, 1¼ lb (625 g), halved, seeded, peeled, and cut into 1-inch (2.5-cm) chunks

6 cups (48 fl oz/1.5 l) chicken stock

salt and freshly ground pepper to taste

❧ In a large saucepan over medium–low heat, melt the butter. Add the apples, onions, and thyme and cook, stirring frequently, until soft and golden brown, about 15 minutes. Add the squash chunks and stir until fragrant, about 2 minutes. Pour in the stock, raise the heat to high, and bring to a boil. Reduce the heat to low and simmer until the squash and apples are very soft, about 25 minutes.

❧ Remove from the heat and let cool slightly. Working in batches if necessary, purée the soup in a blender until smooth.

❧ Transfer the puréed soup to a clean saucepan and place over medium–low heat. Season generously with salt and pepper to bring out the apple flavor, and heat to serving temperature. Ladle into warmed bowls and serve at once.

serves 8

California

Fritto Misto of Squid, Artichokes, and Lemon

California fishermen find squid all along the state's coast, but the catch is most abundant in Southern and Central California. Local restaurant-goers like to launch a meal with fried calamari or, in the Italian tradition, a mixed fry (fritto misto) with artichokes and paper-thin lemon slices. Onion rings and shrimp (prawns) are other possible additions. Be sure to use plenty of oil when you fry and to maintain the oil temperature at 375°F (190°C). A deep-frying thermometer is critical.

1 lb (500 g) squid

about 2 cups (16 fl oz/500 ml) buttermilk

12 baby artichokes

1 lemon

olive oil or vegetable oil for deep-frying

2 cups (10 oz/315 g) unbleached all-purpose (plain) flour

2 teaspoons sea salt, plus salt to taste

1 teaspoon cayenne pepper

several grinds of black pepper

First, clean the squid: Working with 1 squid at a time, pull the head from the body. Cut off and reserve the tentacles; discard the head. Squeeze out and discard the small, hard "beak" at the base of the tentacles; leave the tentacles whole. Using your fingers, pull out any internal matter from the body, including the quill-like cartilage, and discard. Peel off the mottled skin that covers the body. Rinse the body well. Cut the body crosswise into rings ½ inch (12 mm) wide. Put the rings and tentacles in a bowl and add enough of the buttermilk to coat the squid. Set aside.

Working with 1 artichoke at a time, pull back and snap off the outer leaves until you reach the pale heart. Trim the base of any brown parts and cut about ½ inch (12 mm) off the top. Cut each artichoke into 4 lengthwise slices, each with some stem attached. Put the sliced artichokes in a bowl and add enough buttermilk to coat the slices.

Slice the lemon into very thin rounds, discarding the end pieces. Put the lemon slices in a bowl and add buttermilk to coat the slices.

Pour the oil to a depth of 3 inches (7.5 cm) into a deep saucepan, and heat to 375°F (190°C).

While the oil heats, combine the flour, 2 teaspoons sea salt, cayenne pepper, and black pepper in a pie dish and stir to blend.

Drain the artichokes well in a sieve, then transfer to the pie dish. Toss to coat evenly with the flour mixture. Transfer them to another sieve and shake to remove excess coating.

Fry the artichokes in batches until golden brown outside and tender within, about 1½ minutes. Using a wire skimmer or slotted spoon, transfer the artichokes to paper towels to drain. Repeat the process with the squid, then with the lemon slices. Be sure to let the oil return to 375°F (190°C) before frying each new batch. Each squid batch will take about 1 minute, and the lemon slices about 30 seconds. Drain on paper towels.

Season the artichokes, squid, and lemon slices with salt. Combine in a basket or on a platter, or divide among individual plates, and serve.

serves 4

SAVORING AMERICA

Dairy Land

The lush pasturelands of Illinois, Indiana, Ohio, Michigan, Wisconsin, Minnesota, and Iowa attracted early European immigrants who saw their old-world landscapes in their newly adopted country. Hills of sweet alfalfa tumbled into verdant valleys of grass, ideal for grazing Brown Swiss and Holstein cows. They quickly settled in and began to re-create the dairy tradition that they had left behind, producing rich milk and cream, which they preserved in the form of tangy fresh and mellow aged cheeses, and velvety butter.

Mrs. Anne Pickett, a farm wife who bought milk from her neighbors, opened Wisconsin's first commercial "cheeserie" in 1841, in Lake Mills. Twenty years later, along came another Wisconsin innovator, Chester Hazen. He founded the first true cheese factory in 1864, and is credited with the groundbreaking idea to load railroad cars with cheese for out-of-state customers. Perhaps the most famous of these early Midwest cheeses is Colby, a cousin to cheddar, first developed in the town of Colby, Wisconsin, in 1885. Soon Midwest dairy lands were supplying the growing nation with cheddar, brick, Swiss, and other cheeses.

Although California has since passed Wisconsin as the country's biggest milk-producing state, the Midwest as a whole continues to dominate America's dairy industry, producing nearly half of the nation's butter and cheese. More than 350 varieties, types, and styles of cheese come from Wisconsin alone.

The growing market for artisanal cheeses has helped many new and existing midwestern cheese makers find successful niche markets with specialty cheeses, such as Mexican queso blanco, Italian Gorgonzola, and Greek-style feta. Small-scale producers are turning out more and more handcrafted cheeses, several of which rely on organic milk and are available only within a narrow radius of where they are made. Farmstead cheeses from Wisconsin's "Green Country" just south of Madison are winning both loyal fans and critical accolades with fine Limburger, aged cheddar, Muenster, and Havarti. From Minnesota come creamy fromage blanc and piquant smoked sheep's milk cheese. Regional chefs can find tart and smooth goat's milk cheeses close to home, turned out in limited batches by craftspeople in Missouri and Indiana.

Midwest

Summer Crudités with Ranch Dip

Ranch dressing is America's most popular. Some midwesterners like it so much that they put it on french fries and baked potatoes, as well as crisp vegetables, fresh from the garden.

1 cup (8 oz/250 g) sour cream

1 cup (8 fl oz/250 ml) buttermilk

½ cup (4 fl oz/125 ml) mayonnaise

6 tablespoons (¾ oz/20 g) buttermilk powder

½ teaspoon white wine vinegar

kosher salt and freshly ground pepper to taste

½ teaspoon sugar

4 tablespoons (⅓ oz/10 g) minced fresh flat-leaf (Italian) parsley

12–16 green (spring) onions, trimmed

2 fennel bulbs, trimmed and cut into narrow wedges

4 or 5 small red or orange beets, peeled and sliced paper-thin, or halved if small

½ lb (250 g) sugar snap or snow peas (mangetouts)

12–16 young carrots, tops trimmed

1 small head red cabbage, cut into narrow wedges

2 celery hearts, trimmed with leaves intact

2 yellow or orange bell peppers (capsicums), seeded and cut crosswise into rings

1 small zucchini (courgette) or summer squash, thinly sliced

24 each cherry tomatoes and radishes

❧ In a bowl, combine the sour cream, buttermilk, mayonnaise, buttermilk powder, vinegar, salt, pepper, and sugar. Whisk until smooth. Stir in 3 tablespoons of the parsley. Adjust the seasoning. Cover and refrigerate for 2 hours. Prepare all the vegetables and have them ready in the refrigerator.

❧ Arrange the vegetables on platters. Put the dip in a bowl and sprinkle with the remaining 1 tablespoon parsley. Serve immediately.

serves 12

N

Southwest

Arizona Chile-Cheese Crisps

Unlike bold and highly seasoned Texas cuisine and the fiery, chile-driven dishes of New Mexico, Arizona's table favorites celebrate beef, flour tortillas, and mild cheeses, all imports from Sonora, the Mexican state directly across the border. The rest of the food is intrinsically milder, too, with most spicing added by the spoonful from a bowl of salsa. This appetizer, a restaurant specialty, is among the most distinctive of the region's snacks, based as it is on a dramatic eighteen-inch (45-cm) tortilla and on service that calls for a round metal pan on a rack above a warming candle. Even in Arizona, such megatortillas require a trip to a tortilleria. Elsewhere it is more practical to make your own twelve-inch (30-cm) tortillas, unless you have a huge frying pan or a commercial range with a griddle.

TORTILLA(S)

1 cup (5 oz/155 g) unbleached all-purpose (plain) flour

½ teaspoon baking powder

½ teaspoon salt

2½ tablespoons lard or solid vegetable shortening (vegetable lard)

⅓ cup (3 fl oz/80 ml) warm water

¾ lb (375 g) mild cheese such as Colby or Monterey Jack, or a combination, shredded

2 green New Mexico or Anaheim chiles, roasted and peeled (page 246), then cut lengthwise into strips ¼ inch (6 mm) wide

pico de gallo (page 83) or store-bought salsa

☙ To make the tortilla(s), in a bowl, sift together the flour, baking powder, and salt. Add the lard or shortening to the dry ingredients and, using a pastry blender or 2 forks, cut in the fat until it forms particles the size of small peas. Add the water, stir to moisten, and then briefly knead the dough in the bowl until it begins to come together.

☙ Turn the dough out onto a lightly floured work surface and knead until smooth and elastic, 10–12 times. Enclose the dough in plastic wrap and refrigerate for 1 hour.

☙ For an 18-inch (45-cm) or larger tortilla, keep the dough in 1 piece. To make two 12-inch (30-cm) tortillas, cut the dough in half. On a lightly floured surface, roll out the dough to the desired size. Only

serves 4–6

practice will produce perfectly round tortillas; even misshapen ones taste good. (The tortillas can be rolled out up to an hour in advance. Cover with plastic wrap and then a dampened kitchen towel.)

☙ If cooking 12-inch (30-cm) tortillas, set a heavy, ungreased 12-inch (30-cm) frying pan (one with low sides will make turning the tortillas easier) over medium heat. When the pan is hot, lay a round of dough in the pan. Cook until the tortilla has puffed and the underside is dappled a golden brown, about 2 minutes. Use a spatula to release the tortilla from the pan. Flip it and cook on the other side until no longer raw, another 1–2 minutes. Repeat with the remaining dough. If cooking an 18-inch (45-cm) tortilla, preheat an ungreased griddle to 300°F (150°C) and cook the tortilla in the same way. The tortilla(s) can be used immediately or prepared up to 2 hours ahead. Let cool on a rack and cover with plastic wrap and a kitchen towel to prevent drying out.

☙ Preheat an oven to 325°F (165°C).

☙ Cover an oven rack with aluminum foil. Lay one 12-inch (30-cm) or the 18-inch (45-cm) tortilla on the rack. Scatter half the cheese over the smaller tortilla; use all of it on the larger one. Arrange half the green chile strips in a spoke pattern over the cheese on the smaller tortilla; use all the strips on the larger tortilla. Slide the rack into the upper third of the oven. Bake until the edges of the tortilla are lightly browned and the cheese has melted, about 10 minutes.

☙ Carefully slide the tortilla onto a large serving platter. Serve immediately, accompanied with the salsa. Provide diners with small plates. Diners tear off small pieces, top them with salsa, and roll them into bite-sized bundles. If making 2 crisps, bake the second tortilla while you are eating the first.

A thousand years ago, the ancestors of today's Pueblo Indians were already planting chiles.

SAVORING AMERICA

Hawaii

Ahi Tuna Poke

Once you have tasted this classic Hawaiian dish of cubed raw tuna tossed with a sesame soy dressing, you'll never think about "tuna salad" in the same way again. In some grocery-store deli cases in the islands, you can find a dozen or more versions of poke (pronounced poh-kay). Some are spicy, others are made with tropical fruits, and still others use different exquisitely fresh seafoods such as swordfish. Variations are countless, including green (spring) onion in place of the sweet onion, or the addition of ogo, the crunchy, flavorful seaweed popular in Hawaii.

Be sure to use the best-quality tuna, usually labeled "sashimi grade" and found in well-stocked fish markets or in the fish section of some supermarkets. Ahi, or yellowfin tuna, is the favorite choice, but other fresh tunas such as albacore or bigeye can be used. Poke is best when served within a couple of hours of being made, although it will keep, tightly covered, in the refrigerator for up to a day.

1 lb (500 g) sashimi-grade ahi tuna steaks, skin and bones removed

½ cup (2½ oz/75 g) finely chopped Maui or other sweet onion

3 tablespoons soy sauce

2 tablespoons minced fresh cilantro (fresh coriander), plus sprigs for garnish

2 teaspoons sesame seeds, toasted

few dashes of Asian sesame oil

large pinch of coarse sea salt

pinch of red pepper flakes

Using a sharp knife, cut the tuna into ¾-inch (2-cm) cubes. Place the tuna in a bowl and add the onion, soy sauce, minced cilantro, sesame seeds, sesame oil, salt, and red pepper flakes. Toss the mixture gently to blend evenly. Cover the bowl and refrigerate the poke until well chilled, about 1 hour.

Spoon the poke into individual small bowls. Serve chilled, garnished with cilantro sprigs.

serves 4–6

California

Caesar Salad

Legend has it that the Caesar salad was invented by Caesar Cardini at his restaurant in Tijuana, Mexico, just across the California border. Decades later, it still reigns as one of the most popular restaurant salads, a delightful marriage of crunchy romaine and creamy anchovy dressing.

There have been many variations on the Caesar, some with whole lettuce leaves and others with chopped lettuce, and still others with the addition of chicken, turning the salad into main-course fare.

This straightforward version of the original uses crisp hearts of romaine and croutons that are sautéed briefly in olive oil, then baked until crisp. Trimmed hearts of romaine lettuce are available at many markets, but if you are unable to find hearts, buy whole heads of the lettuce and strip away all the dark green, outer leaves (reserving them for another use) until you reach the pale hearts.

SAVORING AMERICA

DRESSING

1 egg yolk, at room temperature

1 teaspoon warm water

½ cup (4 fl oz/125 ml) extra-virgin olive oil

4 anchovy fillets

1 large clove garlic

large pinch of salt

2 tablespoons fresh lemon juice, or to taste

freshly cracked pepper to taste

CROUTONS

1 tablespoon extra-virgin olive oil

2 cups (4 oz/125 g) bread cubes from day-old coarse country bread (½-inch/12-mm cubes)

salt to taste

1 lb (500 g) romaine (cos) hearts

¼ cup (1 oz/30 g) grated Parmesan cheese

☙ To make the dressing, in a small bowl, whisk the egg yolk with the warm water to thin it, then whisk in the olive oil, drop by drop. Once an emulsion has formed, gradually add the oil a little faster until all of it has been incorporated and a thick sauce has formed. In a mortar, combine the anchovies, garlic,

and salt and pound to a paste. (Alternatively, on a cutting board, mince the anchovies, garlic, and salt to a paste.) Whisk the paste into the dressing. Whisk in the 2 tablespoons lemon juice and season with cracked pepper. Set aside.

☙ To make the croutons, preheat an oven to 400°F (200°C). Heat a frying pan over medium-high heat. Add the olive oil and swirl to coat. When the oil is hot, add the bread cubes. Toss quickly to coat the cubes evenly with the oil. Season with salt, then transfer to a baking sheet.

☙ Bake the cubes, stirring once or twice, until they are crisp and lightly browned, about 10 minutes. Set aside to cool.

☙ Cut the romaine hearts in half lengthwise, then cut crosswise into bite-sized pieces. Transfer them to a salad bowl. Add the dressing and toss to coat the leaves evenly.

☙ Add the Parmesan and croutons and toss again. Taste and adjust the seasoning, adding more lemon juice if desired. Serve immediately.

serves 4

Pacific Northwest

Cheddar and Ale Soup

This easy, flavorful recipe blends the Northwest's beer tradition with that of cheese making, which also goes back more than a hundred years. Two popular cheddars, Tillamook from Oregon and Cougar Gold from Washington, are ideal for this rich, delicious soup. In their place, use any sharp full-flavored cheddar. For a vegetarian version, simply replace the chicken stock with vegetable stock.

Serve the soup with a crisp salad and a loaf of artisanal bread for a hearty meal. If you like, pour the same ale to drink along with the soup.

3 tablespoons unsalted butter

1 large yellow onion, diced

⅓ cup (2 oz/60 g) all-purpose (plain) flour

2 teaspoons dry mustard

3 cups (24 fl oz/750 ml) chicken stock, or as needed

1 bottle (12 fl oz/375 ml) pale ale

2½ cups (10 oz/315 g) shredded sharp cheddar cheese

salt and freshly ground pepper to taste

2 tablespoons chopped fresh chives

In a large saucepan over medium heat, melt the butter. Add the onion and sauté until tender and aromatic, 3–5 minutes. Sprinkle the flour and dry mustard over the onion and stir to coat evenly. Continue cooking, stirring often, until the mixture is quite dry, 2–3 minutes.

Pour in the stock, stirring until well blended. Cover and simmer until somewhat thickened, about 10 minutes. Stir in the ale and then the cheese, and cook, stirring constantly, until the cheese has melted and the soup has a silky texture, 3–5 minutes. Remove from the heat. Working in batches, purée the soup in a blender until smooth. Return to the saucepan and reheat over medium heat, adding stock if the soup is too thick. Season with salt and pepper.

Ladle the soup into warmed bowls, scatter the chives on top, and serve immediately.

serves 4

Northwest Beer

Since the mid-1800s, when Oregon and Washington welcomed their first breweries, people in the Pacific Northwest have been drinking local beer. The European immigrants who came to the area arrived with brewing skills in their blood and built a thriving brewery scene. Then, in the early 1980s, a new wave of small breweries emerged, committed to high-quality beers. These operations, which produced fewer than ten thousand barrels annually, were initially called microbreweries, but today the term "craft brewery" is more common, indicating that quality is more important than production size. Washington and Oregon together are home to some 150 breweries.

At neighborhood brewpubs throughout the region, the house brew is on tap along with beer-friendly fare in a very casual, convivial setting. Bigger breweries can be dazzling in their stainless-steel glory, where the aroma of malted barley and hops wafts through the brewing rooms. Many breweries offer tours and tastings, allowing visitors an up-close appreciation for this age-old craft.

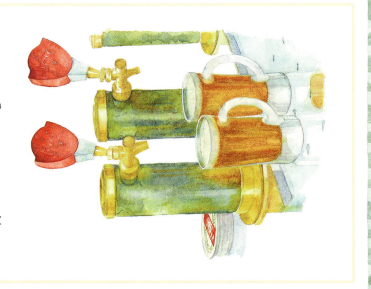

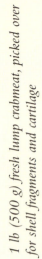

Mid-Atlantic
Crab Cakes with Herbed Tartar Sauce

The Chesapeake Bay area harbors the blue crab, the East Coast's finest crab variety. The name befits this small, dark blue to blue-green crustacean, which turns a brilliant red when boiled. Maryland chefs regularly use the flavorful meat for crab cakes.

CRAB CAKES

⅓ cup (3 fl oz/80 ml) mayonnaise

1 egg

2 teaspoons Worcestershire sauce

1 or 2 dashes Tabasco sauce or other hot-pepper sauce

2 small green (spring) onions, including tender green tops, minced

⅓ cup (1½ oz/45 g) plus 1½ cups (6 oz/185 g) fine dried bread crumbs

3 tablespoons minced red bell pepper (capsicum)

2 tablespoons minced fresh flat-leaf (Italian) parsley

1 lb (500 g) fresh lump crabmeat, picked over for shell fragments and cartilage

¾ teaspoon kosher salt

¼ teaspoon freshly ground pepper

HERBED TARTAR SAUCE

¾ cup (6 fl oz/180 ml) mayonnaise

3 tablespoons drained sweet pickle relish

2 tablespoons minced fresh herbs such as flat-leaf (Italian) parsley, chives, basil, or mint, or a combination

1 tablespoon sour cream

1 tablespoon minced red onion

1 teaspoon fresh lemon juice

1 or 2 dashes Tabasco sauce or other hot-pepper sauce

coarse salt and freshly ground pepper to taste

2 tablespoons unsalted butter

2 tablespoons canola oil

lemon wedges

☙ To make the crab cakes, in a bowl, stir together the mayonnaise, egg, Worcestershire sauce, and hot-pepper sauce until well blended. Add the green onions, ⅓ cup (1½ oz/45 g) bread crumbs, bell pepper, and parsley and mix until blended. Add the crabmeat, salt, and pepper and mix gently. Pour the remaining 1½ cups (6 oz/185 g) bread crumbs onto a plate. Divide the crabmeat mixture into 8 equal portions. Lightly dampen your hands and shape each portion into a patty about 3 inches (7.5 cm) in diameter. Coat the patties with the bread crumbs. Place on a clean plate, cover with plastic wrap, and refrigerate for at least 2 hours or for up to 8 hours before cooking.

☙ Meanwhile, make the tartar sauce: In a bowl, stir together the mayonnaise, relish, herbs, sour cream, red onion, and lemon juice until well blended. Season to taste with hot-pepper sauce, salt, and pepper. Cover and refrigerate until ready to serve.

☙ In a large frying pan over medium heat, combine the butter and the canola oil. Heat until the butter is melted and foaming and then add half of the crab cakes. Cook, turning once or twice, until browned, about 5 minutes on each side. Transfer to a clean plate and cover with aluminum foil. Repeat with the remaining crab cakes. Divide the cakes among individual plates. Place 1 or 2 lemon wedges alongside and pass the tartar sauce at the table.

serves 8 as a first course, or 4 as a main course

Midwest

Pickled Cucumber Salad

America's summer cucumber choices are growing. Thanks to local farm stands, progressive truck farmers, and a growing interest in gardening, many heirloom varieties are available. Some have strange shapes. Others come in unusual colors and sizes. Nearly all take to a short treatment with brine, even the customary "pickling" varieties.

¼ cup (2 fl oz/60 ml) safflower oil

3 tablespoons cider vinegar

1 tablespoon water

1 tablespoon sugar

½ teaspoon kosher salt or coarse sea salt

2½–3 lb (1.25–1.5 kg) cucumbers

1 teaspoon chopped fresh dill, or ½ teaspoon dried dill

1 small red onion, cut into paper-thin rings (optional)

In a small stainless-steel or enameled saucepan over medium-low heat, combine the safflower oil, vinegar, water, sugar, and salt. Heat just until the mixture begins to bubble. Keep warm.

If the skins of the cucumbers are waxed or thick, peel them. If you are not peeling the cucumbers, you can score the skins with a citrus stripper, if desired. Slice the cucumbers crosswise into pieces about ½ inch (12 mm) thick. Place in a heatproof glass or ceramic bowl. Sprinkle with the dill.

Pour the warm dressing over all and toss to coat for several seconds. Allow to cool, then cover and refrigerate. Chill for at least 2 hours or for up to 2 days, stirring often. The cucumbers will continue to absorb more flavor, although they will become somewhat more limp.

Just before serving, taste and adjust the seasoning. Line individual plates with the onion rings, if using, and top with the cucumbers and dressing.

serves 4–6

Pacific Northwest
Wild Mushroom Tart

One of the prime fall foods of the Northwest, wild mushrooms show up in an endless variety of dishes in the region's restaurant and home kitchens. Simple quichelike tarts such as this recipe are one option. The cream cheese in the filling gives the tart a slightly firmer texture than most quiches, and the addition of hazelnuts adds a welcome nuttiness to this tasty starter. Serve the tart with a simple salad of mixed greens tossed with a classic vinaigrette in which hazelnut oil replaces some of the olive oil.

CRUST

½ cup (2½ oz/75 g) hazelnuts (filberts), toasted and skinned

1½ cups (7½ oz/235 g) all-purpose (plain) flour

½ teaspoon salt

6 tablespoons (3 oz/90 g) chilled unsalted butter, cut into ½-inch (12-mm) pieces

1 egg yolk

3–4 tablespoons (1½–2 fl oz/45–60 ml) ice water

FILLING

1 tablespoon unsalted butter

½ cup (2½ oz/75 g) minced shallot or yellow onion

1½ lb (750 g) fresh wild mushrooms such as chanterelle, hedgehog, oyster, and/or lobster, brushed clean and coarsely chopped

salt and freshly ground pepper to taste

¼ lb (125 g) cream cheese, at room temperature

2 eggs

1 cup (8 fl oz/250 ml) half-and-half (half cream)

2 tablespoons minced fresh flat-leaf (Italian) parsley

serves 8

❧ To make the crust, in a food processor, combine the hazelnuts and 2 tablespoons of the flour and pulse until the nuts are very finely ground. Add the rest of the flour with the salt and pulse a few times to blend evenly. Add the butter pieces and pulse until the butter is finely chopped and the flour mixture has a coarse, sandy texture. Add the egg yolk and pulse once. Add the water 1 tablespoon at a time, pulsing once or twice after each addition and using only as much as needed for the dough to hold its shape when pinched between your fingers. It should be soft but not sticky. Do not overmix the dough, or it will be tough rather than flaky. Turn the dough out onto a work surface and form it into a ball. Enclose in plastic wrap and refrigerate for at least 30 minutes or for up to 1 day.

❧ Preheat an oven to 375°F (190°C).

❧ Remove the dough from the refrigerator and let sit for a few minutes. On a lightly floured work surface, roll out the dough into a 12-inch (30-cm) round. Drape around the pin and carefully ease into a 10-inch (25-cm) tart pan with a removable bottom. Lay the overhang over the edge of the pan, and roll the rolling pin over the dough to trim it. Following the fluted edge of the pan, gently crimp the pastry rim. Line the tart shell with a piece of aluminum foil, fill with pie weights or a combination of un-cooked rice and dried beans, and bake until set to the touch, 8–10 minutes. Remove the weights and foil and bake the shell until golden, about 5 minutes. Transfer to a rack and let cool. Reduce the oven temperature to 350°F (180°C).

❧ To make the filling, in a large frying pan over medium-high heat, melt the butter. Add the shallot or onion to the pan and sauté until tender and aromatic, 1–2 minutes. Add the mushrooms and sauté until tender and the liquid that they give off has evaporated, 5–7 minutes. Remove from the heat, season lightly with salt and pepper, and let cool completely.

❧ Put the cream cheese in a bowl. Using a wooden spoon, lightly cream the cheese until smooth. Add the eggs and beat to combine. Pour in the half-and-half and continue to beat until smooth. Season with salt and pepper.

❧ Pour the cream cheese mixture into the pastry shell, then evenly scatter with the cooled mushrooms, gently pressing them into the mixture. Sprinkle the mushrooms with the parsley.

❧ Bake the tart until the pastry edges are browned and the filling is set, about 30 minutes. Transfer to a rack and let cool completely. Remove the pan sides and place the tart on a serving plate. Serve at room temperature, cut into wedges.

California
Green Onion Focaccia

San Francisco's Liguria Bakery, in the heart of North Beach, is justly famous for its focaccia. The proprietors make it in large trays, slathering some with tomato sauce, garnishing others with sliced green onion. Homemade focaccia makes an informal hors d'oeuvre to accompany marinated olives and the evening's first glass of wine.

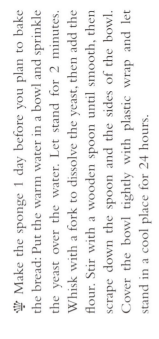

SPONGE

1 cup (8 fl oz/250 ml) warm water

1 package (2½ teaspoons) active dry yeast

1 cup (5 oz/155 g) unbleached all-purpose (plain) flour

DOUGH

½ cup (4 fl oz/125 ml) water

⅓ cup (3 fl oz/80 ml) each dry white wine and extra-virgin olive oil

1 tablespoon sea salt

2¾ cups (14 oz/435 g) plus 2 tablespoons unbleached all-purpose (plain) flour

2 teaspoons extra-virgin olive oil

TOPPING

18–20 green (spring) onions

3½ tablespoons extra-virgin olive oil

scant 1 teaspoon coarse sea salt, lightly crushed

⚜ Make the sponge 1 day before you plan to bake the bread: Put the warm water in a bowl and sprinkle the yeast over the water. Let stand for 2 minutes. Whisk with a fork to dissolve the yeast, then add the flour. Stir with a wooden spoon until smooth, then scrape down the spoon and the sides of the bowl. Cover the bowl tightly with plastic wrap and let stand in a cool place for 24 hours.

⚜ To make the dough, put the sponge in a heavy-duty mixer fitted with the paddle attachment. Add the water, wine, olive oil, sea salt, and 1 cup (5 oz/155 g) of the flour. Mix on low speed, gradually adding the remaining 1¾ cups (9 oz/280 g) plus 2 tablespoons flour to make a soft, sticky dough. Knead in the mixer for 5 minutes with the paddle attachment. Scrape down the paddle and the sides of the bowl, cover the bowl tightly with plastic wrap, and let rise in a cool place until doubled, about 1½ hours.

⚜ Generously grease a 12-by-17-inch (30-by-43-cm) rimmed baking sheet with the 2 teaspoons olive oil. Transfer the dough to the baking sheet and, with well-oiled fingers, pat and prod it to cover the bottom completely. It will be very elastic and will want to bounce back. Let the dough rest for 5 minutes, then pat and prod again. If the dough still refuses to cover the sheet completely, let rest for another 5–10 minutes and try again.

⚜ Cover the dough loosely with oiled plastic wrap to prevent it from drying out. Let rise in a cool place until puffy, about 1½ hours. While the dough rises, line the center rack of an oven with baking tiles or a baking stone and preheat the oven to 550°F (290°C), or the highest setting, for at least 45 minutes.

⚜ Meanwhile, make the topping: Unless the green onions are very slender, cut them in half lengthwise. Then cut crosswise into pieces ½ inch (12 mm) thick, using all the white and pale green parts and one-third of the dark green tops. You should have about 2 cups (6 oz/185 g). In a frying pan over medium-high heat, warm 1½ tablespoons of the olive oil. Add the green onions and sauté briskly until slightly softened, about 1 minute. Let cool.

⚜ Carefully lift the plastic wrap off the dough. Drizzle the surface with the remaining 2 tablespoons olive oil. Scatter evenly with the green onions, then sprinkle with the coarse salt. Dimple the dough vigorously all over with oiled fingertips. Bake until lightly browned and firm to the touch, 12–14 minutes. Remove from the oven and slide out of the baking sheet onto a rack. Let cool. Use a serrated knife to cut the focaccia into pieces of the desired size.

serves 8

Hot-Pepper Jelly Turnovers

These turnovers make the perfect starter or a quick bite when you are faced with unexpected company. Rather than chill the turnovers for an hour, freeze them on the baking sheet, transfer them to a container, arranging in layers separated by waxed paper, and freeze for up to 2 months. Bake the turnovers straight from the freezer, increasing the baking time by 5 minutes. Hot-pepper jelly, a tasty condiment with a long history in the South, was first made with the addition of chopped apples, probably because of their high level of natural pectin. If you are short on time, hot-pepper jelly is available at grocery stores.

southern pie pastry (page 250)

½ cup (5 oz/155 g) hot-pepper jelly (page 248)

½ cup (2 oz/60 g) shredded mild cheddar or hoop cheese

1 egg beaten with 1 tablespoon water

❧ Lightly butter a baking sheet. On a lightly floured work surface, roll out the pastry into a round about 12 inches (30 cm) in diameter.

❧ Using a 2-inch (5-cm) round fluted cookie cutter, cut out as many rounds as possible. Place about 1 teaspoon of the hot-pepper jelly and 1 teaspoon of the cheese in the center of each round. Fold the round in half, enclosing the jelly and cheese completely, and seal the edge with the tines of a fork that have been dipped in water.

❧ Place the turnovers on the prepared baking sheet and refrigerate. Gather together the pastry scraps, reroll the pastry, and cut out as many additional rounds as possible. Repeat the filling and folding, place on the baking sheet, and refrigerate all the turnovers for 1 hour.

❧ Preheat an oven to 425°F (220°C). Brush each turnover with some of the egg-water mixture. Bake the turnovers until golden brown, 22–25 minutes.

❧ Transfer the turnovers to a rack to cool. Serve warm or at room temperature.

makes about 24 turnovers

Mid-Atlantic

Heirloom Tomato Salad with Basil Vinaigrette

The rich, loamy soil of Long Island, New York, and New Jersey supports many crops, including plenty of tomatoes. Some varieties are more than a century old, heirlooms in distinctive and diverse sizes, shapes, colors, and flavors. Most folks are lured to these gems because of their unusual colors and shapes, but it is their flavor that truly sets them apart. Produced primarily on small farms, the stunning, vine-ripened fruits can be found in abundance at local farmers' markets and roadside stands. For an eye-catching assortment, choose Red Brandywines, Big Rainbows, and Black Krims, all of them large, tasty tomatoes perfect for slicing. Or use just a single Mortgage Lifter, a big specimen that typically tips the scales at more than two pounds (1 kg).

½ cup (½ oz/15 g) firmly packed fresh basil leaves

1 small clove garlic

3 tablespoons red wine vinegar

1 tablespoon Dijon mustard

⅔ cup (5 fl oz/160 ml) olive oil

kosher salt and freshly ground pepper to taste

2 lb (1 kg) mixed heirloom tomatoes

3 large balls fresh mozzarella cheese, about 3 oz (90 g) each, drained

kosher salt and freshly ground pepper to taste

6 fresh basil sprigs

🌿 To make the vinaigrette, in a food processor, combine the basil leaves, garlic, vinegar, and mustard. Process briefly to combine. With the machine running, gradually add the olive oil through the feeding tube, processing until completely incorporated. Season with salt and pepper. Pour the vinaigrette into a small serving pitcher or bowl, cover, and refrigerate until ready to serve or for up to 2 days.

🌿 Cut the tomatoes and mozzarella into ¼-inch (6-mm) slices. Arrange the tomato and cheese slices on a chilled large plate or individual plates. Sprinkle with salt and pepper. Drizzle with some of the basil vinaigrette and garnish with the basil sprigs. Pass the remaining vinaigrette at the table.

serves 6

Heirloom Vegetables

No one has come up with a solid definition for the heirloom vegetable. Must it first have been planted more than a century ago, or can it simply predate the arrival of hybrids on the scene? The toughest judges are the ones who insist that a true heirloom can never originate from a commercial source. For these inflexible people, heirlooms must be planted only from seeds handed down through the generations. What everyone can agree on is that heirloom vegetables are increasingly popular. Most home gardeners and small farmers are interested in these old-timers for their flavor, but a handful of garden historians seek them out for what they can reveal about the farms and backyards of an earlier time.

Tomatoes are arguably the most common of the heirloom vegetables, but keep an eye out for the many others worth sampling, such as Early Jersey Wakefield cabbage, which sports mild, crisp leaves in the first weeks of summer, or Early Scarlet Horn carrots, tasty roots that date back to seventeenth-century gardens. Seeds for these survivors and others can be purchased from specialty-seed catalogs. If you lack your own garden plot, look for the time-honored beauties at roadside farm stands.

California
Frittata with Spring Herbs and Leeks

Because of California's large Italian American population, frittatas are almost as common as omelets in the state's home cooking. Italian delicatessens in many neighborhoods sell thick frittatas by the slice for picnics or take-home suppers. Made with the fresh, tender herbs and young leeks that flood local farmers' markets in spring, this frittata has a distinctly California accent.

Use whatever delicate, nonwoody herbs are in your garden or in the market. Consider parsley, basil, mint, chervil, tarragon, dill, or chives. Leftover frittata makes a delicious sandwich on toasted bread.

2 tablespoons unsalted butter

4 cups (12 oz/375 g) thinly sliced leeks, including tender green tops

salt to taste, plus pinch of salt

freshly ground pepper to taste

6 eggs

½ cup (¾ oz/20 g) mixed minced fresh flat-leaf (Italian) parsley, basil, and mint

¼ cup (1 oz/30 g) grated Parmesan cheese

In a flameproof 10-inch (25-cm) nonstick frying pan over medium heat, melt the butter. Add the leeks, season with salt and pepper, and sauté until softened, about 15 minutes. Reduce the heat if needed to keep the leeks from browning.

In a large bowl, whisk the eggs to break them up. Whisk in the herbs, cheese, and pinch of salt. Add the eggs to the frying pan, stirring for just a few seconds to distribute the leeks evenly. Reduce the heat to low and cook very slowly until the eggs are set around the sides but still a little moist in the center, about 15 minutes.

Meanwhile, preheat a broiler (grill). When the eggs are ready, slip the frying pan under the broiler several inches from the heat source and broil (grill) until the top is lightly colored and the center is firm to the touch, 1 minute or less. Slide the frittata onto a cutting board. Serve warm, cut into wedges.

serves 4

Southwest

Tortilla Soup

Easy to make, tortilla soup consists of little more than a rich broth embellished with various garnishes as the diner sees fit. Serve it as the main course for a lunch or light supper, following cheese crisps (page 55) or guacamole (page 37) and preceding Orange Flan (page 237) or fresh fruit.

1 chicken, about 3½ lb (1.75 kg)

3 tablespoons corn oil, plus oil for deep-frying

2 tablespoons olive oil

2 large yellow onions, finely chopped

2 carrots, peeled and finely chopped

2 celery stalks, finely chopped

8 cloves garlic, finely chopped

2 teaspoons dried Mexican oregano

3 qt (3 l) water

1 can (14 oz/440 g) whole plum (Roma) tomatoes, drained and chopped

1 teaspoon salt, plus salt to taste

½ teaspoon freshly ground black pepper

6 blue or yellow corn tortillas, or a combination, each 6 inches (15 cm) in diameter

½ lb (250 g) Monterey jack cheese, diced

1 avocado, halved, pitted, peeled, and sliced

4 green (spring) onions, including tender green tops, sliced

½ cup (¾ oz/20 g) finely chopped fresh cilantro (fresh coriander)

2 limes, quartered

red pepper flakes

🌿 Cut the chicken into 5 pieces: 2 breast halves with wings, 2 whole legs, and the back. In a soup pot over medium heat, warm the 3 tablespoons corn oil. Working in batches, fry the chicken pieces until well browned on both sides, 12–14 minutes total. Transfer to a plate. Discard the oil.

🌿 Return the pot to medium-low heat and add the olive oil. Add the yellow onions, carrots, celery, garlic, and oregano. Cover and cook, stirring occasionally and scraping up any browned bits on the pan bottom, until the vegetables begin to soften, 10–12 minutes. Return the chicken to the pan. Add the water, tomatoes, 1 teaspoon salt, and black pepper and bring to a simmer. Cover partially and cook for 20 minutes.

Remove the white-meat pieces and reserve. Re-cover partially and simmer for another 20 minutes. Remove the dark-meat pieces and reserve. Re-cover partially and simmer for another 20 minutes. Remove from the heat and strain the broth, discarding the solids. Skim off as much fat from the surface as possible. You should have 2½ qt (2.5 l) broth. Skin the chicken pieces, then pull the meat from the bones and shred it. Add the shredded chicken to the broth.

🌿 Cut the tortillas in half. Cut each half crosswise into strips ¼ inch (6 mm) wide. Pour corn oil to a depth of 2 inches (5 cm) into a deep, heavy frying pan and heat over medium-high heat. Working in 2 batches, fry the strips, stirring once or twice, until crisp, about 1 minute. Using a slotted spoon, transfer to paper towels to drain. Season lightly with salt.

🌿 Bring the soup to a simmer. Taste and adjust the seasoning. Divide the cheese and tortilla strips evenly among warmed soup bowls. Put the avocado, green onions, cilantro, limes, and red pepper flakes in separate small bowls and place on the table. Ladle the simmering soup into the soup plates. Diners garnish their servings as desired.

serves 6

Main Dishes

Regional classics —
pot roast, chiles rellenos,
cracked crab, barbecue —
prevail at the table.

THE CHRISTMAS GIFTS have been opened in a flurry of wrapping paper and ribbon. The kids have paraded their new bikes around the block a dozen times, and the grandparents have used up all the film in their cameras. It must be lunchtime.

From the kitchen come the meaty, mouth-watering aroma of roasted meat and the sound of fat sizzling in a roasting pan. The dining-room table wears holiday dress: a heavy, white linen cloth, special-occasion china, and cut-crystal goblets. When the excited youngsters finally take their seats alongside parents, aunts, uncles, and grandparents, the celebratory roast is already on the table, an enormous, seven-bone prime rib of beef, its well-browned surface glistening, its rosy juices puddling on the platter. Could there be a more stately cut of meat, a more worthy candidate for the Christmas table? Let the carving begin.

Although beef dominates the American table today, not only for special occasions but at everyday meals, its widespread popularity is a modern phenomenon. Early settlers raised primarily pigs and chickens, which were easier to feed and manage. With the discovery of the

Preceding pages: Cattle graze in a Colorado pasture. This scenic state offers travelers a varied landscape of dramatic canyons, towering mountains, steep-sided mesas, vast plains, and swift-flowing rivers. **Top:** In 1782, Benjamin Franklin, statesman, inventor, and publisher, lobbied hard to have the wild turkey named the national bird of the United States. He lost the fight to the bald eagle. Despite that early slight, the turkey has become the centerpiece of the Thanksgiving table. **Above:** *Ristras* of chiles hung to dry in the hot Southwest sun will be used in sauces that flavor such dishes as enchiladas and *carne adovada*. **Right:** As the sign promises, Amarillo, located in the Texas Panhandle, is a perfect stop for folks with a hearty appetite. The town's restaurants and diners feature local beef in the form of hamburgers fresh off the grill, heaping bowls of chili con carne, and thick sirloin steaks.

wide-open West, cattle ranching took off in Texas and Arizona, and beef was brought to eastern markets slowly, via arduous cattle drives. One can only imagine how tough those longhorns were when they reached Chicago.

The arrival of the railroad and refrigerated railcars profoundly changed the future for beef. Chicago and Kansas City were the centers of a giant meat-packing industry that could ship fresh, high-quality western beef to the East Coast quickly and cheaply. Americans remain enthusiastic beef eaters, but they are choosing poultry and seafood more often, most likely with an eye on their health.

In modern New England, main-course cooking exhibits the no-nonsense practicality that one associates with the Yankee character. Revered dishes like pot roast and potpies reflect the down-to-earth hand of the region's cooks and a sensibility that scorns embellishment. A taste for pork persists in New England, a legacy of frontier days when the accommodating pig, which survived on scraps from the table, made the difference between having meat and not. Packed in deep barrels of salt, pork lasted through the long winter to

Left: A collection of colorful buoys, used to mark the location of lobster traps beneath the water's surface, hangs on a wall in Rock Harbor, Maine. **Top:** Full lobster traps are a regular sight off the New England coast. While more and more boats with state-of-the-art equipment are now seen, older vessels outfitted with traditional wooden traps are still popular. **Above:** Steamer clams, which flourish in cold northern waters, are a delicious treat in a clambake, quickly steamed, or breaded and deep-fried.

flavor innumerable pots of baked beans and clam chowder. Lawmakers accused today of playing "pork barrel politics" are typically trying to steer some funds to constituents, akin to reaching a little too deeply into the precious cold-weather stash.

The seafood rituals practiced up and down the Atlantic Coast become summer highlights for many families. Around Chesapeake Bay, on the Maryland coast, a blue-crab feast can materialize anywhere: at a park, in a backyard, at the shore. Picnic tables are draped with newspaper, and crab pots are filled with a spicy mixture of beer, vinegar, and Old Bay seasoning. When the hot shellfish arrive at the table, diners roll up their sleeves, and the messy picking begins.

The New England equivalent is a clambake or lobster boil, the former based on methods the early settlers learned from the Native Americans. An authentic clambake transpires at the shore, in a pit lined with hot stones and seaweed. For many current and former New Englanders, childhood memories include family trips to the Massachusetts

shore for a clambake or to Maine to eat lobster cooked in seawater and drenched in drawn butter.

Far from the coasts, the Midwest is proudly meat-and-potatoes country, from Chicago's famed steakhouses to Kansas City's barbecue joints to Milwaukee's outposts for bratwurst and beer. Calvin Trillin, the New York humorist and Kansas City native, raised eyebrows everywhere when he named Arthur Bryant's, a barbecue house in his hometown, "the single best restaurant in the world." Many pilgrims have trekked there since, but the truth is that Kansas City boasts dozens of worthy barbecue meccas, and this barbecue-revering community supports them all.

The signature dish of Kansas City is surely burnt ends, the bits and scraps of beef brisket that get singed in the smoking process. They're cut off, thrown back on the smoke, then chopped up and sauced to produce a local version of a sloppy joe.

In the South, where culinary trends get little respect, tradition rules, especially as southern cooks begin to realize that they are the

last repository of dying home arts, like how to make biscuits from scratch or deep-fry a chicken. Indeed, unlike many other Americans, most southerners have no fear of frying. They understand it, do it often, and relish the results. Local catfish farms provide one of the most popular candidates for southerners' cast-iron frying pans. Cooks dip the fillets in cornmeal, or in egg and fine cracker meal, then fry them crisp in hot, deep lard. Coleslaw and hush puppies—deep-fried balls of well-seasoned cornmeal batter—complete a catfish feast.

One modern southern cookbook writer takes more than two pages to instruct readers how to fry a chicken. The detailed method begins with a fresh-killed bird, meticulously cleaned and cut up at home. The frying itself is a carefully choreographed ballet, a rhythmic interplay of cook, pan, bird, and batter. A skillful performance requires complete focus, good timing, and patience.

Although southern fried chicken and Yankee pot roast clearly have regional roots,

Left: Sheep make up a minor part of the American livestock profile, with many of the animals raised for their wool and smaller numbers for their milk for cheese. **Top:** In Pennsylvania Dutch Country, known for its Amish residents and its traditional lifestyle, a farmer frees an eager chicken from its cage. **Above:** A stack of Navajo blankets awaits interested shoppers in Sedona, Arizona.

The corn-based *antojitos* of Mexico—the snack and street foods such as tacos, enchiladas, and tamales—have evolved into southwestern main dishes that would probably not be recognized below the border. In New Mexico, a cook might use blue corn tortillas to prepare enchiladas and the tortillas might be stacked with cheese rather than rolled. An Arizona enchilada would likely be made with a flour tortilla, with *carne seca* rolled up inside and a mild, flour-thickened red chile sauce on top.

Even in their Arizona renditions, which typically omit hot chiles, these ebullient dishes are indisputably beer food. No wine lover would seriously debate whether *chimichangas* go with red wine or white. In the Pacific Northwest, however, home to a burgeoning wine industry, such pleasurable discussions are occurring all

people everywhere have embraced these dishes and make them at home. The same can't be said for many of the main dishes that typify southwestern cooking, such as *carne adovada*, green corn tamales, and *chimichangas*. These regional specialties have traveled little, so food lovers must travel to them.

For one of the Southwest's great dishes, *chimichangas*, customers flock to El Charro Cafe in Tucson, Arizona. On a flour tortilla nearly the size of a hubcap, the cooks arrange a filling of *carne seca*, air-dried or oven-dried shredded beef that has been rubbed with lime, garlic, salt, and chiles. The tortilla is folded and deep-fried, then bathed in red chile sauce, topped with cheese, and baked. Sometimes the dish is given a caloric boost at the end with dollops of sour cream and guacamole.

the time as cooks try to determine what dishes best complement a Willamette Valley Pinot Noir or a Columbia Valley Merlot. Oregon's cool Willamette Valley has proved hospitable to the finicky Pinot Noir and to its sibling, the white wine–yielding Pinot Gris. In Washington, growers have had notable success with Cabernet Sauvignon, Merlot, and Riesling. Locals are justly proud of these wines, and local restaurants feature them prominently. Nature in its wisdom has provided for some superb food and wine marriages: grilled Pacific salmon with Oregon Pinot Noir, Thai-style mussels with Washington Riesling, steamed local manila clams with Oregon Pinot Gris.

In California, chefs and dinner-party hosts increasingly have to plan for the growing number of people who call themselves

Left: Along California's coastline, windswept bluffs rise above the pounding surf of the Pacific Ocean. **Below:** A seasoned grill master tends a southern barbecue, a culinary tradition with strong regional roots. The meat—usually, but not always, pork—is rubbed with spices and then cooked over a slow fire until it takes on the characteristic deep, smoky flavor of the South's best barbecues. **Bottom:** A tall building in the Windy City reflects a downtown scene. Chicago, the birthplace of the skyscraper, has been called a museum of modern architecture.

vegetarians. Some are strict constructionists, forswearing any animal products, even milk and cheese. Others, motivated more by health than by religion or animal-rights concerns, will readily eat fish and don't mind if the mushroom risotto includes chicken broth. To accommodate these "almost vegetarians," many restaurants regularly include at least one meatless main course on the menu and stand prepared to adapt dishes for customers. Tofu, the soybean curd that is a mainstay of Chinese and Japanese diets, has a large fan club in California, inspiring many restaurants to add tofu burgers, tofu kebabs, and other tofu-based main dishes to the menu.

Most Californians, however, enjoy meat, and some are asking more questions about its provenance. Many markets now offer organic chickens, antibiotic- and hormone-free beef, or meat from suppliers dedicated to humane animal husbandry. A few restaurants even state on their menus that all their meat and poultry comes from such sources.

Top: So famous that it is known worldwide by name, Chicago-style blues can be heard in clubs and concerts throughout the city. **Above:** Small or large, pale or dark, plain or flecked, beans appear in countless American regional dishes, from the Southwest's pot beans and the red beans and rice of New Orleans to New England navy bean soup and Boston baked beans. **Right:** Victorian-era brownstones line the streets of Boston's Back Bay neighborhood fronting the Charles River.

Southwest
Fajitas with Pico de Gallo

This example of how the Texas attitude transforms southwestern fare into something larger than life is based on Mexican arracheras, beef strips rubbed with garlic and lime juice and grilled.

FAJITAS

⅓ cup (3 fl oz/80 ml) fresh orange juice

3 tablespoons fresh lime juice

2 tablespoons each tequila and olive oil

4 cloves garlic, finely chopped

1 tablespoon each honey, soy sauce, and Worcestershire sauce

1 tablespoon minced canned chipotles en adobo

2½ lb (1.25 kg) skirt steaks

PICO DE GALLO

5 tomatoes, halved and seeded

⅔ cup (3½ oz/105 g) finely chopped yellow onion

2 jalapeño chiles, coarsely chopped

3 tablespoons fresh orange juice

2 tablespoons fresh lime juice

3 cloves garlic, coarsely chopped

¾ teaspoon salt, plus salt to taste

4 green New Mexico or Anaheim chiles, roasted and peeled (page 246), then chopped

⅓ cup (½ oz/15 g) chopped fresh cilantro (fresh coriander)

5 tablespoons (2½ fl oz/75 ml) olive oil

4 cloves garlic, finely chopped

2 large red bell peppers (capsicums), seeded and julienned

2 large poblano chiles, julienned

2 large yellow onions, thinly sliced

¾ teaspoon salt

½ teaspoon freshly ground pepper

24 flour tortillas, each 6 inches (15 cm) in diameter

16 large green (spring) onions

guacamole (page 37)

1½ cups (12 oz/375 g) sour cream

🌾 To make the *fajitas*, in a food processor or a blender, combine the orange juice, lime juice, tequila, olive oil, garlic, honey, soy sauce, Worcestershire sauce, and chipotles, and process until smooth.

🌾 Arrange the steaks in a single layer in a shallow dish, and pour the orange juice mixture over them. Cover and marinate, turning occasionally, at room temperature for at least 3 hours, or for up to overnight in the refrigerator. Bring to room temperature before proceeding.

🌾 To make the *pico de gallo*, coarsely chop half the tomatoes and place in a food processor. Add half the yellow onion along with the jalapeño chiles, orange juice, lime juice, garlic, and ¾ teaspoon salt. Process, stopping to scrape down the sides of the bowl, until finely and evenly chopped. Transfer to a bowl. Dice the remaining tomatoes and add to the bowl along with the chiles and the cilantro. Let stand at room temperature, stirring once or twice, for no more than 30 minutes. Taste and adjust the seasoning.

🌾 In a large frying pan over medium heat, warm 3 tablespoons of the olive oil. Add the garlic and cook, stirring once or twice, for about 2 minutes. Add the bell peppers, poblano chiles, yellow onions, salt, and pepper. Raise the heat to high and cook, tossing and stirring the vegetables, until they are lightly browned and becoming tender, 5–7 minutes longer. Remove from the heat and keep warm.

🌾 Prepare a hot fire in a grill with a cover. Preheat an oven to 400°F (200°C). Divide the tortillas into 4 equal stacks of 6 tortillas each. Wrap each stack tightly in aluminum foil. Set the packets in the oven for 10–15 minutes to warm the tortillas.

🌾 Lift the steaks from the marinade, reserving the marinade. Lay them on the grill rack 6 inches (15 cm) from the fire. Cover and grill, basting the meat with the marinade and turning occasionally, until the meat is done to your liking, 8–10 minutes for medium-rare. Stop basting at least 5 minutes before the meat is done. Transfer the steaks to a cutting board and tent loosely with aluminum foil. Brush the green onions with the remaining 2 tablespoons oil. Lay them on the grill rack, cover, and cook, turning once, until lightly marked by the grill rack and beginning to soften, about 4 minutes total.

🌾 Carve the steaks across the grain and on the diagonal into thin strips. Transfer to one end of a large platter. Spoon the reserved bell pepper mixture onto the other end of the platter. Top with the grilled green onions. Serve immediately with the *pico de gallo*, guacamole, sour cream, and tortillas. Diners arrange the steak, bell peppers mixture, *pico de gallo*, guacamole, and sour cream on the tortillas—along with the whole green onions—and fold the tortillas to enclose them.

serves 8

New England
Chicken Potpie

The filling ingredients for a classic New Englander's chicken potpie change little from cook to cook. Creamed chicken, carrots, onions, peas, and mushrooms are the staples in this favorite homey dish, but the choice of topping varies widely from biscuit to pie pastry to mashed potatoes, each of which complements the filling and delivers tasty results. Serving vessels can also vary, from individual crocks to earthenware to glass baking dishes. This potpie with a biscuit topping is served straight from the frying pan in keeping with its rustic New England character.

FILLING

8 tablespoons (4 oz/125 g) unsalted butter

½ lb (250 g) fresh button mushrooms, brushed clean and thinly sliced

2 carrots, peeled and diced

1 yellow onion, chopped

1 small red bell pepper (capsicum), seeded and diced

salt and freshly ground black pepper to taste

1 clove garlic, minced

1 teaspoon chopped fresh thyme

1¼ lb (625 g) boneless, skinless chicken breasts or thighs, trimmed of fat and cut into bite-sized pieces

¼ cup (1½ oz/45 g) all-purpose (plain) flour

2 cups (16 fl oz/500 ml) chicken stock

1 cup (8 fl oz/250 ml) heavy (double) cream or half-and-half (half cream)

1 cup (5 oz/155 g) fresh or frozen peas

2 tablespoons dry sherry

2 tablespoons chopped fresh chives

2 tablespoons chopped fresh flat-leaf (Italian) parsley

BISCUIT TOPPING

1 cup (5 oz/155 g) all-purpose (plain) flour

1 tablespoon sugar

2 teaspoons baking powder

½ teaspoon salt

pinch of ground cayenne pepper

5 tablespoons (2½ oz/75 g) unsalted butter, chilled, cut into ½-inch (12-mm) pieces

½ cup (4 fl oz/125 ml) buttermilk

❧ To make the filling, in an ovenproof frying pan 11 inches (28 cm) in diameter and 2½ inches (6 cm) deep, melt 2 tablespoons of the butter over medium heat. Add the mushrooms, carrots, onion, and bell pepper and season with salt and black pepper. Cook, stirring occasionally, until lightly browned and just barely tender, about 10 minutes. Add the garlic and thyme and cook, stirring, until fragrant, about 1 minute. Transfer to a large plate.

❧ Raise the heat to medium-high and add another 2 tablespoons butter to the frying pan. When the butter is melted, add the chicken and season with salt and black pepper. Cook, stirring often, until the chicken is lightly browned and barely cooked through, about 4 minutes. Scoop out the chicken and pile onto the plate with the vegetables.

❧ Reduce the heat to medium-low and melt the remaining 4 tablespoons (2 oz/60 g) butter in the pan. Add the flour and whisk constantly until bubbling but not browned, about 1 minute, scraping up any browned bits on the pan bottom. Pour in the stock and the cream, raise the heat to medium-high, and bring to a boil. Reduce the heat to low and simmer, stirring occasionally, until thickened, about 3 minutes. Add the reserved vegetables and chicken and the peas, sherry, chives, and parsley. Season with salt and black pepper. Remove from the heat and leave the filling in the pan. Cover with aluminum foil and set aside while you make the topping. (You may make the recipe up to this point, and refrigerate the filling for up to 6 hours. Uncover and reheat gently, stirring frequently, while making the biscuit dough.)

❧ Preheat an oven to 400°F (200°C).

❧ To make the biscuit topping, in a bowl, whisk together the flour, sugar, baking powder, salt, and cayenne pepper until well blended. Add the butter and, using a pastry blender, cut in the butter until the pieces are no larger than peas. Add the buttermilk and stir gently with a rubber spatula until a soft dough forms.

❧ Uncover the filling. Bring to a boil over medium-high heat, stirring occasionally, about 3 minutes. Reduce the heat to medium-low. Using 2 tablespoons, scoop up small amounts of the biscuit dough and drop onto the hot filling. The topping will almost completely cover the filling.

❧ Bake the potpie until the biscuits are lightly browned and a toothpick inserted into the center of one comes out clean, about 25 minutes. Spoon immediately onto warmed plates and serve.

serves 6

SAVORING AMERICA

Pacific Northwest
Steamed Thai
Red Curry Mussels

Mussels are among the most prolific wild seafoods of the Northwest, but virtually all of the mussels sold in the area are farm-raised and are primarily blue mussels, with shells that are deep blue-black on the outside and pearlescent on the inside. The abundant seafood melds well with the Asian influences that have become part of Northwest cooking. Here, Thai flavors dress up the plump shellfish.

1 tablespoon olive oil

½ cup (1½ oz/45 g) chopped green (spring) onion, including tender green tops

2 teaspoons Thai red curry paste

¾ cup (6 fl oz/180 ml) unsweetened coconut milk

¾ cup (6 fl oz/180 ml) dry white wine

3 lb (1.5 kg) mussels, scrubbed and debearded

coarse country bread

※ In a large pot over medium heat, warm the olive oil. Add the green onion and sauté until tender, 2–3 minutes.

※ Add the curry paste and cook, stirring, until aromatic and softened, about 1 minute. Stir in the coconut milk and wine and raise the heat to medium-high. Bring just to a boil, stirring to blend the ingredients evenly.

※ Add the mussels, discarding any that do not close to the touch, and cover the pot. Cook, occasionally shaking the pot gently for even cooking, until the mussels open, 3–5 minutes.

※ Using a slotted spoon, divide the mussels evenly among individual bowls, discarding any mussels that failed to open. Spoon the cooking liquids over the mussels, again dividing evenly.

※ Serve immediately, and pass the bread at the table. Place an empty bowl or two on the table for discarded shells.

serves 4

Petrale Sole Doré with Meyer Lemon–Caper Butter

A specialty of San Francisco's oldest seafood restaurants, sole doré is coated with egg before frying to give it a gilded (doré) appearance. Many knowledgeable diners consider the petrale—which is technically flounder, not sole—one of the best West Coast fish because of its fine texture and delicate flavor, but any small flatfish fillets will work in this preparation. You can also make the recipe with whole petrale sole or sand dabs, although the fish will take longer to cook. Serve it with steamed creamer potatoes and buttered fresh spinach. A glass of California Sauvignon Blanc or dry Chenin Blanc would be an ideal companion.

2 petrale sole fillets, about ¾ lb (375 g) total weight

salt and freshly ground pepper to taste

about ¼ cup (1½ oz/45 g) unbleached all-purpose (plain) flour

2 eggs

2 teaspoons olive oil

2 teaspoons plus 3 tablespoons unsalted butter

sweet paprika

2 tablespoons capers, coarsely chopped

1 tablespoon chopped fresh flat-leaf (Italian) parsley

1 tablespoon fresh Meyer lemon juice

2 Meyer lemon wedges

☙ Season the fillets on both sides with salt and pepper. Spread the flour on a sheet of waxed paper. Crack the eggs into a large, shallow bowl and beat until well blended. Place a large nonstick frying pan over medium-high heat. When it is hot, add the olive oil. When the oil is hot, add the 2 teaspoons butter. Do not allow it to burn.

☙ Working quickly, dip the fillets in the flour, coating both sides lightly and shaking off any excess. One at a time, dip the floured fillets in the beaten egg. Coat them thoroughly, allowing excess egg to drip back into the bowl. Place the fillets in the hot pan. Reduce the heat to medium-low.

☙ Cook until the underside is nicely browned, about 5 minutes. Turn carefully with an offset spatula.

serves 2

with lemon wedges and serve immediately.

☙ Transfer the fish to a warmed platter. Wipe out the frying pan with paper towels and return to low heat. Add the remaining 3 tablespoons butter, capers, parsley, and lemon juice. Swirl the pan until the butter melts. Pour the pan sauce over the fish. Garnish

Season the browned side with paprika. Continue cooking until the fish is opaque throughout when tested with a knife, 3–4 minutes longer.

Italian immigrants dominated California's fishing industry in its early years.

Basque Leg of Lamb with Peppers and Garlic

The Basque cuisine of the Mountain States, primarily Nevada, is distinct and distinctive but not as well known as other culinary specialties of the West. Coming here from their home region in Spain, the Basques worked—and still work—as shepherds, tending flocks that graze over mountain meadows. Served in hotel and boardinghouse dining rooms, in towns like Elko, Winnemucca, and Reno, Basque food is bold and rugged, like the Basques themselves.

Often featuring mutton or lamb and frequently seasoned with herbs and spices that recall those of Euskadi, the Basque homeland, this is simple, rib-sticking fare that is easy to like.

Given that lamb is also prized by Hispanic and Native American diners, that fragrant rosemary is a popular herb growing unattended in the Southwest and West, and that paprika is a close cousin of chile powder, this recipe seems right at home in the region. Serve the lamb and its accompaniment of meltingly tender roasted peppers with Pot Beans (page 171) and Green Rice (page 171).

1 leg of spring lamb, about 5½ lb (2.75 kg)

2 large cloves garlic, each cut into about 12 slivers, plus 18 whole large cloves, unpeeled

about 24 small fresh rosemary sprigs

2 tablespoons sweet Spanish or Hungarian paprika or medium-hot pure chile powder

6 tablespoons (3 fl oz / 90 ml) olive oil

8 large red bell peppers (capsicums), seeded and quartered lengthwise

½ teaspoon salt, plus salt to taste

½ teaspoon freshly ground pepper, plus pepper to taste

¾ cup beef stock or chicken stock

½ cup (4 fl oz / 125 ml) medium-dry red wine

SAVORING AMERICA

❧ Ask the butcher to remove the aitchbone, or hip-bone, from the lamb leg for easier carving, or do it yourself. Set the lamb, skin side down, on a roasting rack on a work surface. Using a paring knife, make a deep slit in the meaty portion of the upper surface of the lamb. Insert a sliver of garlic and a sprig of rosemary in the slit. Repeat, making 11 more evenly spaced slits and inserting a garlic sliver and a rosemary sprig in each one. Evenly dust the upper surface of the lamb with 1 tablespoon of the paprika, patting it firmly to encourage it to adhere. Turn the lamb skin side up on the rack and repeat the process of making evenly spaced slits and filling them with the remaining garlic slivers and rosemary sprigs. Dust the upper surface with the remaining 1 tablespoon paprika, and pat it into place. Set the rack in a shallow, flameproof roasting pan large enough to hold all the bell peppers without excessive crowding. Drizzle the upper surface with 1 tablespoon of the oil. Cover loosely with aluminum foil and let come to room temperature, about 1½ hours.

❧ Position a rack in the lower third of an oven and preheat to 450°F (230°C).

❧ Uncover the lamb, place in the oven, and roast for 15 minutes. Scatter the bell pepper quarters and garlic cloves in the roasting pan around the rack. Drizzle with the remaining 5 tablespoons (2½ fl oz / 75 ml) olive oil and sprinkle with the ½ teaspoon salt and the ½ teaspoon pepper. Stir well to coat evenly with the oil. Return the pan to the oven, reduce the oven temperature to 350°F (180°C), and continue to roast, stirring the bell peppers and garlic every 10–15 minutes to promote even cooking, until an instant-read thermometer inserted into the thickest part of the lamb away from the bone registers 135°–140°F (57°–60°C) for rare to medium-rare, about 1 hour, or until done to your liking. The bell peppers will be tender and lightly browned, and the garlic cloves will be soft inside their peels. Transfer the lamb to a platter, tent with aluminum foil, and let rest for 10 minutes. Using a slotted spoon, transfer the bell peppers and garlic to the platter, arranging them around the lamb.

❧ Set the roasting pan over medium-high heat on the stove top and add the stock and the wine. Bring to a brisk simmer and deglaze the pan, stirring to scrape up any browned bits from the pan bottom. Cook until the liquid is reduced by half and is becoming syrupy, about 5 minutes. Taste and adjust the seasoning. Pour through a fine-mesh sieve into a warmed gravy boat.

❧ Carve the lamb into thick slices and arrange on individual plates. Mound some of the bell peppers and garlic over the lamb. Drizzle with a bit of the pan sauce and serve immediately, passing the remaining sauce at the table.

serves 8

SAVORING AMERICA

The Corn Belt

Throughout the summer, fields of corn wrap the nation's midsection in a shimmering golden band. The term "corn belt" was born in the early twentieth century, when corn for livestock was the predominant crop in Iowa, Illinois, and Indiana, and in parts of Ohio, Minnesota, South Dakota, Nebraska, Kansas, and Missouri. Corn is now cultivated in nearly every state, and the Midwest has diversified into other feed crops. At the same time, the market for just-picked sweet corn has been steadily growing. In summer, the farm stands that dot highways and country lanes across America are stacked high with heirloom varieties alongside new "super-sweets," and the colors of the kernels vary from yellow, white, and checkerboard yellow and white to all shades of red and blue.

Midwestern cooks take advantage of the brief sweet corn season to make traditional dishes such as succotash, corn pudding, corn chowder, and covered-dish casseroles of every configuration. But one of the best ways to cook corn is the simplest: Peel back the tops of the husks, remove the silks, re-cover the kernels, tie the husks in place, and soak the ears in salted water for half an hour. Turn the ears over a charcoal fire for several minutes, and they are ready for a swabbing with butter and eating.

Midwest

Chicken and Cornmeal–Cheddar Dumplings

This version of chicken and dumplings adds a little texture to the dumplings with cornmeal and enriches them with cheddar cheese. As a first choice, use a stewing hen or roasting chicken, both of which are larger and more flavorful than young fryers.

CHICKEN

1 chicken (see note), 6–7 lb (3–3.5 kg)

3 carrots, peeled and cut into chunks

3 celery stalks, cut into chunks

2 yellow onions, quartered

1 head garlic, unpeeled, with top sliced off to reveal cloves

4 bay leaves

1 small bunch fresh flat-leaf (Italian) parsley

2 teaspoons black peppercorns

2 teaspoons kosher salt or coarse sea salt

1 teaspoon coriander seed

1 bunch fresh chives

DUMPLINGS

1¼ cups (6½ oz/200 g) stone-ground yellow cornmeal

1¼ cups (6½ oz/200 g) all-purpose (plain) flour

1½ teaspoons baking powder

¼ teaspoon baking soda (bicarbonate of soda)

½ teaspoon kosher salt or coarse sea salt

¼ teaspoon freshly ground white pepper

¼ cup (2 oz/60 g) chilled unsalted butter

¼ lb (125 g) sharp cheddar cheese, shredded

½ cup (4 fl oz/125 ml) buttermilk

2 eggs

☙ Several hours before serving, rinse the chicken and place in a large stockpot. Add the carrots, celery, onions, garlic, bay leaves, parsley, peppercorns, salt, and coriander seed. Add water to cover the chicken. Cover with a lid and bring to a boil. Pick out several chives and add to the pot. Reserve the remainder for the dumplings. When the chicken reaches a boil, reduce the heat to medium-low, cover partially, and cook until the meat starts to fall off the bone, about 2 hours. Remove from the heat, uncover, and let the chicken rest in the liquid for 30–60 minutes.

Lift the bird from pot, leaving all the seasonings and vegetables behind, and set aside to cool. Strain the broth through a fine-mesh sieve into a saucepan and skim off the fat. Place the pan over low heat and bring the broth to a simmer. Cook, uncovered, to reduce a little and concentrate the flavor. Remove the meat from the chicken carcass in large pieces. Set aside in a bowl, or refrigerate if dinner is more than a couple hours away.

About 30 minutes before serving, start the dumplings: Chop the reserved chives. You should have about ½ cup (⅔ oz/20 g). Pour 1 cup (8 fl oz/250 ml) of the broth into a large, deep frying pan with a tight-fitting lid. Add water to bring the depth to 2 inches (5 cm). Add the chicken meat to the remaining broth and heat through. Taste and adjust the seasoning. Keep warm.

In a large bowl, combine the cornmeal, flour, baking powder, baking soda, salt, white pepper, butter, and all but ¼ cup (1 oz/30 g) of the cheese. Using a pastry blender, cut the butter and the cheese into the dry ingredients until the mixture resembles coarse meal. In a bowl, beat the buttermilk and the eggs

until well blended. Stir in ¼ cup (⅓ oz/10 g) of the chives. Fold the buttermilk mixture into the dry ingredients and stir just until moistened. The dough will be firm but not dry. Adjust the flour and the buttermilk as needed.

Gently press the dough into a large disk about 1 inch (2.5 cm) thick. Using a 2-inch (5-cm) biscuit cutter or drinking glass, cut out the dumplings. Gather the scraps and cut out more dumplings. You should have 12–14. Bring the liquid in the frying pan to a slow boil over medium heat. Carefully slip in the dumplings in a single layer. They can get a little crowded, as they will remain separate. Set any extra dumplings aside for a second batch, which can be cooked after the first batch is served.

Reduce the heat to a steady gentle boil, cover, and cook until the dumplings puff up and are light and a toothpick inserted into the center comes out clean, 10–15 minutes. Sprinkle with the remaining cheese and chives and cover while you serve the chicken. In each bowl, put a little broth and some chicken pieces. Top with 1 or 2 dumplings and serve.

SAVORING AMERICA

South

Seafood Gumbo

Gumbo, a Creole dish that carries evidence of Spanish, French, and African kitchens, is synonymous with the cuisine of New Orleans. Recipes for gumbo vary from cook to cook, but good gumbos all have one thing in common: a dark roux. A roux is an equal combination of a fat—oil, butter, lard—and flour. The longer it is cooked, and thus the darker it becomes, the less thickening capabilities it will have, but the deeper its flavor will be. The roux defines the character of the gumbo, but the thickening of the stew is left to the addition of okra, also known as ladies' fingers, or gumbo filé, ground sassafras leaves usually found in small packets in well-stocked food stores.

½ cup (4 fl oz/125 ml) peanut oil

½ cup (2½ oz/75 g) all-purpose (plain) flour

2 celery stalks, chopped

2 yellow onions, chopped

1 green bell pepper (capsicum), seeded and chopped

3 cloves garlic, chopped

½ lb (250 g) okra, sliced

8 cups (64 fl oz/2 l) chicken stock

1 smoked ham hock, about 10 oz (315 g)

2 tablespoons Worcestershire sauce

1 teaspoon Tabasco sauce or other hot-pepper sauce, plus hot-pepper sauce for serving

½ cup (4 oz/125 g) bottled chili sauce or ketchup

1 bay leaf, crumbled

2 teaspoons chopped fresh sage

2 teaspoons chopped fresh rosemary

salt and freshly ground pepper to taste

1 lb (500 g) andouille or other spicy smoked sausage, sliced

3 cups (21 oz/655 g) long-grain white rice

6 cups (48 fl oz/1.5 l) water or chicken stock

1 tablespoon unsalted butter

½ lb (250 g) shrimp (prawns), peeled and deveined

½ lb (250 g) claw crabmeat, picked over for shells

½ lb (250 g) crayfish tails, peeled and deveined

½ cup (¾ oz/20 g) chopped fresh flat-leaf (Italian) parsley

filé powder (see note)

☙ In a large dutch oven or heavy stockpot over medium heat, combine the peanut oil and the flour to make a roux. Cook, stirring constantly, until the roux is a dark caramel color, 30–35 minutes. Be careful not to burn the roux, or a scorched taste will develop throughout the gumbo.

☙ Stir in the celery, onions, bell pepper, and garlic and cook, stirring occasionally, until thick and creamy, about 20 minutes longer. The mixture tends to seize up, but it will become smooth again once the vegetables release their natural moisture. Add the okra and cook until crisp-tender, about 3 minutes. (At this stage the mixture can be cooled and refrigerated for up to 3 days or frozen for up to 1 month).

☙ Add the 8 cups (64 fl oz/1 l) chicken stock to the pot along with the ham hock, Worcestershire sauce, 1 teaspoon Tabasco sauce, chili sauce or ketchup, bay leaf, sage, rosemary, salt, and pepper. Stir in the sausage and cook, uncovered, until the vegetables are tender, about 30 minutes. Retrieve the ham hock and set aside to cool.

☙ Meanwhile, place the rice in a fine-mesh sieve and rinse under running cold water to remove any impurities. Place the rice in a large saucepan with the 6 cups (48 fl oz/1.5 l) water or chicken stock, the butter, and salt and pepper to taste. Bring to a boil over high heat. Stir the rice, reduce the heat to low, cover, and cook, without removing the lid, until the liquid is absorbed, about 20 minutes. Remove from the heat and let stand for 10 minutes. Uncover and, using a fork, gently fluff the rice to separate the grains.

☙ Stir the shrimp, crabmeat, crayfish tails, and parsley into the gumbo. Remove from the heat, cover, and let stand until the shrimp begin to curl and turn pink, about 5 minutes.

☙ Remove the meat from the ham hock and shred, discarding the fat and bone. Stir the shredded meat into the gumbo, place over low heat, and bring to a gentle simmer.

☙ Divide the rice among warmed individual bowls. Ladle the gumbo over the rice. Sprinkle the filé powder on top and serve at once. Pass the Tabasco sauce at the table.

serves 8–10

SAVORING AMERICA

Carne Adovada

One way to understand the mystique of the red chile, which permeates the cooking of northern New Mexico, is to simmer up a batch of this specialty. Consisting of cubed pork, marinated and braised to falling-apart tenderness in puréed red chiles, the dish brims with a sweetly fiery essence. Serve the pork accompanied with Posole (page 166) and Green Rice (page 171), or use in an enchilada (page 103) in place of the chicken.

4 lb (2 kg) well-trimmed boneless pork shoulder, cut into ¾-inch (2-cm) cubes

3 cups (24 fl oz/750 ml) red chile purée (page 246)

3 cups (24 fl oz/750 ml) chicken stock

1 yellow onion, chopped

1 cup (8 fl oz/250 ml) amber beer

8 cloves garlic, chopped

1 tablespoon red wine vinegar

1 teaspoon salt, plus salt to taste

1 teaspoon dried Mexican oregano

¾ teaspoon red pepper flakes, or to taste (optional)

½ teaspoon each ground cumin, ground coriander, and freshly ground black pepper

※ In a large, nonaluminum bowl, stir together the pork cubes and the chile purée. Cover and refrigerate, stirring once or twice, for 24 hours.

※ Position a rack in the lower third of an oven and preheat to 325°F (165°C).

※ In a large, heavy nonaluminum pot over medium heat, combine the marinated pork, stock, onion, beer, garlic, vinegar, salt, oregano, red pepper flakes (if using), cumin, coriander, and black pepper. Bring to a simmer, stirring occasionally. Cover partially and bake, stirring once or twice, for 1 hour. Adjust the oven temperature as necessary to maintain a steady simmer. Uncover and continue to bake, stirring occasionally, until the meat is tender and the braising liquid has thickened, another 2 hours. Taste and adjust the seasoning. Divide among warmed individual plates and serve.

serves 6–8

Mustard and Peppercorn
Beef Filets

This recipe calls for one of the South's most prized products, bourbon, the only corn-based distilled liquor to have originated in the United States. It takes its name from Bourbon County, Kentucky, where it was first made in the 1800s and where it is still made today. Connoisseurs attribute bourbon's smooth, mellow flavor to the charred wood barrels in which it is aged and to the pure spring water that is mixed with the corn mash.

Here, a bourbon-laced sauce spiced with Dijon mustard cloaks beef filets that are seasoned with cracked pepper before being panfried. The savory Twice-Baked Stuffed Sweet Potatoes (page 190) make a wonderful accompaniment for this easy-to-prepare main dish.

2 teaspoons salt, plus salt to taste

3 tablespoons freshly cracked pepper, plus pepper to taste

1 tablespoon dry mustard

6 filets mignons, each about 6 oz (185 g) and 1¼ inches (3 cm) thick

¼ cup (2 oz/60 g) unsalted butter

2 tablespoons olive oil

2 cloves garlic, chopped

1 yellow onion, halved and thinly sliced

⅓ cup (3 fl oz/80 ml) aged Kentucky bourbon

½ cup (4 fl oz/125 ml) water

1 cup (8 fl oz/250 ml) beef stock

1 tablespoon fresh thyme leaves

½ cup (4 oz/125 g) sour cream

2 teaspoons coarse-grain Dijon mustard

1 can (10 oz/315 g) hearts of palm, drained and sliced on the diagonal ½ inch (12 mm) thick

2 tomatoes, seeded and diced

☙ In a small bowl, stir together the 2 teaspoons salt, 3 tablespoons pepper, and dry mustard. Sprinkle the mixture evenly over both sides of the steaks, pressing it into the meat with your hands.

☙ In a deep frying pan over medium-high heat, melt the butter with the olive oil. Add the filets and cook for 2 minutes. Reduce the heat to medium, turn the filets, and cook for 2 minutes longer.

Continue to cook, turning the steaks every 2 minutes, until done as desired, about 6 minutes longer for rare, 8 minutes longer for medium-rare, and 10 minutes longer for well done. Transfer the steaks to a platter and tent with aluminum foil to keep warm.

☙ Add the garlic and the onion to the pan over medium heat and cook, stirring occasionally, until the onion is soft, about 5 minutes. Add the bourbon (being careful, as the pan might flame), and deglaze the pan, scraping any browned bits on the pan bottom. Add the water and the beef stock and simmer until reduced by half, about 5 minutes.

☙ Add the thyme and the sour cream and cook, stirring, for 1 minute. Stir in the Dijon mustard and any accumulated juices from the cooked steaks. Add the hearts of palm and heat through, about 1 minute. Season with salt and pepper.

☙ Spoon the warm sauce over the steaks. Garnish with the tomatoes and serve at once.

serves 6

California

Grilled Salmon with Shaved Fennel Salad

Commercially fished in waters from Central California to the northern border, wild salmon arrives in markets in late spring and summer, conveniently coinciding with barbecue season.

2 fennel bulbs, plus ¼ cup (⅓ oz/10 g) chopped leaves

2 large shallots, halved and very thinly sliced

8 tablespoons (4 fl oz/125 ml) extra-virgin olive oil

1½–2 tablespoons fresh lemon juice

1 side of salmon, about 3½ lb (1.75 kg), with skin intact

1 lemon, very thinly sliced

❀ Cut the fennel bulbs in half through the core, then slice crosswise as thinly as possible. Put the fennel in a bowl along with the fennel leaves, shallots, and 6 tablespoons (3 fl oz/90 ml) olive oil. Add 1½ tablespoons lemon juice, salt, and pepper. Toss well, taste, and add more lemon juice if desired. Let marinate at room temperature for 45 minutes.

❀ Rub your fingers along the surface of the salmon, and then use needle-nose pliers or tweezers to remove any fine pin bones. Rub the flesh side with the remaining 2 tablespoons olive oil. Season generously with salt and pepper. Arrange the lemon slices down the center of the flesh side of the salmon, overlapping them.

❀ Prepare a hot fire in a grill. When the coals are gray, arrange them in 2 piles on either side of the grill bed, leaving a space between them large enough for the salmon. Put the salmon on the grill, skin side down. Cover the grill, leaving the vents wide open. Cook until the salmon is firm to the touch, 20–25 minutes.

❀ Serve the fish directly from the grill. Use a long offset spatula to lift portions of the salmon from the skin, leaving the skin on the grill and dividing the fish evenly among individual plates. With a slotted spoon, put some of the fennel salad alongside the salmon, dividing it evenly. Serve immediately.

serves 8

Pacific King Salmon

The salmon, with its distinctive orange-pink flesh, is a West Coast icon—a fish that seduces both the eye and the palate. From Alaska to California, salmon fishermen maintain an age-old way of life, going out into Pacific Coast waters to retrieve the glistening, silvery fish for salmon lovers across the country. Five species are native to the Pacific Coast: king (Chinook), sockeye (red), coho (silver), pink (humpback), and chum (keta). But the king is easily the most sought after, with anglers and eaters quick to praise its natural richness—thanks to a high fat content—and its impressive size—an average weight between twenty and twenty-five pounds (10 and 12.5 kg) each.

The most prized kings are those caught in the wild runs that begin in late spring and continue into early fall. Lucky West Coast residents can buy the salmon directly from fishing boats at key docks, including San Francisco's Fishermen's Wharf, the port of Astoria, Oregon, and Seattle's Fishermen's Terminal. This celebrated fish needs only the simplest treatment. Locals like to grill or panfry king salmon and serve it with fresh salsa, a scattering of herbs, or a fruit chutney. Because of their richness, kings are also ideal for the smoker: typically, the fillets are brined and then are set over smoldering wood chips that infuse them with flavor and gently cook the flesh.

New England
Roast Turkey

The stuffing for this Thanksgiving bird calls for apples and apple cider, two pantry items stocked in nearly every New England kitchen come fall.

APPLE STUFFING

½ cup (4 oz/125 g) unsalted butter, plus extra for dotting top

2 yellow onions, chopped

4 large celery stalks, chopped

2 large red apples, cored and chopped

2 cloves garlic, minced

½ cup (¾ oz/20 g) chopped fresh flat-leaf (Italian) parsley

3 tablespoons chopped fresh sage

2 tablespoons chopped fresh thyme

1½ cups (12 fl oz/375 ml) apple cider

1 loaf coarse country bread, about ¾ lb (375 g), cut into small cubes and lightly toasted

2½ teaspoons kosher salt, or to taste

1 teaspoon freshly ground pepper, or to taste

1 turkey, 13–14 lb (6.5–7 kg)

10–12 fresh sage leaves

1 large navel orange, very thinly sliced crosswise

kosher salt and freshly ground pepper to taste

½ cup (4 oz/125 g) unsalted butter

2 large carrots, peeled and quartered crosswise

2 yellow onions, each quartered lengthwise

1½ cups (12 fl oz/375 ml) apple cider, plus extra for drizzling

GRAVY

2–3 cups (16–24 fl oz/500–750 ml) chicken stock

½ cup (2½ oz/75 g) all-purpose (plain) flour

❧ To make the stuffing, in a large, heavy frying pan over medium heat, melt the ½ cup (4 oz/125 g) butter. Add the onions, celery, and apples and cook, stirring frequently, for 10–12 minutes. Stir in the garlic, parsley, sage, and thyme and sauté for about 3 minutes. Transfer to a bowl. Pour the apple cider into the pan, raise the heat to high, and bring to a boil, stirring to loosen any brown bits on the pan bottom. Boil until reduced to 1 cup (8 fl oz/250 ml), about 2 minutes. Add the reduced cider to the vegetables along with the bread cubes, 2½ teaspoons salt,

and 1 teaspoon pepper. Toss to coat. The stuffing should just hold together when mounded on a spoon. Adjust the seasoning. Cover and refrigerate until cold.

❧ Position an oven rack in the lower third of an oven and preheat to 325°F (165°C). Remove the neck, giblets, and liver from the turkey and reserve for stock or gravy, if desired. Rinse the turkey inside and out and pat dry. Beginning at the tail cavity, gently slide your fingers under the skin to loosen it. Place a sage leaf on each orange slice and slide each slice and leaf under the skin, sage leaf up, spacing them evenly to cover the entire breast. Season both cavities with salt and pepper, then loosely stuff with the stuffing. Return any leftover stuffing to the refrigerator. Fold the wings back to secure the neck skin and loosely tie the legs together with kitchen string.

❧ Place the stuffed bird in a large, heavy roasting pan with sides no higher than 2 inches (5 cm). Sprinkle with salt and pepper and smear with the butter. Scatter the carrots and onions around the bird. Pour in the 1½ cups (12 fl oz/375 ml) apple cider. Bake, basting every 30 minutes, until the thigh juices run clear when pierced and an instant-read thermometer inserted into the thickest part of the thigh away from the bone registers 175°F (80°C), 4–4½ hours.

❧ Spoon the reserved stuffing into a buttered baking dish, drizzle with apple cider, and dot with butter. Cover and bake alongside the turkey during the last hour of roasting. For a crispy topping, uncover during the last 30 minutes.

❧ When the turkey is done, transfer it to a platter. Spoon the stuffing from the cavities into a serving dish and keep warm. If the separately cooked stuffing is ready, remove from the oven and keep warm. Tent the bird loosely with aluminum foil and let rest for 15 minutes before carving.

❧ To make the gravy, pour the juices from the roasting pan through a large sieve set over a 2-qt (2-l) glass measuring pitcher. Allow the fat to rise to the top. Spoon off ½ cup (4 fl oz/125 ml) of the fat into the roasting pan, then spoon off and discard the remaining fat. Add enough chicken stock to the reserved juices to total 6 cups (48 fl oz/1.5 l). Set the roasting pan over medium heat, whisk in the flour, and whisk constantly for about 3 minutes. Pour in the juices-stock mixture and whisk until blended. Cook, whisking frequently, until the gravy boils and thickens, about 5 minutes. Adjust the seasoning.

❧ Carve the turkey. Pour the gravy into a serving bowl. Serve the gravy and stuffing alongside.

serves 10–12

New England

Fish and Chips

Sprinkle a little malt vinegar on this batter-fried fish, and you will have a dish worthy of serving in any London pub, which is where this classic combination made its name. Of course, many New England "pubs" opt for lemon wedges and tartar sauce rather than malt vinegar. Wrapping the fish and chips—also known as french fries—in paper will add a further touch of New England authenticity to the recipe.

Cod were once plentiful in the icy ocean waters off New England, but overfishing has depleted their numbers. This might explain some of the confusion over what constitutes true scrod, as it is sometimes sold as or confused with pollack, haddock, or other fish. Scrod is the official term for the smallest of the Atlantic cods. If it is unavailable, choose any white fish with medium-firm flesh, such as cod, pollack, or haddock, while avoiding their more delicate-fleshed relatives, such as flounder, sole, whiting, or hake.

corn oil for deep-frying
4 large russet potatoes, unpeeled
salt to taste, plus 1 teaspoon

1 cup (5 oz/155 g) all-purpose (plain) flour

1½ teaspoons baking powder

½ teaspoon freshly ground pepper

½ cup (4 fl oz/125 ml) water

½ cup (4 fl oz/125 ml) milk

1 egg, lightly beaten

2½ lb (1.25 kg) scrod or other firm white fish fillets, cut into strips 4 inches (10 cm) long by 2 inches (5 cm) wide

lemon wedges, malt vinegar, or tartar sauce (page 60) (optional)

☙ Pour the corn oil to a depth of 3 inches (7.5 cm) into a deep-fat fryer or deep, heavy saucepan and heat over medium-high heat to 375°F (190°C).

☙ Meanwhile, prepare the potatoes: Have ready a large bowl of cold water. Cut the potatoes into strips 2½ inches (6 cm) long by ⅜ inch (1 cm) wide by ⅜ inch (1 cm) thick. As they are cut, immerse them in the water. Leave the potatoes to soak while the oil heats. Preheat an oven to 225°F (110°C). Line a large baking sheet with paper towels or brown paper.

☙ When the oil is almost up to temperature, drain the potatoes and dry well with paper towels. It is important to dry thoroughly, or the oil will spatter. Add one-third of the potatoes to the hot oil and cook until golden brown, about 4 minutes. Using a slotted spoon, transfer the potatoes to the prepared baking sheet and sprinkle generously with salt. Place in the oven to keep warm. Repeat with the remaining potatoes in 2 batches, allowing the oil to regain its correct frying temperature between the batches.

☙ While the potatoes are cooking, in a bowl, sift together the flour, baking powder, 1 teaspoon salt, and pepper. Once the potatoes are cooked, whisk the water, milk, and egg into the dry ingredients until smooth and well blended.

☙ Pat the fish strips dry. Dip a strip into the batter and carefully slip into the hot oil. Repeat with a few more pieces, dipping only 1 strip at a time. Do not crowd the pot or the fish will not brown. Cook, carefully turning the fish as needed with the slotted spoon, until golden brown, about 4 minutes. Transfer to the baking sheet, sprinkle with salt, and keep warm in the oven. Repeat with the remaining fish in batches, allowing the oil to regain its correct frying temperature between the batches.

☙ Serve the fish and chips in napkin-lined bowls with lemon wedges, malt vinegar, or tartar sauce.

serves 6

Midwest
Beer-Braised Bratwursts

Beginning in the mid-1800s, German immigrants settled throughout the Midwest, where pockets of their culinary influence still thrive, as in this signature dish of bratwursts and sauerkraut from Milwaukee.

6 cups (3 lb/1.5 kg) sauerkraut

2 tablespoons safflower oil

3 yellow onions, chopped

3 cloves garlic, crushed (optional)

1 teaspoon paprika

½ teaspoon caraway seed

1 tablespoon light brown sugar

pinch of cayenne pepper (optional)

1 bottle (12 fl oz/375 ml) beer, preferably ale

8 bratwursts, 1½–2 lb (750 g–1 kg) total weight

kosher salt or coarse sea salt and freshly ground white pepper to taste

꽃 Preheat an oven to 375°F (190°C). Place the sauerkraut in a colander, rinse briefly, and drain. Rinse again if you prefer a milder taste. In a large, deep ovenproof frying pan over medium-high heat, warm the safflower oil. Add the onions and fry, stirring often, for 3–4 minutes. Stir in the garlic (if using), reduce the heat to medium-low, and cook, stirring occasionally, for 10 minutes. Sprinkle with the paprika, caraway, brown sugar, and cayenne pepper (if using). Toss to coat and heat until fragrant. Stir in the sauerkraut and beer, raise the heat to medium-high, bring to a boil, and remove from the heat.

꽃 Using a fork, prick each bratwurst in a couple of places. Arrange on top of the sauerkraut, pushing them into the mixture a bit. Cover tightly, place in the oven, and oven-braise until most of the liquid is absorbed and the sausages are plump, 40–45 minutes. Taste and adjust the seasoning with salt and white pepper.

꽃 To reduce the juices further, remove the sausages and keep warm. Place the frying pan over medium-high heat and cook the sauerkraut, stirring often, until the juices have thickened. Divide the sausages and sauerkraut among individual plates and serve.

serves 6–8

Southwest

Red Chile Chicken–Cheese Enchiladas

Constructed of corn tortillas; filled with cheese, ground beef or shredded chicken; rolled or stacked, flat; sauced with chiles; and topped or not with a sunny-side-up egg, enchiladas are a case study in proportion, balance, and quality—in other words, elegance on the plate.

CHICKEN FILLING

1 chicken, about 3½ lb (1.75 kg), quartered

about 2½ qt (2.5 l) water

1 small yellow onion, sliced

1 carrot, peeled and chopped

4 cloves garlic, finely chopped

1 teaspoon each dried Mexican oregano and salt

½ teaspoon ground coriander

1 bay leaf

½ teaspoon freshly ground pepper

RED CHILE ENCHILADA SAUCE

3 tablespoons olive oil

⅔ cup (3½ oz/105 g) finely chopped yellow onion

3 cloves garlic, finely chopped

¾ teaspoon dried Mexican oregano

2 tablespoons unbleached all-purpose (plain) flour

3 cups (24 fl oz/750 ml) red chile purée (page 246)

1 teaspoon salt

½ teaspoon freshly ground pepper

corn oil for frying

12 yellow or blue corn tortillas, each 6 inches (15 cm) in diameter

1 small yellow onion, finely chopped

salt to taste

¾ lb (375 g) Monterey jack or mild cheddar cheese, coarsely shredded

2 green (spring) onions, thinly sliced

shredded crisp lettuce such as romaine (cos)

To make the sauce, in a heavy saucepan over medium-low heat, warm the olive oil. Add the onion, garlic, and oregano, cover, and cook, stirring once or twice, for 10 minutes. Uncover, stir in the flour, and cook without browning, stirring frequently, for 2 minutes. Whisk in the chile purée and the reserved 2 cups (16 fl oz/500 ml) cooking liquid, and add the salt and the pepper. Bring to a simmer, cover partially, and cook, stirring occasionally, until reduced to 4 cups (32 fl oz/1 l), about 30 minutes. The sauce can be used immediately, but will improve in flavor if made in advance. Let cool, cover, and refrigerate for up to 3 days.

Position a rack in the upper third of an oven and preheat to 375°F (190°C). Pour corn oil to a depth of 1 inch (2.5 cm) into a frying pan and place over medium-low heat. One at a time, lower a tortilla into the oil. The aim is to make the tortillas tender, not to cook them until crisp. They should bubble gently around the edges in the oil, not blister. This will take about 2 minutes. Using tongs, transfer the tortillas to paper towels to drain.

Spread the bottoms of 4 round, 8-inch (20-cm) ovenproof dishes with a bit of the sauce. Transfer the remaining sauce to a wide, shallow dish. One at a time, dip 4 tortillas in the sauce and transfer to the individual baking dishes. Divide half the chicken evenly among the 4 sauced tortillas. Sprinkle half the yellow onion over the chicken, dividing it evenly. Season with salt. Scatter one-third of the cheese over the chicken, dividing it evenly. Sauce 4 more tortillas and set on top of the cheese layers. Add the remaining chicken and yellow onion and top with half the remaining cheese. Sauce the last 4 tortillas and set on top of the cheese layers. Drizzle the enchilada stacks with any remaining sauce. Scatter the remaining cheese evenly over the stacks.

Bake until the sauce is bubbling, the cheese has melted, and the enchiladas are piping hot, 10–12 minutes. Transfer the enchiladas to individual plates. Scatter the green onions and lettuce on top of each stack, and serve immediately.

serves 4

To make the chicken filling, rinse the chicken quarters. In a deep frying pan large enough to hold the chicken in a single layer, arrange the quarters and pour in the water to cover. Add the onion, carrot, garlic, oregano, salt, coriander, bay leaf, and pepper. Place over medium heat and bring slowly to a simmer,

turning once or twice. Cover partially and cook until the chicken is just cooked through but the meat is still moist and tender, about 5 minutes. Let cool to room temperature in the cooking liquid. Remove the chicken from the pan, then pour the contents of the pan through a sieve, reserving 2 cups (16 fl oz/500 ml) of the liquid for the chile sauce. Remove and discard the skin from the chicken quarters. Remove the meat from the bones and shred it.

Olives and Olive Oil

Franciscan friars planted the first olives in California and used the precious oil for cooking, lighting, and soap. As the monks moved northward from San Diego, they planted olives at each newly established mission. Some of those historic trees still stand today. The Mission olive, named for these origins, remains a major variety, along with the Ascolano, Sevillano, and Manzanillo. California's mild Mediterranean climate proved hospitable to the olive, and over time, the state established a thriving canning industry. Most of the production today is in the warm inland valleys, and 90 percent of the crop is processed as ripe black olives. That name is a misnomer, however, because the olives are actually picked green, or underripe. During the curing process, the olives are oxygenated to turn them a deep, shiny black familiar to consumers.

In the 1980s and 1990s, several pioneers with a passion for fine olive oil began importing and planting trees from France, Italy, and Spain. Others restored neglected old trees with an eye to oil production. Because the United States has no legal definition for extra-virgin olive oil, some of the new producers banded together in 1992 to form the California Olive Oil Council (COOC), which soon developed stringent standards for the state's extra-virgin oil. Today, a highly trained panel of COOC tasters certifies California-grown oils as extra virgin. In 2002, the COOC panel received official recognition from the International Olive Oil Council, an important acknowledgment of the panel's standards and tasting skills.

With this new spotlight on the state's olive oil, some property owners with a few inherited olive trees have begun picking and processing their fruit for the first time. In the Sonoma County town of Glen Ellen, homeowners can bring their harvest, however small, to the local mill on designated community pressing days. While the olives are pooled and washed, then crushed and kneaded in a state-of-the-art Italian mill, the participants sip wine and share harvest stories. After a river of green oil flows from the centrifuge, harvesters head home with their proportion of the oil produced.

California

Golden Beet Risotto

Golden beets, cooked and grated, make a lovely if unconventional addition to risotto, a way of showcasing the multicolored harvest of California's small farms.

6 golden beets, about 1½ lb (750 g) total weight

6 tablespoons (3 fl oz/90 ml) extra-virgin olive oil

½ yellow onion, minced

7–8 cups (56–64 fl oz/1.75–2 l) chicken stock

1 clove garlic, minced

2 cups (14 oz/440 g) Arborio rice

½ cup (4 fl oz/125 ml) dry white wine

salt and freshly ground pepper to taste

❧ Preheat an oven to 400°F (200°C). Remove the beet tops, if attached, leaving ½ inch (12 mm) of the stem. Put the beets in a baking dish and add water to a depth of ¼ inch (6 mm). Cover and bake until a knife pierces the beets easily, about 50 minutes.

Remove the beets from the oven and, when cool enough to handle, peel and grate coarsely.

❧ Warm 2 tablespoons of the olive oil in a large pot over medium-low heat. Add the onion and sauté until soft, about 8 minutes. In a saucepan, bring the stock to a simmer over medium heat. Adjust the heat to keep the liquid just below a simmer.

❧ Add the garlic to the onion and sauté for about 1 minute. Add the rice and raise the heat to medium. Cook, stirring, for about 2 minutes. Add the wine and simmer until it has been absorbed, about 1 minute. Begin adding the hot stock ½ cup (4 fl oz/125 ml) at a time, stirring often and adding more stock only when the previous addition has been absorbed. After 10 minutes, stir in the grated beets. Continue adding hot stock until the rice is tender but firm and the risotto is creamy, 10–12 minutes longer. If you need more liquid, use boiling water.

❧ Cover the pot, remove from the heat, and let stand for 2 minutes. Uncover and stir in the remaining 4 tablespoons (2 fl oz/60 ml) olive oil. Season with salt and pepper. Serve the risotto in warmed shallow bowls.

serves 6

Great Plains

Slow-Smoked Brisket with Homemade BBQ Sauce

Texas may have staked a claim on BBQ beef, but people in the Great Plains will never cede the right to call pit-cooked tender smoked brisket a local specialty. The recipe may seem long and complicated, but the process makes for a rewarding day, especially if you build a social gathering around the event.

BRINE

1 cup (8 oz/250 g) kosher salt

1 head garlic, unpeeled, with top sliced off to reveal cloves

8 bay leaves

1 whole trimmed beef brisket, 7–9 lb (3.5–4.5 kg)

SAUCE

½ cup (4 fl oz/125 ml) corn oil

2 large white onions, chopped

1 teaspoon kosher salt or coarse sea salt

1 tablespoon New Mexico chile powder

2 teaspoons freshly ground black pepper, plus pepper to taste

½ teaspoon each celery seed and ground allspice

¼ teaspoon ground mace

¼ teaspoon ground cayenne pepper, or to taste

¼ cup (2 fl oz/60 ml) each distilled white vinegar and Dijon mustard

2 tablespoons light brown sugar

1 tablespoon molasses

2 cans (28 oz/875 g each) whole plum (Roma) tomatoes with juice

granulated sugar and salt to taste

RUB

1 tablespoon each black peppercorns, white peppercorns, celery seed, caraway seed, and mustard seed

1 loaf soft, white sandwich bread (optional)

❧ Begin brining the brisket 1 or 2 days before smoking. Select a stockpot or other vessel large enough to hold the brisket and about 4 qt (4 l) of water. Pour in 2 qt (2 l) of water. Add the salt, garlic, and bay leaves. Stir to dissolve the salt. Rinse the brisket under running cold water and place in the brine. Add water just to cover. Cover and refrigerate for 24–36 hours, turning the meat once or twice.

❧ The day before smoking the meat, make the sauce: In a large, heavy nonaluminum pan over medium-high heat, warm the corn oil. Add onions and salt and sauté, stirring often, for 3 minutes. Add the chile powder, 2 teaspoons black pepper, celery seed, allspice, mace, and cayenne pepper and stir and toss to coat the onions. Cook until fragrant, about 1 minute. Pour in the vinegar and stir to scrape up any browned bits on the pan bottom. Stir in the mustard, brown sugar, and molasses. When the mixture comes to a boil, add the tomatoes and return to a boil. Reduce the heat to very low, cover partially, and cook, stirring occasionally and mashing the tomatoes, for 3–3½ hours. Using a blender and working in batches, purée the sauce, adding water as needed to reach the desired consistency. It should be thick but pourable. Adjust the seasoning with sugar, salt, and black pepper. Cover and refrigerate until ready to use.

❧ On the morning you will begin smoking, make the rub: In a spice mill or clean coffee grinder, combine the black and white peppercorns, celery seed, caraway seed, and mustard seed and grind finely. Remove the meat from the brine and rinse thoroughly. Pat dry with paper towels and rub with the spice mixture, coating well on all sides. Set aside for 1–2 hours to come to room temperature.

❧ Prepare a fire for indirect-heat cooking in a covered grill, building it on one side of the grill bed and starting with about 2 qt (2 l) hardwood charcoal. Light the fire, and open the vent beneath it. Place a drip pan on the other side of the grill bed. When the coals are almost all white, spread them a little but keep them to one side. Add a handful of fresh charcoal. Replace the grill rack.

❧ Place the brisket, fat side up, on the rack over the drip pan. The fire should not be under the meat. Close the lid and open the vent on the lid so an opening is over the meat. Check the fire every 30 minutes to make sure it is still hot, adding 6 or 7 coals at a time. The goal is to keep the temperature inside the grill around 220°F (105°C). If it is too high, the meat will be dry; if it is too low, microbial growth will occur. Continue smoking the brisket for 8–10 hours. Do not worry if the crust turns very dark. The brisket is ready when it is tender and firm but not dry when cut into at the center and an instant-read thermometer inserted into the thickest part resisters at least 160°F (71°C). Remove from the grill and let rest for 15 minutes.

❧ Gently reheat the barbecue sauce. Slice the brisket thinly against the grain and serve with the sauce and with the sandwich bread, if desired.

serves 16

To make the teriyaki sauce, in a small saucepan over medium-high heat, combine the soy sauce, mirin, minced green onion, and ginger and bring just to a boil. Let cool completely. Transfer 1 cup (8 fl oz/250 ml) of the cooled sauce to a shallow dish. Add the halibut steaks, turning to coat. Marinate for about 30 minutes at room temperature, turning the steaks once or twice.

Prepare a fire in a grill. Reheat the remaining teriyaki sauce over medium heat, then add the cornstarch mixture, and stir until the sauce has thickened, about 2 minutes. Set the teriyaki glaze aside.

Brush the grill rack lightly with oil. Lift the steaks from the marinade, allowing the excess liquid to drip off, and set on the grill. Grill, turning once, until there is a touch of translucency at the center of the steaks when tested with a knife (the steaks will continue to cook through once taken from the grill), 3–5 minutes on each side. Remove the steaks from the grill, brush both sides with the teriyaki glaze, and divide among warmed individual plates. Scatter the sliced green onion over the tops.

serves 4

Pacific Northwest
Grilled Halibut Teriyaki

Halibut is one of the most distinctive fish of the Pacific Northwest, with much of the catch coming from the deep, frigid waters of the Gulf of Alaska. The large flatfish is related to flounder and sole but is unique in its potential size, which can reach well over a hundred pounds. Serve these teriyaki-glazed halibut steaks with steamed white rice with toasted sesame seeds stirred in just before serving.

¾ cup (6 fl oz/180 ml) each soy sauce and mirin

2 tablespoons minced green (spring) onion, including tender green tops, plus sliced green onion for garnish

1 tablespoon peeled and minced or grated fresh ginger

4 halibut steaks, about ½ lb (250 g) each

2 teaspoons cornstarch (cornflour) dissolved in 1 tablespoon water

SAVORING AMERICA

Southwest

Tequila Shrimp Pasta with Tomato-Cream Sauce

One reason southwestern food has gained wide acceptance is because local cooks mingle its traditional flavors and essential ingredients with the dishes of other cultures. There is no history behind this hybrid pasta, but shrimp from the gulfs on both sides of Mexico, tequila, chipotles, pumpkin seeds, and slow-roasted tomatoes make it a modern classic.

1½ lb (750 g) plum (Roma) tomatoes (8 or 9 large), halved lengthwise

3 tablespoons olive oil

¾ teaspoon salt, plus salt to taste

1¼ lb (625 g) shrimp (prawns), peeled and deveined

¼ cup (2 fl oz/60 ml) fresh tangerine or orange juice

3 tablespoons good-quality tequila

⅓ cup (2 oz/60 g) raw hulled green pumpkin seeds

4 cloves garlic, finely chopped

2 minced chipotle chiles en adobo, plus 1–2 teaspoons sauce from the chiles

1 cup (8 fl oz/250 ml) heavy (double) cream

¾ lb (375 g) bow tie pasta

2 green (spring) onions, including tender green tops, thinly sliced

grated Parmigiano-Reggiano cheese

Preheat an oven to 400°F (200°C). Arrange the tomatoes, cut sides up, in a 9-inch (23-cm) glass baking dish. Drizzle with 1 tablespoon of the olive oil, and season with ¼ teaspoon of the salt. Place in the oven and bake for 30 minutes. Turn the tomatoes cut sides down and continue to bake until the tomatoes are soft and lightly browned and most of their juices have evaporated, 25–30 minutes longer. Let cool and transfer the tomatoes and any remaining juices to a food processor. Process until fairly smooth.

In a nonaluminum dish, combine the shrimp, tangerine or orange juice, tequila, and ¼ teaspoon of the salt. Let stand at room temperature, stirring once or twice, for 30 minutes. Spread the pumpkin seeds in a small metal pan, place in the oven, and toast for 5 minutes. Stir and continue to toast, stirring every 2 or 3 minutes, until the seeds are lightly browned, 10–12 minutes. Let cool and coarsely chop.

Drain the shrimp, reserving the marinade. Set a large frying pan over high heat and add the remaining 2 tablespoons olive oil. When it is hot, add the shrimp and cook, tossing and stirring, until the shrimp are pink and partially curled but not done through, about 2 minutes. Transfer to a bowl. Reduce the heat to low and add the garlic to the pan. Cook, stirring often, until fragrant and golden, about 2 minutes. Add the puréed tomatoes, the reserved marinade, the chipotles and their sauce to taste, and the remaining ¼ teaspoon salt. Raise the heat slightly and simmer until thick, about 5 minutes. Add the cream and stir in the shrimp and any juices from the bowl. Bring to a simmer and cook, stirring occasionally, until the shrimp are just cooked through but still moist and the sauce is thick, 3–5 minutes. Taste and adjust the seasoning.

Bring a large pot three-fourths full of water to a boil over high heat. Salt generously. When the water returns to a boil, add the pasta, stir well, and cook until al dente, about 10 minutes or according to package directions. Drain the pasta and add to the sauce in the frying pan. Heat briefly, tossing and stirring, until well combined. Divide the pasta among individual plates. Scatter the pumpkin seeds and green onions over the top, dividing evenly. Serve immediately, passing the cheese at the table.

serves 4

Southwest

Chiles Rellenos with Green Chile Sauce

There are lovers of red chile, and there are lovers of green, and for such single-minded types, only the favorite will do. Knowing that red chiles are merely ripe versions of green ones can lead the non-native to wonder what the fuss is about, but locals know.

It is the difference between night and day; Chile lovers have their benchmarks. Those who champion red chiles use enchiladas (page 103) as their litmus test, while diners who like it green seek out the best chiles rellenos—whole chiles stuffed with cheese, then coated with batter and fried.

GREEN CHILE SAUCE

3 tablespoons olive oil

1 yellow onion, finely chopped

6 cloves garlic, finely chopped

1 teaspoon dried Mexican oregano

3 tablespoons unbleached all-purpose (plain) flour

4 cups (32 fl oz/1 l) chicken stock

1 can (14½ oz/455 g) plum (Roma) tomatoes, drained and chopped

12 large, green New Mexico or Anaheim chiles, roasted and peeled (page 246), then chopped (about 2 cups/16 oz/500 g)

1 teaspoon salt, plus salt to taste

½ teaspoon freshly ground pepper, plus pepper to taste

CHILES RELLENOS

10 large, green, thick-walled New Mexico or Anaheim chiles, roasted and peeled (page 246)

½ lb (250 g) Monterey jack cheese, cut into 8 strips each ½ inch (12 mm) wide, ¼ inch (6 mm) thick, and 4 inches (10 cm) long

6 eggs, at room temperature

2 tablespoons water

7 tablespoons (2¼ oz/70 g) unbleached all-purpose (plain) flour

½ teaspoon salt

corn oil for frying

❧ To make the green chile sauce, in a nonaluminum saucepan over medium-low heat, warm the olive oil. Add the onion, garlic, and oregano, cover, and cook, stirring once or twice, until they begin to soften, about 10 minutes. Add the flour and, stirring

frequently, cook without browning for 2 minutes. Gradually whisk in the stock and the tomatoes, and stir in the green chiles, 1 teaspoon salt, and ½ teaspoon pepper. Raise the heat to medium, bring to a brisk simmer, and cook uncovered, stirring occasionally, until the sauce has thickened and is reduced to 5 cups (40 fl oz/1.25 l), about 45 minutes. Taste and adjust the seasoning. The sauce can be used immediately but will improve upon standing. Let cool to room temperature, cover, and refrigerate for up to 3 days or freeze for up to 1 month.

❧ To make the *chiles rellenos*, reserve any roasted chiles with holes for another use. Beginning at the stem end, gently make a lengthwise slit 2 inches (5 cm) long in each chile. With the tip of your little finger, and without enlarging the slit, scrape out as many seeds inside each chile as possible. Gently tuck a strip of cheese into each of the 8 chiles with the shortest slits. The remaining 2 chiles are for insurance; reserve them for another use. Lay the cheese-stuffed chiles on a baking sheet, cover with plastic wrap, and refrigerate for 4 hours.

❧ Preheat an oven to 200°F (95°C). Line a baking sheet with paper towels.

❧ Separate the eggs, putting the yolks in a wide, shallow dish, and the whites in a deep bowl. Whisk the water into the yolks, then whisk in the flour and the salt. Using an electric mixer or a large whisk, whip the whites until soft peaks form. Stir one-third of the whites into the yolk mixture to lighten it, then gently fold in the remaining whites just until combined. Do not overmix.

❧ Pour corn oil to a depth of 2 inches (5 cm) into a wide, deep frying pan and heat to 380°F (195°C).

❧ Dip a chilled stuffed chile into the batter, then, with a spatula, carefully transfer, seam side up, to the hot oil. Using a spoon, immediately baste the top of the chile with hot oil to seal the batter over the slit. Batter a second chile, add it to the pan, and baste it as well. Cook the chiles until lightly browned on the bottom, then turn and continue to cook until browned on the second side, about 5 minutes total. Using the spatula, transfer the chiles to the prepared baking sheet and keep them warm in the oven. Repeat with the remaining chiles.

❧ While the last of the chiles are frying, reheat the green chile sauce over low heat until simmering. Spoon about ¾ cup (6 fl oz/180 ml) of the hot sauce onto each of 4 warmed plates. Set 2 stuffed chiles into each puddle of sauce. Serve immediately.

serves 4

SAVORING AMERICA

California
Grilled Ahi Tuna Niçoise

California cooks often adapt the familiar salade niçoise by making it with fresh Pacific tuna instead of the traditional canned tuna. Ahi, a meaty, red-fleshed tuna from the waters off Hawaii and Southern California, works beautifully in this French classic. Serve the salad with a chilled dry rosé.

DRESSING

2 large cloves garlic, peeled but left whole

8 anchovy fillets

large pinch of salt, plus salt to taste

3 tablespoons red wine vinegar

½ cup (4 fl oz/125 ml) plus 1 tablespoon extra-virgin olive oil

freshly ground pepper to taste

4 ahi tuna steaks, about 6 oz (185 g) each

2 tablespoons extra-virgin olive oil

½ teaspoon fennel seed, crushed in a mortar

salt and freshly ground pepper to taste

4 eggs

¾ lb (375 g) small boiling potatoes

½ lb (250 g) slender green beans, ends trimmed

½ red onion, very thinly sliced

½ fennel bulb, very thinly sliced crosswise

2 tablespoons capers, coarsely chopped

¼ cup (⅓ oz/10 g) coarsely chopped fresh basil

3 small tomatoes, cut in half or into wedges

24 Niçoise olives

❧ To make the dressing, combine the garlic, anchovies, and pinch of salt in a mortar and pound to a paste. Transfer to a bowl. Whisk in the vinegar, then whisk in the oil. Season with pepper and more salt to taste. Set aside to allow the flavors to mellow.

❧ Prepare a medium-hot charcoal fire, preheat a gas grill, or preheat a broiler (grill). Rub the tuna all over with the olive oil. Season with the fennel seed, salt, and pepper. Grill or broil on both sides until opaque throughout, 6–8 minutes. Set aside to cool.

❧ Put the eggs in a small saucepan and add water to cover by 1 inch (2.5 cm). Bring to a boil over high heat, cover, and remove from the heat. Let stand for 8 minutes, then drain and place under running cold water until cool. Drain again, then peel and set aside.

❧ Put the potatoes in a saucepan and add salted water to cover by 1 inch (2.5 cm). Bring to a boil over high heat, then adjust the heat to maintain a gentle simmer. Cook, uncovered, until the potatoes are just tender when pierced, about 15 minutes. Drain and, when cool enough to handle, peel the potatoes. Bring a saucepan three-fourths full of salted water to a boil. Add the green beans and boil until tender, about 5 minutes. Drain and place under running cold water until cool. Drain again and pat dry. Cut in half.

❧ Put the tuna in a large bowl, breaking it up with your hands. Halve or slice the potatoes and add to the bowl along with the green beans, red onion, fennel, capers, and basil. Add the dressing and toss gently. Add the tomatoes and toss again gently. Adjust the seasoning. Transfer the salad to a shallow serving bowl. Cut the eggs lengthwise into quarters and arrange around the edge of the salad. Scatter the olives over all.

serves 6

Pacific Northwest

Flank Steak with Walla Walla Sweets

Walla Walla onions are grown in eastern Washington State. Merlot, the state's top red wine, is an ideal partner for this steak-and-onion recipe.

1 flank steak, about 2 lb (1 kg)

2 cups (16 fl oz/500 ml) Merlot

2 cloves garlic, minced

large pinch each of salt and freshly ground pepper, plus salt and pepper to taste

2 large Walla Walla onions, cut into slices ½ inch (12 mm) thick

2 tablespoons olive oil

☙ Lightly score both sides of the steak in a diamond pattern. In an oblong, nonaluminum dish, combine ½ cup (4 fl oz/125 ml) of the Merlot, the garlic, and the pinch each of salt and pepper. Add the steak, turn to coat, cover, and refrigerate.

☙ Separate the onion slices into individual rings. In a large frying pan over medium-high heat, warm the olive oil. Add the onions and cook, stirring often, until they just begin to soften, about 5 minutes. Reduce the heat to medium and add the remaining 1½ cups (12 fl oz/375 ml) Merlot. Cover the pan loosely and braise the onions, stirring occasionally, until they are very tender and most of the Merlot has been absorbed or has evaporated, 30–40 minutes. Season with salt and pepper. Keep the onions warm.

☙ Preheat a broiler (grill). Line a broiler pan with aluminum foil. Lift the steak from the marinade, allowing the excess liquid to drip off, and set on the foil-lined pan. Slip under the broiler 5 inches (13 cm) from the heat source and broil (grill), turning once, for 3–5 minutes on each side for rare to medium-rare, 6–8 minutes for medium to medium-well. Transfer the steak to a cutting board, tent loosely with aluminum foil, and let stand for a few minutes.

☙ Carve the steak on the diagonal against the grain into slices about ½ inch (12 mm) thick. Arrange on warmed individual plates, spoon the braised onions alongside, and serve at once.

serves 4

California

Pizza with Broccoli Rabe and Olives

Broccoli rabe (also known as rapini), long available only in Italian-American communities, now has a broader audience. Many non-Italians have come to appreciate its pleasantly bitter taste and its affinity for strong seasonings like garlic, anchovies, and hot red pepper. Although it resembles broccoli, with thinner stems and smaller florets, broccoli rabe is botanically closer to turnips. Cooked and chopped, it makes an appealing topping for pizza. If you like anchovies, add them to taste with the greens.

DOUGH

¾ cup (6 fl oz/180 ml) warm water

1½ teaspoons active dry yeast

1 tablespoon extra-virgin olive oil

1 teaspoon salt

about 1¾ cups (9 oz/280 g) unbleached all-purpose (plain) flour

2 tablespoons extra-virgin olive oil

1 large clove garlic, minced

¼ teaspoon red pepper flakes

pinch of salt

1 bunch broccoli rabe, about ¾ lb (375 g), thick stems removed

cornmeal for dusting

½ lb (250 g) low-moisture mozzarella cheese, coarsely shredded

3 tablespoons pitted Niçoise olives

🔱 To make the dough, put the warm water in a large bowl and sprinkle the yeast over the surface. Let stand for 2 minutes. Whisk with a fork to dissolve. Let stand until bubbly, about 10 minutes.

🔱 Whisk in the olive oil and salt. Add 1½ cups (7½ oz/235 g) of the flour, stirring with a wooden spoon. Turn the dough out onto a lightly floured work surface and knead gently until the dough is smooth and elastic, about 5 minutes, adding as much of the remaining ¼ cup (1½ oz/45 g) flour as needed to keep the dough from sticking to the board or your hands. Shape into a ball, transfer to an oiled bowl, turn to coat the dough with oil, and then tightly cover the bowl with plastic wrap. Let rise in a cool place for 2 hours.

🔱 Punch the dough down, reshape into a ball, re-cover the bowl, and let the dough rise again in a cool place for 4 hours.

🔱 Position a rack in the bottom of an oven. Line the rack with baking tiles or a baking stone. Preheat the oven to 550°F (290°C), or the highest setting, for at least 45 minutes. Punch the dough down and turn it out onto a work surface. Shape into a ball. Cover with a clean kitchen towel and let rest for 30 minutes.

🔱 In a small bowl, combine the olive oil, garlic, red pepper flakes, and salt. Let stand for 30 minutes to marry the flavors.

🔱 Bring a large pot three-fourths full of salted water to a boil over high heat. Add the broccoli rabe and cook until tender, 2–3 minutes. Drain and cool under running cold water. Gently squeeze out excess water. Cut the broccoli rabe up a little, if desired, but leave in fairly large pieces.

🔱 To assemble the pizza, lightly flour a work surface. Roll out the dough into a round 13–14 inches (33–35 cm). Generously dust a pizza peel or rimless baking sheet with cornmeal and transfer the round to it. Working quickly, spread the cheese evenly over the pizza dough, leaving a ¾-inch (2-cm) rim uncovered. (If you don't work quickly, the dough may stick to the peel or sheet.) Top evenly with the broccoli rabe (you may not need it all) and the olives. Brush the rim with some of the seasoned oil, then drizzle more oil, including the garlic and red pepper flakes, evenly over the pizza. Reserve a little oil for brushing on the rim after baking.

🔱 Immediately slide the pizza from the peel or bak-ing sheet onto the baking tiles or stone and bake until the crust is crisp and browned, about 8 minutes. Remove from the oven. Brush the rim of the crust with the remaining olive oil. Serve immediately.

serves 2 generously

California's Central Valley has been called the "world's most fertile farmland."

New England

Clambake Dinner

The first New England clambake dates back to the early 1600s, when Native Americans demonstrated hot-pit cooking to the Massachusetts Bay colonists. The spirit of this seaside dinner, plain or fancy, still draws New Englanders to the summer table.

4 live lobsters, 1 lb (500 g) each

8 small red potatoes, each about 2 inches (5 cm) in diameter, unpeeled

4 ears corn, husks and silk removed

2 small white onions, each about 2½ inches (6 cm) in diameter, halved

48 small hard-shelled clams such as littleneck or mahogany, scrubbed

1½ cups (11 oz/345 g) salted or unsalted butter

2 lemons, quartered

¼ cup (⅓ oz/10 g) chopped fresh flat-leaf (Italian) parsley

☙ Set a large steaming rack in the bottom of a large lobster kettle or other large, wide pot. Fill the pot about one-third full with water. Cover and bring to a boil over high heat. Plunge the lobsters, headfirst, into the boiling water. Cover and boil until the lobsters are partially cooked and their shells are beginning to turn bright red, about 3 minutes. Using long tongs, transfer the lobsters to a large plate.

☙ Return the water to a boil, and add the potatoes, corn, and onions. Return the lobsters to the pot along with any accumulated juices. Cover the pot tightly with a double layer of aluminum foil and the lid. Cook for 10 minutes. Uncover and scatter the clams around the lobsters, discarding any clams that fail to close to the touch. Re-cover with the foil layers and the lid and continue cooking until the lobsters are bright red, the potatoes are tender when pierced, and the clams have opened, 6–8 minutes longer. In a small saucepan, melt the butter and keep warm.

☙ Using the tongs, remove the lobsters, clams, corn, potatoes, and onions to a large platter or cutting board. Discard any clams that failed to open. Ring the edge of the platter with lemon wedges, and sprinkle the entire platter with the parsley. Divide the melted butter among small ramekins. Serve at once.

serves 4

Clams and Lobster

The rough waters of the Atlantic harbor two of New England's most cherished natural resources, clams and lobsters. Two main types of clams are harvested along the coast. Small hard-shelled clams, such as the littleneck, cherrystone, and Maine mahogany, are excellent raw, steamed, or added to soups and sauces. Larger hard-shelled species, known as quahogs or chowder clams, are meatier, but also tougher and usually processed for use in chowders, stuffings, and savory pies. Soft-shelled clams have oval shells and a telltale black "foot," or neck, protruding from one end. These sweet clams are the first choice for steaming and are also delicious battered and fried.

Until the early 1800s, lobsters were so ordinary that they were fed to children, prisoners, and servants, or used as fertilizer. Although tastes have changed, the local lobstering industry has altered little. In the predawn hours, hardy New England lobstermen head out to sea in search of a good day's haul, many choosing to follow the livelihood of their fathers and grandfathers.

Pacific Northwest

Duck Breasts with Cherry-Syrah Sauce

The Northwest's sweet cherries peak in late June to mid-July. Off-season, you could use frozen dark sweet cherries or ¼ cup (1 oz/30 g) dried cherries, plumped in hot water and well drained.

2 duck half breasts, ½–¾ lb (250–375 g) each

salt and freshly ground pepper to taste

1 cup (8 fl oz/250 ml) Syrah or other medium-bodied red wine

⅓ cup (2 oz/60 g) pitted and halved Bing cherries

2 tablespoons red currant jelly

2 teaspoons minced fresh chervil or flat-leaf (Italian) parsley

☙ With the tip of a sharp knife, score the duck skin in a diamond pattern, slashing not quite to the flesh. Season the breasts with salt and pepper. Place a heavy frying pan over medium-high heat. When it is well heated, add the duck breasts, skin side down, and cook until the skin is well browned and much of the fatty layer has been rendered, about 5 minutes. Turn the breasts over, partially cover the pan, reduce the heat to medium, and continue cooking until the duck is just pink when cut into at the center, 4–5 minutes longer. Transfer the duck breasts to a cutting board and tent loosely with aluminum foil.

☙ Pour out and discard the duck fat from the frying pan. Add the wine to the pan, place over high heat, bring to a boil, and deglaze the pan, stirring to scrape up any browned bits on the pan bottom. Boil the wine until reduced by about three-fourths and slightly thickened, 3–4 minutes.

☙ Add the cherries and jelly to the pan and stir to blend evenly, about 1 minute. Taste and adjust the seasoning with salt and pepper.

☙ Carve each of the duck breasts on the diagonal into slices about ½ inch (12 mm) thick. Arrange the slices in a slightly fanned pattern on individual plates. Spoon the pan sauce over the duck, sprinkle with the chervil or parsley, and serve immediately.

serves 2–4

Southwest

Buffalo Chili

In Texas, exuberantly seasoned versions of south-western classics, dubbed Tex-Mex, are at their best when the subject is chili, or, more precisely, chili con carne—"with meat." Reputed to have originated in San Antonio, where women street vendors, known as chili queens, served up a similarly spicy stew, chili is a dish for the independent-minded cook, who is encouraged, within limits, to improvise. The line is drawn, however, when meat (red meat) is replaced with poultry or seafood or omitted altogether. Buffalo, on the other hand, with its deep traditions in the West and Southwest, is perfectly at home in a pot of chili. Lean and ever so slightly gamy, buffalo contributes another layer of flavor to what has to be the most vividly tasty dish anywhere in America. Coarse, or "chili-grind," meat is commonly found in many southwestern supermarkets. Elsewhere, it can also be ordered from a good butcher.

3 lb (1.5 kg) coarsely ground (minced) buffalo or lean beef, at room temperature

1 tablespoon salt

5 slices thick-cut bacon, about ¼ lb (125 g) total weight, chopped

2 large yellow onions, chopped

8 cloves garlic, chopped

3 jalapeño chiles, chopped

⅓ cup (3 oz/90 g) mild, pure powdered red chile

2 tablespoons ground cumin

1 tablespoon dried Mexican oregano

1 tablespoon freshly ground black pepper

1 teaspoon ground coriander

½ teaspoon red pepper flakes, or to taste

5 cups (40 fl oz/1.25 l) beef stock

1 can (28 oz/875 g) whole tomatoes, finely chopped, with juice

2 tablespoons cornmeal

2 cans (15 oz/470 g each) black beans, rinsed and drained

sour cream; sliced green (spring) onions, including tender green tops; chopped tomatoes; and shredded Monterey jack cheese

☙ Place the ground meat in a large frying pan over medium heat and season with the salt. Cook, breaking up any clumps of meat and stirring as needed, until it is uniformly gray, 12–15 minutes.

☙ Meanwhile, in a large, nonaluminum pot over medium-low heat, fry the bacon, stirring often, until lightly browned, 8–10 minutes. Add the onions, garlic, and jalapeños, cover, and cook, stirring occasionally without browning, until almost tender and golden, about 10 minutes. Add the powdered red chile, cumin, oregano, black pepper, coriander, and red pepper flakes and cook, stirring constantly, for 2 minutes to blend the flavors. Gradually stir in the beef stock, then add the tomatoes and the meat, including any juices, from the frying pan. Bring to a simmer, cover partially, and cook, stirring the chili occasionally, until it has thickened and the meat is tender, about 2 hours. (At this point, the chili can be completed and served immediately, but it will improve in flavor if cooled, covered, and refrigerated overnight. Reheat the chili to simmering over low heat before proceeding.)

☙ Sprinkle the cornmeal over the chili, then stir it in. Stir in the beans and heat through. Taste and adjust the seasoning.

☙ Place the sour cream, green onions, tomatoes, and cheese in separate small bowls and bring to the table for garnishing. Spoon the chili into warmed bowls. Diners add the garnishes as desired.

serves 8–10

South

Lemon Catfish with Slaw in Parchment

Catfish is the South's most versatile freshwater catch, turning up on dinner tables fried, steamed, poached, baked, grilled, wrapped in parchment, or "dished up" in soups and stews. Today, most of the catfish sold in markets and appearing on menus are farmed-raised. Mississippi is the uncontested Catfish Capital of the World, raising more of this lean, mild-tasting fish than any other place on earth. Pour a young, fruity Chardonnay or an ice-cold beer to accompany this dish, and you will have a meal to remember.

8 catfish fillets, 6–8 oz (185–250 g) each, skinned

salt and freshly ground pepper to taste

VINAIGRETTE

¼ cup (2 fl oz/60 ml) dry white wine

¼ cup (2 fl oz/60 ml) fresh lemon juice

finely grated zest of 1 lemon

2 teaspoons Dijon mustard

1 teaspoon Asian sesame oil

⅓ cup (3 fl oz/80 ml) canola oil

1 teaspoon salt

1 teaspoon freshly ground pepper

1 teaspoon sugar

2 tablespoons sesame seeds

COLESLAW

½ small head red cabbage, thinly sliced (about 2 cups/6 oz/185 g)

½ small head green cabbage, thinly sliced (about 2 cups/6 oz/185 g)

6 green (spring) onions, including tender green tops, chopped

1 tablespoon peeled and chopped fresh ginger

1 carrot, peeled and shredded

1 red bell pepper (capsicum), seeded and cut into 2-inch (5-cm) matchsticks

1 yellow bell pepper (capsicum), seeded and cut into 2-inch (5-cm) matchsticks

½ cup (⅔ oz/20 g) chopped fresh dill

16 thin lemon slices

fresh dill sprigs

❧ Preheat an oven to 400°F (200°C). Pat the catfish fillets dry with paper towels. Season on both sides with salt and pepper.

❧ To make the vinaigrette, in a bowl, whisk together the wine, lemon juice and zest, and mustard. In a small measuring pitcher, combine the sesame oil and the canola oil. Slowly add the oil to the bowl in a thin, steady stream, whisking constantly, until the vinaigrette is thick and emulsified. Whisk in the salt, pepper, and sugar. Stir in the sesame seeds.

❧ To make the coleslaw, in a large bowl, toss together the red cabbage, green cabbage, green onions, ginger, carrot, red and yellow bell peppers, and half of the chopped dill. Add half of the vinaigrette and toss to coat the vegetables evenly.

❧ Preheat an oven to 400°F (200°C).

❧ Cut 8 pieces of parchment (baking) paper, each about 12 by 18 inches (30 by 45 cm). Lay the pieces on a work surface and lightly oil the top surface of the parchment.

❧ Divide the coleslaw evenly among the pieces of parchment, placing each portion slightly off center. Place a catfish fillet over each mound of slaw. Lay 2 lemon slices over each catfish fillet. Drizzle the remaining vinaigrette evenly over each portion, then top with the remaining chopped dill, dividing evenly.

❧ Fold the parchment in half over the fish by bringing the short sides together and folding them to seal. Fold in the sides so that none of the juices or steam can escape. (The packets can be refrigerated for up to 4 hours before continuing.)

❧ Place the packets on a baking sheet and place in the oven. Bake until the paper begins to brown and puff, 22–25 minutes. Remove from the oven and let sit for 5 minutes.

❧ Place the packets on warmed individual plates. Carefully slit an X in the top of each packet to let the steam escape.

❧ Garnish each packet with a sprig of fresh dill, then serve at once.

serves 8

SAVORING AMERICA

Mountain States

Panfried Trout with Mushrooms and Bacon

With ingredients like wine, fish stock, and cream, this dish is obviously a modern invention. But it does take its inspiration from the past and from three of the Mountain States' indigenous ingredients—trout, mushrooms, and pine nuts—transforming (but not disguising) them into something fresh and new. Made up of elements that once would have been captured or foraged and then combined and fried over an open flame, the trout and its creamy French-inspired mushroom sauce are sophisticated enough to serve company. At the dinner table, pour a white wine much like the one you use in the dish.

4 slices thick-cut bacon

2 tablespoons pine nuts

¾ lb (375 g) full-flavored fresh mushrooms such as cremini, brushed clean and thickly sliced

¼ teaspoon salt, plus salt to taste

¼ teaspoon freshly ground pepper, plus pepper to taste

½ cup (4 fl oz/125 ml) fish stock

⅓ cup (3 fl oz/80 ml) medium-dry white wine such as Chardonnay

⅓ cup (3 fl oz/80 ml) heavy (double) cream

2 tablespoons corn oil

⅓ cup (2 oz/60 g) yellow cornmeal

2 rainbow trout, about ¾ lb (375 g) each, cleaned

1 tablespoon minced fresh chives

◈ In a frying pan over medium heat, fry the bacon slices, turning once or twice, until browned and almost crisp, about 8 minutes. Transfer to paper towels to drain; keep warm.

◈ Pour off all but about 2 tablespoons of the bacon drippings. Return the pan to medium-low heat. Add the pine nuts to the bacon drippings and cook, stirring occasionally, until crisp and lightly browned, 3–4 minutes. Using a slotted spoon, transfer the nuts to a plate and reserve.

◈ Return the pan to medium heat. Add the mushrooms to the bacon drippings and add the ¼ teaspoon salt and the ¼ teaspoon pepper. Cover and cook, stirring once or twice, until the mushrooms render their juices and are beginning to soften, about 5 minutes. Uncover, add the stock and the wine, and raise the heat to high. Bring to a brisk simmer and deglaze the pan, stirring to scrape up any browned bits on the pan bottom. Cook, stirring occasionally, until the liquid is reduced by half, 3–4 minutes. Stir in the cream, reduce the heat to medium, and simmer, uncovered, until the sauce thickens slightly and coats the mushrooms, about 3 minutes. Stir the pine nuts into the sauce. Keep the sauce warm.

◈ Meanwhile, in a large frying pan over medium-high heat, warm the corn oil. Spread the cornmeal on a plate. One at a time, dip the trout in the cornmeal, coating them evenly on both sides. Again one at a time, shake off the excess cornmeal and carefully lower the trout into the hot oil. When both are in the pan, cook until browned on the first side, about 5 minutes. Using a large spatula, carefully turn the trout. Cook until browned on the second side and opaque throughout but still moist, 4–5 minutes longer.

◈ Transfer the trout to warmed individual plates. Taste the sauce and adjust the seasoning. Spoon the sauce around (not over) the trout, dividing it evenly and using it all. Sprinkle the sauce with the chives. Top each trout with 2 bacon slices and serve.

serves 2

Pork Chops with Vidalia Onion Gravy

The southern fondness for gravy is manifested in many dishes, such as this pairing of pork chops and onions, which are often referred to as "smothered."

2 cups (10 oz/315 g) all-purpose (plain) flour

3 tablespoons cornstarch (cornflour)

1 teaspoon each onion powder and garlic powder

1 teaspoon each salt and freshly ground black pepper, plus salt and black pepper to taste

¼ teaspoon ground cayenne pepper

6 bone-in loin pork chops, about ½ lb (250 g) each

⅓ cup (3 oz/90 g) unsalted butter

⅓ cup (3 fl oz/80 ml) olive oil

3 Vidalia onions, chopped

2 celery stalks, chopped

1 large carrot, peeled and chopped

3 cups (24 fl oz/750 ml) chicken stock

🦐 In a large, lock-top plastic bag, combine the flour, cornstarch, onion powder, garlic powder, 1 teaspoon each salt and black pepper, and cayenne pepper. Seal and shake the bag to mix. Add the pork chops, then seal and shake the bag to coat the chops. In a large frying pan over medium-high heat, melt the butter with the olive oil. Reduce the heat to medium, add the chops (reserving the seasoned flour), and cook, turning once, until browned, about 5 minutes on each side. Transfer to a plate and keep warm.

🦐 Add the onions, celery, and carrot to the frying pan over medium heat and cook for 5–7 minutes. Add ½ cup (2½ oz/75 g) of the reserved seasoned flour and cook, stirring occasionally, for 3 minutes. Raise the heat to medium-high and add the stock. Bring to a boil, stirring constantly and scraping up any browned bits on the pan bottom. Reduce the heat to low, stir in any accumulated juices from the chops, and nestle the meat in the gravy. Cover and simmer over very low heat until the gravy is very thick and the meat is fork-tender, about 1 hour.

🦐 Transfer the chops to a warmed platter. Season the gravy with salt and black pepper. Spoon the gravy over the chops and serve.

serves 6

Roast Chicken with Acorn Squash

Hearty vegetables played a crucial role in the early Great Plains farm diet. This cold-weather classic can move easily into more temperate-weather months. Simply substitute summer squashes, asparagus, or stuffed tomatoes for the acorn squash and adjust the cooking times accordingly:

1 chicken, 3–4 lb (1.5–2 kg)

1 tablespoon each olive oil and melted unsalted butter

1 tablespoon kosher salt

several fresh thyme sprigs

2 shallots, peeled but left whole

2 acorn squashes

1½ cups (12 fl oz/375 ml) fresh orange juice

🌿 Rinse the chicken and pat dry. Set in a large roasting pan. In a bowl, combine the olive oil, butter, and salt. Coat the chicken, inside and outside, with the mixture. Stuff the thyme sprigs and shallots into the cavity. Remove the wing tips and truss or tie the legs together. Position the bird, breast side down, in the pan and let come to room temperature. Preheat an oven to 425°F (220°C). Cut the squashes lengthwise into quarters or eighths and remove the seeds.

🌿 Place the pan in the oven and roast the chicken until lightly browned, 15–20 minutes. Turn the bird and pour ½ cup (4 fl oz/125 ml) of the orange juice into the pan. Add the squashes, skin side down, and brush with the pan juices. Reduce the oven temperature to 400°F (200°C). Continue to roast, brushing the chicken and the squash with the pan juices every 15 minutes and adding more orange juice if the pan is dry, until an instant-read thermometer inserted into the thickest part of the thigh away from the bone registers 165°F (74°C), 50–60 minutes. Transfer the chicken and squashes to a warmed platter. Place the roasting pan over medium-high heat, pour in the remaining orange juice, and stir to scrape up any browned bits on the pan bottom. Pour the pan juices through a fine-mesh sieve placed over a serving bowl, and skim off any fat from the surface.

🌿 Carve the chicken and serve with the squashes. Pass the pan juices at the table.

serves 4

Southwest

Indian Fry-Bread Tacos

Sometimes called Navajo fry bread, but in fact prepared by a number of the region's tribes and pueblos, these breads are made from essentially the same dough used for sopaipillas. Formed into disks and fried until golden and puffy, the breads can be served sweet with a drizzle of honey or a dusting of cinnamon-sugar, but they are at their best in this savory taco preparation.

dough for Sopaipillas (page 189)

about 4 lb (2 kg) solid vegetable shortening (vegetable lard) for deep-frying

3 cups (21 oz/655 g) Pot Beans (page 171), heated to a simmer

6 ounces (185 g) cheddar cheese, shredded

2 cups (4 oz/125 g) finely shredded crisp lettuce

4 pickled jalapeño chiles

about 1 cup (8 fl oz/250 ml) store-bought hot salsa

☙ Divide the sopaipilla dough into 4 equal portions. Shape each portion into a ball, and let rest on a floured work surface, covered with a kitchen towel, for 20 minutes. Using your fingertips, shape each ball into a rough round 6 inches (15 cm) in diameter.

☙ Preheat an oven to 250°F (120°C). Cover a baking sheet with paper towels. In a large, deep frying pan, melt enough shortening to fill the pan no more than halfway full but at least 3 inches (7.5 cm) deep, and heat to 375°F (190°C). When it is hot, one at a time, gently lower the rounds into the pan. Cook, turning once, until golden and puffed, about 3 minutes total. Using a slotted spoon, transfer the fry bread to the prepared baking sheet and keep warm in the oven. Repeat until all the breads are fried, arranging them on the baking sheet in a single layer.

☙ Divide the breads among individual plates. Divide the beans over the breads. Top with the cheese, again dividing evenly, and top the cheese evenly with the lettuce. As you make each layer, spread it in a slightly smaller round than the previous one, so the edges of the layers below remain visible. Serve the tacos, and pass the pickled jalapeños and salsa at the table.

serves 4

Southwestern Chiles

Found in a range of brilliant colors and in widely varying heat levels, modern chiles are descendants of an ancient vine that originally grew in the Amazon forest. Compared with subtropical Mexico, the arid and sometimes chilly American Southwest relies on only a crucial handful of chile varieties. New Mexico produces the most chiles in the region, particularly in the south, along the Rio Grande, around the village of Hatch, "Chile Capital of the World." Medium-sized or larger, medium hot or hotter, these shiny green pods, six to eight inches (15–20 cm) long, are the workhorse chiles of the Southwest.

When the harvest reaches its peak in late summer, many native cooks stock their freezers for the coming year. Along the roadsides, in grocery store parking lots, and at farmers' markets, a fragrant smoke rises as cylindrical wire-mesh roasters the size of oil drums turn above propane-fired burners, charring the peels of prime chiles, which are then packed into plastic bags and frozen. Later, the tough peels easily slip off the chiles as they thaw, leaving them ready to be used whole in such dishes as *chiles*

rellenos, or chopped and added to everything from green chile sauce to cheeseburgers.

The same chile varieties may also ripen to bright red. As hot as the green, red chiles possess an added and attractive sweetness. They are dried whole and strung in decorative but useful bunches, called *ristras,* or are ground to powder or flaked. Whole dried red chiles must be soaked, puréed, and sieved before using. The resulting crimson paste flavors, fires, and colors the sauces and stews that are the heart of southwestern cooking.

Other essential favorites include small, thin serranos and slightly larger and plumper jalapeños, which are mostly used raw, in sauces and salsas, or are pickled. They run from hot to very hot and are found in brilliant green mounds in markets throughout the region. Pungent chipotles from Mexico are popular newcomers to the Southwest. Actually red-ripe jalapeños that have been smoked, chipotles are most useful *en adobo,* that is, canned in a tart, brick red sauce. A few go a long way, creating a fiery flavor that is habit-forming.

South

Pulled Pork with Tabasco-Mustard Sauce

People in the lower United States love barbecue. South of the Mason-Dixon line, every state, city, county, township, community, village, and even where two country roads cross seem to boast the best. At the top barbecue joints in the South, you will see thick plumes of hickory smoke rising from the smoldering fire inside. In this version, the smoke is omitted, but the pulled (shredded) pork, doused in a not-too-sweet, not-too-sour soaking sauce, is just right.

1 bone-in pork shoulder, about 6 lb (3 kg)

2 teaspoons red pepper flakes

1 tablespoon salt

1 tablespoon freshly ground black pepper

1 tablespoon mustard seed

1 cup (8 fl oz/250 ml) water

1 cup (8 fl oz/250 ml) cider vinegar

4 yellow onions, thinly sliced

1 green bell pepper (capsicum), seeded and finely chopped

SAUCE

½ cup (4 oz/125 g) unsalted butter

3 yellow onions, chopped

3 cloves garlic, chopped

2 cups (16 fl oz/500 ml) canned whole tomatoes, puréed

2 tablespoons tomato paste

1 cup (10 oz/315 g) peach preserves

½ cup (4 oz/125 g) coarse-grain Dijon mustard

½ cup (4 fl oz/125 ml) aged Kentucky bourbon

½ cup (6 oz/185 g) honey

⅓ cup (2½ oz/75 g) firmly packed dark brown sugar

1 cup (8 fl oz/250 ml) cider vinegar

2 tablespoons Worcestershire sauce

1 tablespoon Tabasco sauce or other hot-pepper sauce

salt and freshly ground black pepper to taste

1 tablespoon chopped fresh rosemary

12 sesame seed–topped sandwich buns, warmed

bread-and-butter pickle slices

♨ Preheat an oven to 300°F (150°C). Lightly oil a large baking pan.

♨ Place the pork shoulder in the prepared pan and rub with the red pepper flakes, salt, black pepper, and mustard seed. Pour the water and the vinegar over and around the pork. Scatter the onions and the bell pepper over and around the meat. Cover with aluminum foil and roast in the oven for 4 hours. Remove the foil and continue to roast until an instant-read meat thermometer inserted into the thickest part of the pork away from the bone registers 180°F (82°C) and the juices run clear, about 1 hour longer. Remove the pork from the pan and let stand for 1 hour. Using 2 forks, shred the pork by steadying the pork shoulder with 1 fork and pulling the meat away with the other, discarding any fat as you shred. Place the pork in a bowl. Using a slotted spoon, lift the roasted vegetables from the baking pan and ladle over the pork, then mix well.

♨ Meanwhile, make the sauce: In a saucepan over medium heat, melt the butter. Stir in the onions and the garlic and cook, stirring occasionally, until the onions are soft and beginning to brown, about 10 minutes. Add the puréed tomatoes, tomato paste, peach preserves, mustard, bourbon, honey, brown sugar, vinegar, Worcestershire sauce, Tabasco sauce, salt, and black pepper. Bring to a boil, then reduce the heat to very low and simmer gently, uncovered, stirring occasionally to prevent sticking, until the sauce is very dark and thick, about 2 hours. Stir in the rosemary and cook for 10 minutes to blend the flavors. Remove from the heat and let cool for 15 minutes.

♨ Mix half of the sauce with the shredded pork. Mound on a large serving platter with the sandwich buns and the pickle slices on the side. Pass the remaining sauce at the table. Diners make their own sandwiches, topping them with pickle slices.

serves 12

Ask a dozen southerners who makes the best barbecue, and you'll get a dozen different answers.

Remove any remaining white muscle from the side of each scallop. If using sea scallops, cut each in half horizontally to form 2 rounds. Rinse the scallops and pat dry, then sprinkle with the flour, coating evenly. In a large frying pan over medium-high heat, melt the 2 tablespoons butter until hot and foamy. Add the scallops and cook, stirring frequently, until slightly browned on the edges, about 3 minutes. Transfer to a plate and cover with aluminum foil.

Add the wine and shallot to the same pan, bring to a boil over medium-high heat, and deglaze the pan, scraping up any browned bits on the pan bottom. Boil, stirring occasionally, until reduced to 2 tablespoons, about 4 minutes. Remove from the heat and gradually whisk in the butter, a few pieces at a time, until emulsified, about 3 minutes. Return the scallops and any accumulated juices to the pan and stir in the tarragon. Gently warm over very low heat until the scallops are heated through. Do not overheat, or the sauce will separate and the scallops will toughen. Season with salt and pepper.

Spoon the scallops and sauce onto individual plates. Sprinkle with the pine nuts and serve.

serves 4

New England

Scallops with White Wine and Herbs

Bay scallops are found in the calm waters that border Long Island, New York, and Massachusetts, but most New Englanders agree that the best scallops are harvested just off Nantucket Island. Commercial scallopers are joined by locals (and some savvy visitors) who gather their equipment and set off at low tide in search of the treasured shellfish.

¾ lb (375 g) bay scallops or sea scallops

1 tablespoon all-purpose (plain) flour

2 tablespoons plus ¼ cup (4 oz/125 g) unsalted butter

½ cup (4 fl oz/125 ml) dry white wine

1 shallot, minced

1 tablespoon minced fresh tarragon

kosher salt and freshly ground pepper to taste

3 tablespoons pine nuts, lightly toasted

Golden Cornmeal-Crusted Fried Chicken

Ask nearly anyone to name the quintessential dish of the South, and "fried chicken" will invariably be the answer. Every cook in the region claims to have the ultimate recipe for this centerpiece of the southern Sunday dinner, which usually involves little more than dredging the pieces in flour, dipping them in egg, rolling them in cornmeal, and then frying them, sometimes covered, sometimes not. The two most important qualities of the best fried chicken? A crisp crust and a moist interior are vital.

1 chicken, 4 lb (2 kg), cut into 8 serving pieces

8 cups (64 fl oz/2 l) water

½ cup (4 oz/125 g) kosher salt

¼ cup (2 oz/60 g) sugar

2 cups (16 fl oz/500 ml) buttermilk

1 egg, beaten

1 teaspoon Tabasco sauce or other hot-pepper sauce

1 cup (5 oz/155 g) yellow cornmeal

2 cups (10 oz/315 g) all-purpose (plain) flour

1 teaspoon salt

1 teaspoon freshly ground pepper

1 teaspoon paprika

1 teaspoon celery seed

1 teaspoon garlic powder

1 teaspoon onion powder

2½ cups (1¼ lb/625 g) solid vegetable shortening (vegetable lard)

❦ Rinse the chicken pieces and pat dry. In a large bowl, combine the water, kosher salt, and sugar and stir to dissolve. Place the chicken pieces in the water, and weight down with a small plate to immerse totally. Cover and refrigerate for at least 12 hours or for up to 24 hours.

❦ In a bowl, mix together the buttermilk, egg, and Tabasco sauce. Remove the chicken from the brine and place in the buttermilk mixture, turning to coat evenly. Let stand for 15 minutes.

❦ In a shallow baking dish, stir together the cornmeal, flour, salt, pepper, paprika, celery seed, garlic powder, and onion powder.

❦ Remove each piece of chicken from the buttermilk, allowing the excess to drip away. Dredge the chicken pieces in the seasoned flour and place on a large baking sheet. After 10 minutes, dip each piece into the buttermilk a second time and then dredge in the seasoned flour again. Return to the baking sheet.

❦ In a large, deep frying pan over medium-high heat, melt the shortening and heat to 365°F (185°C). Place the chicken, skin side down, in the hot shortening, putting the pieces of dark meat in the center and the pieces of white along the sides. Allow the pieces to touch slightly, but do not crowd the pan. Reduce the heat to medium and cook the chicken until golden brown on the first side, about 12 minutes. Using tongs, turn over the chicken pieces, cover, and continue to cook for 10 minutes. Uncover, turn the chicken once more and cook until the chicken skin is crisp and the meat is cooked through, 8–10 minutes longer. Using tongs, transfer the pieces to paper towels to drain.

❦ Serve the chicken at once, allow to cool and serve at room temperature, or chill and enjoy cold, straight from the refrigerator.

serves 4

Midwest

Meat Loaf with House Ketchup

Bread crumbs bring together ground meat and seasonings into a fine, firm loaf. But many midwesterners grew up with what is sometimes known as "the oatmeal method." Rolled oats are soaked in scalded milk before mixing them with the meat. The result is a somewhat nutty flavor and creamy texture with no discernable remnants of grain. Homemade chunky ketchup, a piquant sauce passed at the table, pushes this dish toward fancy fare. Serve with Herbed Spaetzle (page 163) or Roasted Garlic Mashed Potatoes (page 187).

KETCHUP

1 tablespoon olive oil

2 cloves garlic, crushed

3 anchovy fillets (optional)

1 teaspoon ground ginger

1 teaspoon dry mustard

1 teaspoon celery seed

2 teaspoons Worcestershire sauce

2 cans (28 oz/875 g each) whole plum (Roma) tomatoes, roughly chopped, with juice

1 cup (10 oz/315 g) light corn syrup

3 bay leaves

kosher salt or coarse sea salt to taste

2 tablespoons sugar (optional)

MEAT LOAF

1 tablespoon olive oil

6 green (spring) onions, including tender green tops, minced

2 teaspoons kosher salt or coarse sea salt

1 teaspoon freshly ground pepper

½ cup (4 fl oz/125 ml) milk

1 cup (3 oz/90 g) old-fashioned rolled oats

1 egg, beaten

1½ lb (750 g) ground (minced) pork

1½ lb (750 g) ground (minced) beef round or sirloin

Several hours or a day before serving the meat loaf, make the ketchup: In a saucepan over medium-low heat, warm the olive oil. Add the garlic and the anchovies, if using, mashing and stirring until soft, about 2 minutes. Add the ginger, mustard, and celery seed and heat until fragrant. Add the Worcestershire sauce and deglaze the pan, stirring to scrape up any browned bits on the pan bottom. Cook until almost fully evaporated.

Stir in the tomatoes and their juice, the corn syrup, and the bay leaves. Raise the heat to high and bring to a boil, then reduce the heat to low so the mixture cooks at a gentle simmer. Cook, uncovered, stirring occasionally, until thickened and shiny, about 1 hour. Season with the salt, and sweeten with the sugar, if desired. Remove from the heat and let cool.

To make the meat loaf, in a small frying pan over medium-high heat, warm the olive oil. Add the green onions and sauté until soft, about 2 minutes. Add 1 teaspoon of the salt and the pepper and stir to distribute evenly. Remove from the heat and let cool.

Place the milk in a small saucepan over medium heat and heat until small bubbles appear along the edges of the pan. Pour the hot milk into a large bowl, and stir in the rolled oats and the remaining 1 teaspoon salt. Let stand until the liquid is absorbed, about 15 minutes.

Preheat an oven to 350°F (180°C).

Add the egg, sautéed green onions, and 1 cup (8 fl oz/250 ml) of the ketchup to the rolled oats and stir to incorporate. Fold in the ground meats and mix gently with your hands just until the liquids are evenly distributed. Do not overmix, or the meat loaf will be tough and crumbly. Sear a small patty of the mixture in a hot frying pan until cooked. Taste and adjust the seasoning with salt and pepper.

Pack the meat mixture into an 8½-by-4½-inch (21.5-by-11.5-cm) loaf pan, mounding it nicely on top. Place in a baking pan to collect any overflowing juices. Bake the meat loaf for 1 hour. Remove from the oven and pour off the fat. Return to the oven until the juices run clear when the meat loaf is pierced in the center with a sharp knife or an instant-read thermometer inserted into the thickest part registers 165°F (74°C), 30–45 minutes longer. If the top of the loaf is browning too quickly, cover loosely with aluminum foil.

Just before the meat loaf is ready, reheat the remaining ketchup. Remove the meat loaf from the oven and let rest for 5 minutes, then cut into slices of desired thickness. Using a flexible metal spatula, carefully remove the slices from the pan and arrange on a warmed platter or individual plates. Pour some of the ketchup around the slices and pass the remaining ketchup at the table.

serves 8–10

Alaska

Salmon Pirog

This traditional Alaskan dish garnished with dilled sour cream reflects the heritage that the Last Frontier shares with Russia, its nearest neighbor to the west.

DOUGH

3 cups (15 oz/470 g) all-purpose (plain) flour

1 teaspoon salt

¾ cup (6 oz/185 g) chilled unsalted butter, cut into ½-inch (12-mm) pieces

1 tablespoon fresh lemon juice

4–6 tablespoons (2–3 fl oz/60–90 ml) ice water

2 tablespoons canola oil

½ small head green cabbage, about ½ lb (250 g), trimmed and finely shredded

2 tablespoons minced fresh flat-leaf (Italian) parsley

4 teaspoons minced fresh dill

salt and freshly ground pepper to taste

¾ lb (375 g) fresh mushrooms, brushed clean and very finely chopped

¾ cup (4 oz/125 g) finely chopped yellow onion

1 piece salmon fillet, 1½ lb (750 g), skin removed

1 egg

1 cup (5 oz/155 g) cooked long-grain white rice

½ cup (4 oz/125 g) sour cream

❦ To make the dough, in a bowl, stir together the flour and the 1 teaspoon salt. Add the butter and toss to coat. Using a pastry blender or 2 knives, cut the butter into the flour mixture until it has a coarse sandy texture. Stir in the lemon juice and then the ice water, 1 tablespoon at a time, using only as much as needed for the dough to hold its shape when pinched between your fingers. Turn the dough out onto a work surface and divide in half. Form each half into a ball, enclose separately in plastic wrap, and refrigerate for at least 30 minutes or for up to 1 day.

❦ In a frying pan over medium heat, warm 1 tablespoon of the canola oil. Add the shredded cabbage and 2 tablespoons water and cook, stirring often, until very tender, 8–10 minutes. Stir in 1 tablespoon of the parsley with 1 teaspoon of the dill and season with salt and pepper. Transfer to a bowl and wipe out the frying pan.

❦ In the frying pan over medium-high heat, warm the remaining 1 tablespoon canola oil. Add the mushrooms and onion and sauté until the mushrooms are tender and the liquid that they give off has evaporated, 5–7 minutes. Season with salt and pepper. Add the remaining 1 tablespoon parsley and 1 teaspoon of the dill. Remove from the heat.

❦ Rub your fingers along the surface of the salmon fillet. Use needle-nose pliers or tweezers to remove any fine pin bones. Cut against the grain into slices about ½ inch (12 mm) thick. In a small bowl, lightly beat together the egg, a pinch of salt, and 2 tablespoons water to make an egg wash.

❦ Preheat an oven to 375°F (190°C).

❦ On a lightly floured work surface, roll out 1 dough ball into a rectangle about 10 inches (25 cm) wide and 14 inches (35 cm) long. Trim the edges. Cut the dough in half lengthwise and then crosswise, making 4 smaller rectangles. Lightly brush the egg wash evenly over the rectangles. Spread one-fourth of the rice over each rectangle, leaving a 1-inch (2.5-cm) border uncovered around the edges. Spoon an even layer of one-fourth of the cabbage over each rice base. Lay the salmon slices on top of the cabbage, cutting and rearranging the pieces as needed so the salmon evenly covers the cabbage and dividing the salmon evenly among the rectangles. Season lightly with salt and pepper. Spread the mushroom mixture evenly over the salmon, dividing it among the rectangles.

❦ Roll out the remaining dough ball into a rectangle about 12 inches (30 cm) wide and 16 inches (40 cm) long. Trim the edges. Cut the dough in half lengthwise and then crosswise, making 4 smaller rectangles. Lay these pastry pieces over the filling, lining up the edges with the pastry base as much as possible and very gently stretching the dough a bit if needed. Press firmly along the edges to seal, trim with a small knife to neaten, then use your fingers or the tines of a fork to crimp the edges. Brush the pastry top with egg wash and, using the tip of a sharp knife, cut a few vents in the top of each pastry to allow steam to escape during cooking. Transfer the pastries to an ungreased baking sheet.

❦ Bake until well browned, about 20 minutes. Meanwhile, in a bowl, stir together the sour cream and the remaining 2 teaspoons dill. Cover and refrigerate until ready to serve. Remove the pastries from the oven and immediately divide among individual plates. Spoon some of the dilled sour cream alongside and serve at once.

serves 4

Mountain States

Rack of Venison with Honey-Glazed Vegetables

The tradition of wild game cooking in the West is very old, predating even bows and arrows. European settlers also took advantage of the area's natural bounty to sustain life in a land that, for a very long time, remained starkly undeveloped. Even today, the hunting tradition is vital in the region, but modern life makes the preparation of game meats far more often a choice than a necessity. Local chefs are perhaps the greatest proponents of game cooking, which for most nonhunters is now a novelty, and even a luxury; albeit with a strong link to the past. Meat from farm-raised animals, such as venison, is lean, tender, mildly flavored, low in cholesterol, in predictable supply by mail order, and wholesome, and it makes turning out spectacular main courses like this showstopper relatively effortless. Ask the butcher or supplier to french the rib bones, that is, cut away the thin layers of meat from the top 4 inches (10 cm) or so of each bone.

1½ cups (12 fl oz/375 ml) medium-dry red wine

4 cloves garlic, chopped

5 tablespoons (3 fl oz/80 ml) olive oil

3 tablespoons honey

2 tablespoons red wine vinegar

18 juniper berries, chopped

1 oven-ready 8-chop venison rack, about 2½ lb (1.25 kg), frenched (see note)

2 tablespoons corn oil

12 small, red new potatoes, unpeeled, halved

2½ cups (12 oz/375 g) peeled, cubed butternut squash (½-inch/12-mm cubes)

½ teaspoon freshly ground pepper, plus pepper to taste

¼ teaspoon salt, plus salt to taste

2 Red Delicious apples, peeled, cored, and cut into ½-inch (12-mm) cubes

⅓ cup (½ oz/15 g) finely chopped fresh sage

In a food processor, combine the wine, the garlic, 3 tablespoons of the olive oil, the honey, the vinegar, and the juniper berries. Process until as smooth as possible. Place the venison rack in a shallow, non-aluminum pan or dish and pour the wine mixture over the rack. Cover and let stand at room temperature, turning once or twice, for 2 hours.

Ranching in the West

Columbus brought the first cattle to the New World in 1494, but it wasn't until the early sixteenth century that the Spanish began ranching in Mexico, later expanding the tradition north of the border into New Mexico, Texas, and Colorado. Spanish cowboys, or *vaqueros*, were responsible for much of the early character of ranching, right down to the word *rodeo*, from the Spanish for "to go around."

Following the Civil War, Anglo ranchers ran giant herds freely on public land throughout the region. The cattle grazed for months on natural grassland virtually untended, with a single large house, barn, bunkhouse, and corrals serving as headquarters. Once fattened, the herds were rounded up by cowboys and driven to railheads, then taken by train to Chicago and other eastern markets.

From this rich mixture of the Spanish *cocina*—rough fare from trail-drive chuckwagon cooks and home cooking from the ranch-house kitchen—was forged a tradition of hearty eating that lives on in the West of today.

SAVORING AMERICA

❧ Position a rack in the upper third of an oven and preheat to 400°F (200°C).

❧ In a large frying pan over medium-high heat, warm the corn oil. Lift the venison from the marinade, reserving the marinade, and pat the rack dry. Lay in the hot oil and cook until browned on the first side, about 4 minutes. Turn and cook on the other side until browned, 3–4 minutes. Transfer the rack to a shallow roasting pan, positioning it bone side up. Discard the oil from the frying pan but do not clean the pan.

❧ Place the frying pan over medium heat and add the remaining 2 tablespoons olive oil. Add the potatoes and cook, stirring once or twice and scraping the browned bits from the pan bottom, until lightly browned, about 7 minutes. Add the squash cubes and cook, stirring once or twice, until they begin to brown, about 7 minutes longer. Stir the ½ teaspoon pepper and the ¼ teaspoon salt into the vegetables and remove from the heat. Stir the apples into the vegetables, then spoon the mixture around the venison in the roasting pan.

❧ Place the roasting pan in the oven and roast for 8 minutes. Pour the marinade through a fine-mesh sieve and discard the solids. Baste the venison with about one-third of the marinade and stir the vegetable mixture. Return the venison to the oven and roast for another 8 minutes. Then baste the roast with half the remaining marinade and again stir the vegetables. Roast for another 8 minutes, then baste with the remaining marinade and stir the vegetables again. If the vegetables are tender, remove them from the pan and reserve. Continue to roast the venison until an instant-read thermometer inserted into the thickest part of the rack away from the bone registers 120°–125°F (49°–52°C) for rare, about 5 minutes longer, or until done to your liking.

❧ Transfer the venison to a platter, tent loosely with aluminum foil, and let rest for 5 minutes. If the vegetables are not yet tender, continue to roast for a few more minutes, then arrange on the platter.

❧ Carve the rack of venison between the bones into chops. Arrange the chops on warmed individual plates, and season lightly with salt and pepper. Stir the sage into the vegetables, then taste and adjust the seasoning. Spoon the vegetables and any pan juices over the venison chops. Serve immediately.

serves 4

Green Corn Tamales

Arizona's indigenous dishes are fewer and subtler than those of Texas or New Mexico, but no less worthy. Tamales made from green (unripe) corn are among the tastiest and most unusual of them. Composed of a main ingredient with limited seasonal availability and characterized by a sturdy simplicity of flavor that is the very essence of comfort food, the tamales appeal most readily to those who grew up eating them. Others will become converts in time, assisted perhaps by this streamlined recipe, which replaces the traditional starchy, yellow field corn with a mixture of tender sweet corn and masa harina, the specially treated corn flour used in making tortillas. In Arizona, the appearance of green corn in the fields, which precedes the arrival of green corn tamales on the plate, is also a precursor of the cooling monsoon rains, a sign that the brutal summer will soon end. Dried corn husks, soaked in hot water for 15 minutes, may be used in place of fresh.

6 or 7 ears very sweet, tender corn, with husks

½ cup (4 oz/125 g) solid vegetable shortening (vegetable lard), at room temperature

4 teaspoons sugar

1½ teaspoons baking powder

1 teaspoon salt

1½ cups (7½ oz/235 g) masa harina

about 6 ounces (185 g) Monterey jack cheese, coarsely shredded

1 or 2 green New Mexico or Anaheim chiles, roasted and peeled (page 246), then cut into 16–18 strips 3 inches (7.5 cm) long by ¼ inch (6 mm) wide

about 2 cups (16 fl oz/500 ml) Green Chile Sauce (page 111) (optional)

SAVORING AMERICA

Remove and discard the toughest outer husks from each ear of corn. Using a sharp knife, cut around the base of each ear to release the remaining husks. Sort through the husks, picking out 2 or 3 of the largest and most intact from each ear, and reserve. The goal is to secure 16–18 husks (1 for each tamale) to use as wrappers. Remove the silks from the ears. Stand each ear of corn on its stem end on a cutting board. Using a sharp knife and a downward motion, cut off the kernels. With the blunt edge of the blade, scrape down the ears, removing any remaining corn juices. Measure out 2½ cups (15 oz/470 g) corn kernels and juice. Reserve any remaining corn for another use.

In a food processor, combine the corn kernels and their juice, shortening, sugar, baking powder, and salt and process until fairly smooth. Add the *masa harina* and process until a damp dough forms and adheres to the blade. Remove the dough from the processor, place in a bowl, and stir in the cheese. Cover and let rest at room temperature for 20 minutes.

One at a time, lay a reserved corn husk on the work surface, with the wide end toward you. Using a small, narrow spatula or a table knife, spread a layer of the corn dough about ¼ inch (6 mm) thick over the lower two-thirds of the corn husk, smoothing it to the edges. Rotate the husk so its pointed end is facing you. Center a strip of green chile lengthwise on the corn dough. Fold in the sides of the corn husk and overlap them slightly, enclosing the chile; press gently to seal. Spread a small dab of corn dough at the base of the tapered end of the corn husk up over the dab of corn dough; press gently to adhere. Use another dab of corn dough to seal the remaining open end of the tamale. Be sure no chile filling is visible. (If desired, tear any unused corn husks lengthwise, along their natural fiber lines, into thin ribbons. Tie a ribbon around each tamale to hold the folded end in place.) Transfer the tamale, sealed end up, to a steamer basket. Repeat with the remaining corn husks, corn dough, and chile strips. If the tamales are not tied, pack them close together, seam to seam, in the steamer basket to prevent them from unwrapping. You should have between 16 and 18 tamales.

Fill a pot about one-third full with water and bring to a boil over high heat. Set the steamer basket in place on the pot (not touching the water) and cover. If water enters the steamer basket, pour some water out of the pot. Adjust the heat so that the pot maintains a brisk simmer. Timing from when the water simmers, steam the tamales until they are firm but still moist, about 1 hour. Unwrap a tamale to check the interior. (At this point, the tamales can be allowed to cool, wrapped tightly, and refrigerated for up to 2 days. To serve, unwrap the chilled tamales and rewarm them in a steamer over simmering water until just heated through, about 20 minutes.)

To serve, divide the tamales among individual plates. Open up the corn husk packets, but do not unwrap fully. Spoon some of the green chile sauce over each tamale, if desired, and pass the remaining sauce at the table.

Makes 16–18 tamales, serves 4–6

California
Soba with Shiitake and Mustard Greens

Served hot in soup, Japanese soba, noodles made primarily from buckwheat, satisfy many Californians seeking a quick, healthful meal. Look for soba and the other ingredients in Japanese markets.

one 4-inch (10-cm) square dried konbu

⅔ cup (⅓ oz/10 g) dried bonito flakes

¼ lb (125 g) young, tender mustard greens, ribs removed

½ lb (250 g) dried soba

7 oz (220 g) Japanese-style firm tofu

3 tablespoons mirin

2 tablespoons soy sauce

1 cup (3 oz/90 g) sliced fresh shiitake mushroom caps without stems

2 green (spring) onions, thinly sliced

shichimi

❀ In a saucepan, combine the *konbu* and 4 cups (32 fl oz/1 l) water. Bring to a simmer, add the bonito flakes, and let stand for 1–2 minutes. Strain the broth through a fine-mesh sieve.

❀ Bring a large saucepan three-fourths full of salted water to a boil. Cut the mustard greens in half if large, or leave whole. Add to the pan and boil just until tender, about 1 minute. Lift out with a wire skimmer and place under running cold water. Gently squeeze to remove excess water. Add the soba to the boiling water and cook until al dente, 8–10 minutes. Drain and rinse with warm water.

❀ Bring another large saucepan three-fourths full of water to a boil. Cut the tofu into ½-inch (12-mm) cubes. Place the broth in a clean saucepan and add the tofu, *mirin*, soy sauce, and mushrooms. Bring to a simmer and simmer gently until the mushrooms are tender, about 3 minutes. Dip the sieve containing the soba into the boiling water. Lift the sieve, let the water drain, then divide the hot noodles between 2 bowls. Top with the mustard greens. Ladle the hot broth with the mushrooms and tofu over all. Garnish with the green onions and a sprinkle of *shichimi*.

serves 2

Pork Roast with Apples and Cream

Apples regularly turn up on the Northeast table in preparations both savory and sweet. Here they are paired with pork and cream in a main dish that owes its inspiration to the kitchens of Normandy, a French coastal region famous for its dairy farms, apple orchards, and apple brandy: Winesap, Empire, and Jonathan apples are among the many apple varieties that thrive in the orchards of the Mid-Atlantic states, from Rhode Island and Connecticut to Delaware and Maryland.

6 large shallots, halved lengthwise

2 tablespoons canola oil

3 lb (1.5 kg) boneless pork loin, trimmed of fat and tied

2 tablespoons plus 2 teaspoons minced fresh sage

2 cloves garlic, minced

1 tablespoon Dijon mustard

¾ teaspoon kosher salt, plus salt to taste

¼ teaspoon freshly ground pepper, plus pepper to taste

1½ cups (12 fl oz/375 ml) apple cider

2 tablespoons unsalted butter

2 large, firm, red apples (see note), cored and cut into wedges ½ inch (12 mm) thick

½ cup (4 fl oz/125 ml) heavy (double) cream

Preheat an oven to 450°F (230°C).

Place the shallots in a roasting pan, drizzle with 1 tablespoon of the canola oil, and push to the edges of the pan. Set the pork loin in the center of the pan. In a small bowl, mix together the 2 tablespoons sage, garlic, mustard, remaining 1 tablespoon canola oil, ¾ teaspoon salt, and ¼ teaspoon pepper until well blended. Smear the paste evenly over the top of the pork loin.

Roast the pork and shallots for 15 minutes. Reduce the heat to 325°F (165°C). Pour 1 cup (8 fl oz/250 ml) of the apple cider into the pan, and shake the pan to coat the shallots with the cider. Roast, basting the pork and shallots occasionally, until an instant-read thermometer inserted into the thickest part of the loin reads 150°F (65°C),

55–65 minutes. Transfer the roast and shallots to a platter. Pour any pan juices into a cup and reserve. Tent the meat loosely with aluminum foil.

Set the roasting pan on the stove top over medium heat and add the butter. When the butter is melted and foaming, add the apple wedges and cook, turning frequently, until tender and browned, about 10 minutes. Transfer the apples to the platter.

Spoon off any fat from the reserved pan juices and add the juices to the pan with the remaining ½ cup (4 fl oz/125 ml) cider and the cream. Bring to a boil and deglaze the pan, stirring to scrape up the browned bits on the pan bottom. Boil the liquid until slightly thickened, about 4 minutes.

Return the apple slices and the shallots to the pan and gently reheat. Season with the remaining 2 teaspoons sage and salt and pepper. Using a slotted spoon, transfer the apples and shallots to the platter, arranging them around the pork. Pour the sauce into a bowl.

Snip the strings and carve the pork into thin slices. Serve on warmed individual plates with the apples, shallots, and sauce.

serves 6

SAVORING AMERICA

Pacific Northwest

Dungeness Crab Boil with Shallot Butter

Most Northwest crab recipes are insistently devoid of too many additional flavorings, all the better to let the delicious, sweet flavor of the crab shine through. It's true of crab cakes, where "just enough other stuff to hold the cakes together" is the best recipe of all. The same can be said of the region's crab boil dinners, which typically focus on piles of steaming crabs in the middle of a big table covered with newspapers. Accompaniments include melted butter, lemon wedges, and maybe cocktail sauce, along with crusty bread, a crisp green salad or coleslaw, and chilled beer or white wine. Here, that basic idea has been embellished, with some lemon and herbs added to the cooking water, and the butter blended with the sweetness of roasted shallot.

If you can find live Dungeness crabs, they are by far the best choice. If only precooked crabs are available, skip the step of boiling with herbs and instead steam just long enough to heat the meat through, and then serve with the shallot butter. The serving size can range from half a crab per person to a whole crab for true devotees.

SHALLOT BUTTER

1 shallot, peeled but left whole

1 teaspoon olive oil

¾ cup (6 oz/185 g) unsalted butter, melted

pinch of salt

salt

1 lemon, sliced

handful of fresh herb sprigs such as flat-leaf (Italian) parsley, chervil, tarragon, and/or chives

2 live Dungeness crabs, about 2½ lb (1.5 kg) each

☙ To make the shallot butter, preheat an oven to 400°F (200°C). Set the shallot on a piece of aluminum foil, drizzle the olive oil over the shallot, and wrap the foil around it to seal securely. Roast the shallot until aromatic and very tender when squeezed, about 30 minutes. Remove from the oven, unwrap, and let cool.

☙ Coarsely chop the shallot and place in a food processor or blender. Add the melted butter and process until the shallot is puréed. Add the pinch of salt and continue processing until the mixture is very smooth. Pour into a small saucepan and set aside.

☙ Fill a large pot three-fourths full of water, salt generously, and add the lemon slices and herbs. Bring to a boil over high heat. (If you don't have a pot large enough to cook both crabs at the same time, cook them one at a time.) When the water is at a full rolling boil, grab each of the crabs securely at the back of the carapace (top shell) and gently, but swiftly, drop them headfirst into the boiling water. Cover the pot, return to a boil, and then reduce the heat to medium-high. Cook the crabs for 20 minutes, counting from the time that the water returns to a boil. Keep an eye on the pot during cooking; the liquid may bubble up and over the edge, so you might want to set the lid askew to allow steam to escape.

☙ Drain the crabs well. When they are just cool enough to handle, and working with 1 crab at a time, lift off and discard the carapace. Turn the crab over and lift off the "apron," or small, narrow triangular shell flap. Pull or scrape out the dark gray intestines and the liver from the body section and discard. The crab "butter," a yellowish amber mass, can be scooped out and saved for eating along with the crabmeat. Also lift off and discard the feathery gills on either side of the cavity. Use a large, heavy knife to cut the body in half where it narrows at the center.

☙ Arrange the hot crabs on a large platter and serve with crab crackers for cracking the shells and with seafood forks for picking the meat from the shells. Gently reheat the shallot butter and pour it into individual bowls for dipping the sweet crabmeat. Place an empty bowl on the table for discarded shells.

serves 2–4

Meat-rich Dungeness crab, unique to America's West Coast, has been harvested commercially since the late 1800s.

Pot Roast with Vegetables

Transforming an inexpensive, tough piece of beef into a hardy, tender stew through slow cooking is just one of the great culinary lessons New Englanders learned from their colonial forefathers, who passed on the secret to coaxing flavor and texture from even the most sinewy meat. This version of pot roast also reflects the colonists' reliance on the larder. Roots and tubers like potatoes, parsnips, and carrots, stored for use during the winter, were often added to the pot.

bouquet garni of 3 large fresh flat-leaf (Italian) parsley sprigs, 1 fresh rosemary sprig, 2 fresh thyme sprigs, and 1 small bay leaf

1 large yellow onion

1 boneless beef bottom round or rump roast, 3½ lb (1.75 kg), tied

1½ teaspoons kosher salt

¼ teaspoon freshly ground pepper

2 tablespoons all-purpose (plain) flour

2 tablespoons canola oil

6 cloves garlic, peeled but left whole

1 can (14 oz/440 g) whole tomatoes, drained and diced

1 cup (8 fl oz/250 ml) beef stock

1 bottle (12 fl oz/375 ml) beer

3 Yukon gold or other boiling potatoes, peeled and halved

2 tablespoons light brown sugar

2 large sweet potatoes, peeled and cut into 3-inch (7.5-cm) chunks

3 carrots, peeled and cut into 1½-inch (4-cm) lengths

2 parsnips, peeled and cut into 2-inch (5-cm) lengths

☙ Preheat an oven to 325°F (165°C).

☙ Put the bouquet garni ingredients on a square of cheesecloth (muslin), bring the corners together, and tie with kitchen string; set aside. Starting at the stem end, cut the onion into 6 wedges, stopping just short of the root end. Set aside. Rub the roast with the salt and pepper. Dust the entire surface of the roast with the flour and tap off any excess.

☙ In a large dutch oven or other heavy, lidded, oven-proof pot over medium-high heat, warm the canola oil until hot but not smoking. Add the roast and brown well on all sides, about 15 minutes. Transfer to a plate and set aside. Add the garlic, onion, and bouquet garni and cook, stirring frequently, until fragrant, about 2 minutes. Add the tomatoes, beer, beef stock, and brown sugar. As the foam subsides, scrape up the browned bits on the pot bottom. When the liquid is boiling, return the roast to the pot, cover, and bake for 2 hours, turning the roast every 30 minutes.

☙ Remove the pot from the oven and lift off the lid. Scatter the carrots, potatoes, sweet potatoes, and parsnips around the roast and baste with the juices. Cover the pot and return to the oven. Bake, basting the roast and vegetables occasionally, until the vegetables and meat are tender when pierced with a fork, 1–1½ hours longer.

☙ Transfer the meat to a large carving board and snip off the strings. Using a slotted spoon, arrange vegetables on one side of the carving board. Tent the meat and vegetables with aluminum foil. Remove and discard the bouquet garni. Spoon off any fat from the pan juices, then taste and adjust the seasoning. Pour into a warmed serving bowl.

☙ Slice the meat and serve on warmed individual plates with the vegetables and some of the pan juices. Pass the remaining juices at the table.

serves 6

SAVORING AMERICA

The varied New England landscape embraces tall mountains, broad valleys, dense woodlands, and a long, craggy seacoast.

California

Braised Lamb Shanks with Zinfandel

Zinfandel is grown all over California, but regions particularly renowned for it include the Sierra Nevada foothills, Sonoma County, Lodi, and Napa Valley's Howell Mountain. The state's zesty Zinfandels pair beautifully with slow-cooked lamb, both in the sauce and on the table. And because this sauce requires only a small amount of wine, you will have plenty left to pour with the dinner. Serve the lamb with fresh egg noodles or polenta.

California is the nation's second largest sheep producer, after Texas, with the mild weather and lush pasturage that sheep prefer. For some ranchers, sheep are a seasonal business, economical only when the grass is flourishing. Others move their stock from south to north to follow the green fields. When California's dry summer weather sets in and pastures throughout the state turn brown, the sheep must be fed far more costly grain.

4 lamb shanks, 2¾–3 lb (1.4–1.5 kg) total weight

salt and freshly ground pepper to taste

1 tablespoon extra-virgin olive oil

¾ lb (375 g) plum (Roma) tomatoes

½ yellow onion, finely minced

1 small carrot, peeled and finely chopped

1 celery stalk, finely chopped

2 cloves garlic, finely minced

2 teaspoons minced fresh rosemary

½ cup (4 fl oz/125 ml) Zinfandel

½ cup (4 fl oz/125 ml) water

2 tablespoons chopped fresh flat-leaf (Italian) parsley

❦ Season the lamb with salt and pepper. In a high-sided frying pan or dutch oven over medium-high heat, warm the olive oil. When the oil is hot, add the lamb, reduce the heat to medium-low, and brown on all sides, about 30 minutes. Using tongs, transfer the lamb shanks to a plate.

Meanwhile, halve the tomatoes. With your fingers, scoop out and discard the seeds. Grate the tomatoes using the large holes on a box shredder-grater, positioning the cut side of each half against the grater. Discard the tomato skins. You should have about 1 cup (8 fl oz/250 ml) purée.

Add the onion, carrot, celery, garlic, and rosemary to the pan. Sauté until soft, about 10 minutes. Add the wine, raise the heat to high, and simmer until the pan is almost dry, about 1 minute. Add the tomato purée and the water and return the lamb shanks to the pan. Bring to a simmer, cover, and adjust the heat to maintain a bare simmer. Cook until the meat is fork-tender and is easy to pull away from the bone, about 2 hours, turning the lamb shanks occasionally in the liquid.

Transfer the lamb to a plate. Pour the braising liquid and vegetables into a large measuring cup and refrigerate until most of the fat rises to the top, about 30 minutes. Spoon off the fat and return the braising liquid and vegetables to the pan. Place over high heat and simmer, uncovered, until thickened to a sauce consistency. Taste and adjust the seasoning.

Return the lamb shanks to the sauce and reheat gently until hot throughout. Stir in 1 tablespoon of the parsley.

Divide the shanks among warmed individual plates. Spoon the sauce over them. Garnish with the remaining parsley and serve at once.

serves 4

Zinfandel boasts ardent fans~ an annual tasting in San Francisco welcomes thousands of "Zinfanatics."

Zinfandel

California's first Cabernet Sauvignon, Pinot Noir, and Merlot vines came from Europe, but historians puzzled for years over the state's Zinfandel. Where did the original vines come from? Certainly, European vintners grew nothing by that name. Finally, in the late 1990s, with the help of DNA fingerprinting, researchers proved that Zinfandel and southern Italy's Primitivo are the same grape. How its name changed en route to America is still unknown; yet by the 1850s, California nursery owners were selling Zinfandel, and for a while it was the most widely planted wine grape in the state. Most growers today train the vines on trellises. Earlier farmers allowed them to sprawl. Some old vines survive, their thick gnarled arms a picturesque sight in winter.

If Cabernet Sauvignon is the serious member of the red wine family, Zinfandel is the fun-loving brother. When made in a light, fruity, zesty style, it complements barbecued ribs, hamburgers, and grilled chicken. Even when made in a weightier, riper style, this California classic seems better suited to informal, straightforward food—a juicy grilled steak, some aged cheese—than it does to a fussy, starched-tablecloth meal.

Side Dishes

As in the past, side dishes mirror seasonal shifts, local harvests, and regional custom.

IT'S SATURDAY MORNING before the Fourth of July, and the farmers' market teems with shoppers. Some grip bulging canvas bags; others pull children's red wagons or even push baby strollers, pressed into service as shopping carts on market day. At one stall, ears of corn spill from the back of a truck, next to a hand-scrawled sign announcing "Picked this A.M." At another, a farmer in overalls slices dripping white peaches for customers imagining fresh peach ice cream on Independence Day. Baskets fill with fingerling potatoes for potato salad, vine-ripened blackberries for pie and cobbler, and sweet white corn for the grill.

From Hollywood, California, to Bangor, Maine, farmers' markets are luring customers eager to buy fresh, local produce direct from the grower. From fewer than one hundred in 1970, farmers' markets have multiplied to twenty-eight hundred today, in reaction to the increasing facelessness of America's farms.

In 1900, 40 percent of Americans worked on farms. Today, only 2 percent do, and many youngsters have no idea what a cornstalk looks like. Over the last century, the country's farms became bigger and more specialized, and their

Preceding pages: Early in the season, a Wisconsin farmer surveys his corn crop. **Left:** A bountiful selection of locally grown greens draws shoppers to San Francisco's Ferry Plaza Farmers' Market. **Top:** In many rural communities, the old-fashioned outdoor clothesline has not been replaced by the indoor dryer. **Above:** In the interests of good flavor and good health, cooks seek out organic produce.

numbers plummeted, from 6 million to 2 million. Modern farms are highly mechanized, efficient, and productive, able to fill supermarkets and export around the world. Ironically, as Americans moved off the farm and lost any connection to farming, they began to care more about the source of their food. The renaissance of farmers' markets speaks to their newfound desire to meet the people who grow their food, to celebrate what's local, and to cook and eat with the seasons.

Before refrigerated shipping and cold storage made it possible to buy raspberries in December and pears in June, Americans ate seasonally by necessity. Today they have more options, but in many homes, the side-dish repertory still reflects the local bounty and custom that inspired cooks a century or more ago. In fact, one could argue that a roast chicken is a roast chicken around the country, but it's in the dishes chosen for accompaniment that their regional differences show.

In New England, on a snowy January evening, the iconic chicken might come to the table wreathed in roasted root vegetables and other good keepers: carrots, parsnips, turnips, rutabagas, and winter squashes, all residents of the root cellar. Although few New Englanders have root cellars any longer, their cooking of winter vegetables recalls their forebears' need to prepare for the lean season. Indeed, the Pilgrims would have failed to survive their first winter if they hadn't learned of their Native American neighbors' caching of dried corn. The early settlers figured out quickly that stockpiling food was key to getting through winter. Four months or more without freshly harvested vegetables forced eastern cooks to explore the potential of parsnips, potatoes, beets, and other long-lasting produce. Today, New Englanders retain a taste for them, evidenced in the region's classic boiled dinner: corned beef—another preserved food of winter—simmered slowly to make a flavorful broth in which cabbage, potatoes, and other vegetables are cooked.

New Englanders no longer have to worry about which apples are good keepers or whether their fall harvest will carry them through winter. Still, they prepare the side

dishes developed in more challenging times, adapting them as befits today's easier circumstances. The roasted carrots and parsnips around their chicken might be glazed with butter and maple syrup, the scalloped potatoes enriched with Vermont cheddar cheese, the acorn squash seasoned with rum and brown sugar.

In America's heartland, side-dish cooking retains the imprint of waves of German and Scandinavian settlers. In the hundred years after 1830, more Germans and Austrians than any other nationality came to America, settling primarily in the Midwest. In the same era, Norwegians and Scandinavians seized the opportunity to farm the upper Mississippi Valley. Their numbers remain strong today in Iowa, Wisconsin, and Minnesota.

So what might accompany a roast chicken in the Midwest? Possibly spaetzle, the German egg noodles, made by pushing a soft dough through a colander into boiling water. Or perhaps Minnesota's nutty wild rice, seasoned with some of the chicken drippings. A cook with German roots would likely braise some red cabbage with apples or prepare a potato

Left: Hawaii's sunny days and warm, blue-green waters provide the ideal setting for windsurfing, snorkeling, and scuba diving. **Top:** With its thick adobe walls and sculptural buttresses, San Francisco de Asis Church in Ranchos de Taos, New Mexico, has been a popular subject for artists and photographers, Georgia O'Keeffe among them. When the church bells are rung, they can be heard across the valley from where the nearly three-centuries-old community of Ranchos de Taos is located. **Above:** Seated in his canoe, a Native American harvester poles his craft through a field of ready-to-pick wild rice on Minnesota's Rice Lake.

salad with hot bacon dressing. For a vegetable lover, an Amish table in Indiana might offer the most appealing side-dish selection in the Midwest. Although the Amish are predominantly plain cooks, they are also dedicated gardeners who rely heavily on home-grown produce. Depending on the season, a supper-time visitor might find a roast chicken paired with creamed garden peas, beets in orange sauce, coleslaw, spiced tomato preserves, baked limas, or homemade egg noodles topped with toasted bread crumbs.

On a gleaming antique dining table in Charleston, South Carolina, the companion to a roast chicken would likely be rice. Although the state's marshy Low Country hasn't been rice country for several generations, a taste for the grain persists, a holdover from the era when Carolina-grown rice dominated the national market and was prized worldwide. In the vast stretches of Carolina wetlands, early settlers saw potential for rice. They maintained immense plantations and built graceful mansions in

Below: In the Southwest, jewel-like Indian corn, here displayed for sale at a New Mexico roadside stand, is typically used to decorate houses during the fall and winter holiday season. **Bottom:** A snow-covered hill provides an afternoon of winter fun. **Right:** At a 1950s-style diner in California, customers sit down to old-fashioned burgers, thick milk shakes, ice-cream sundaes, hot apple pies, and ice-cold sodas, while listening to jukebox hits.

Charleston with their profits. States using more mechanized production put Carolina rice virtually out of business by the early 1900s. For their roast chicken, today's Low Country locals might choose to make red rice, toasting the grains first in bacon drippings before adding tomato and chicken broth.

In the Southwest, the revered trinity of corn, beans, and squash still holds sway, 450 years after Francisco Vásquez de Coronado first saw the Pueblos growing these crops in what is now northern New Mexico. In the modern kitchen, the corn may be fresh sweet corn or blue corn posole (dried kernels). The squashes may be thin-skinned zucchini (courgettes) in summer and hard-shelled pumpkins in winter. The beans will probably be dried pintos, although some cooks are seeking out the heirloom types, such as tepary and Anasazi, that the indigenous people grew. Corn and beans, corn and squash, beans and squash, or all together—southwestern cooks have mastered every permutation. Perhaps a roast chicken will arrive at the table with corn pudding, some meaty tepary beans cooked with garlic and chile, or a bowl of summer squash simmered with green chilies and cheese.

In California, where health-conscious diners often put vegetables center stage, side dishes can constitute a meal. Restaurants often list creative vegetable dishes à la carte, and some diners never venture beyond them. Adventuresome home cooks, inspired by chefs, have learned that the charcoal grill imparts delicious caramelized and smoky flavors to many vegetables, including some, like parsnips or asparagus, that a more conventional cook would never think to grill. On a Los Angeles patio on a balmy evening, guests might well sit down to a store-bought roast chicken picked up on the host's way home from work, served with a bountiful platter of just-grilled vegetables—halved tomatoes, baby squashes, radicchio wedges, and Asian eggplants (slender aubergines)— with a balsamic-vinegar basting or a garnish of chopped garden herbs providing a flavor boost to a side dish that threatens to upstage the bird.

In Seattle, where Asian influences have seeped into the local cooking, a chicken

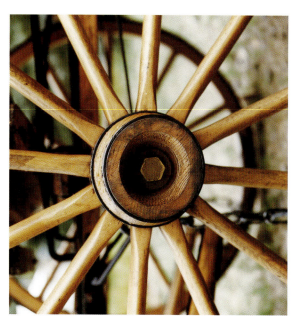

Top: Heads of organic lettuce are packed into boxes at an Oregon farm for transport to local farmers' markets and other retail outlets. The variety of lettuces now available to American cooks has grown dramatically in recent years, with Lollo Rosso, Summer Bibb, and Buttercrunch among the choices. **Above:** Wooden wheels on a Colorado road recall mid-nineteenth-century America, when homesteaders, promised a tract of free public farmland, migrated west by horse-drawn wagon.

might be roasted with lemongrass and kaffir lime leaves and sent to the table with Thai noodles. At the burgeoning farmers' markets in Seattle and Portland, shoppers can find baby bok choy and *gai lan* (Chinese broccoli), Thai basil, and cilantro roots, signs of the region's large and changing Asian population.

The first Chinese arrived in the Pacific Northwest in the mid-nineteenth century to help build the transcontinental railroad, and their culinary ways, especially their stir-fry techniques, left a mark on tasters accustomed to soggy, overcooked vegetables. Before World War II, Japanese farmers had established themselves in Washington's Puget Sound area and were selling produce at Pike Place Market. In recent years, Thai, Vietnamese, Filipino, Korean, and Laotian immigrants have settled in the Pacific Northwest in large numbers. By introducing chefs and home cooks to their palette of ingredients, they guarantee that America's chickens will continue to have a wide array of partners at the table.

Below: In the area around tiny Castroville, California, on Monterey Bay, some three-fourths of the world's globe artichoke crop is now grown, a huge industry started by Swiss-Italian immigrants in the 1880s. **Bottom:** Settled in the 1600s, Cape Cod, a long, narrow, curved peninsula off southern Massachusetts, is a popular summertime vacation destination.

Red Potato Salad with Dill

Whether the occasion is a Sunday afternoon family lunch, a dinner at the beach, or a neighborhood picnic following the local Fourth of July parade, one thing is certain: potato salad will be on the menu. New Englanders love their homegrown potatoes, especially small red and white ones freshly dug in backyard gardens. Dressed with mayonnaise, a few crisp vegetables, and a handful of chopped dill, this homespun version of the ubiquitous salad is a welcome addition to nearly any table.

1½ lb (750 g) red potatoes, preferably small, unpeeled

kosher salt to taste

⅔ cup (5 fl oz/160 ml) mayonnaise

1 tablespoon cider vinegar

1 small red bell pepper (capsicum), seeded and chopped

3 green (spring) onions, including tender green tops, thinly sliced

2 tablespoons chopped fresh dill

freshly ground pepper to taste

☙ In a large saucepan, combine the potatoes with water to cover. Salt lightly and bring to a boil over high heat. Reduce the heat to medium-low and simmer until the potatoes are tender when pierced with a knife, 15–20 minutes; the timing will depend on their size. Drain the potatoes and, when cool enough to handle, cut into halves, quarters, or 1-inch (2.5-cm) chunks, again depending on their size.

☙ In a large bowl, stir together the mayonnaise and cider vinegar until smooth. Add the slightly warm potatoes, bell pepper, green onions, and dill and toss gently to combine the ingredients. Season with salt and pepper.

☙ Spoon the salad into a serving bowl and serve immediately. The salad will keep, covered in the refrigerator, for up to 2 days.

serves 6

Blueberry Muffins

Blueberries are indigenous to New England, where the small, dark, sweet fruits still flourish in the wild on low bushes, especially in Maine. They are difficult to harvest and highly perishable, so their cultivated cousins have replaced them in most kitchens. Cultivated blueberries are larger and sturdier, and their taller bushes make the fruits easier to pick. Some people think of big, juicy blueberry muffins only as a breakfast or teatime treat, but New Englanders take full advantage of the season and serve them alongside grilled chicken or lamb chops and a tangy green salad.

2¼ cups (11½ oz/360 g) all-purpose (plain) flour

½ cup (4 oz/125 g) sugar, plus 2 teaspoons for topping (optional)

1 tablespoon baking powder

½ teaspoon salt

1 cup (8 fl oz/250 ml) milk

1 egg, at room temperature

¾ teaspoon vanilla extract (essence)

½ cup (4 oz/125 g) unsalted butter, melted and cooled slightly

½ pt (4 oz/125 g) blueberries

☙ Preheat an oven to 375°F (190°C). Line 12 muffin-pan cups with foil or paper liners.

☙ In a large bowl, whisk together the flour, ½ cup (4 oz/125 g) sugar, baking powder, and salt until well blended. In a small bowl, whisk together the milk, egg, and vanilla until well blended. Add the milk mixture, melted butter, and blueberries to the flour mixture and stir gently just until combined. Spoon the batter into the prepared muffin cups, dividing evenly. They should be no more than three-fourths full. If desired, sprinkle the tops evenly with the 2 teaspoons sugar.

☙ Bake the muffins until they are golden and a toothpick inserted into the center of a muffin comes out clean, 18–20 minutes. Let the pan sit on a wire rack for 5 minutes, then remove the muffins from the pan and place on the rack. Serve warm or at room temperature.

makes 12 muffins

Pike Place Market

Americans shop differently from much of the rest of the world, relishing the convenience of a big grocery store where they can buy lettuce, rib steaks, and milk along with cleaning supplies, dog food, and a greeting card all in a single stop. At the same time, a second, quite opposite way of stocking the pantry is experiencing a renaissance: the farmers' market. Shoppers in urban centers and small towns across the country are now buying fresh fruits and vegetables directly from growers.

One of the country's oldest and most beloved farmers' markets is Pike Place Market in downtown Seattle. Established in August 1907, it was an economic experiment designed to eliminate the middlemen who were driving down farmers' earnings while driving up consumers' costs. Bringing together growers and shoppers to do business face to face launched a vital institution that has operated without interruption since its opening.

Today more than one hundred farmers from throughout the region sell their produce in the network of stalls along one side of the cobbled street that dissects this nine-acre (3.5-ha)

historic district, with its century-old brick buildings and open-air arcades. On Sundays and Wednesdays during summer and early fall, the growing Northwest organic-farming movement is featured, and shoppers are quick to home in on the two dozen or so stands selling certified organic vegetables and fruits. The market also shelters a bounty of permanent purveyors of produce, seafood, meat, and bread, along with numerous sellers offering ethnic and other specialty foods. Customers can buy everything from freshly steamed tamales, local maple blossom honey, and Asian vegetables to smoked salmon, chewy baguettes, and just-cut flowers.

Everyone who visits Pike Place Market passes Rachel the pig, a strapping 750-pound (375-kg) brass piggy bank that stands just below the large neon-lit clock that dominates the market entrance. Rachel is both the mascot of the market and the drop spot for donations to the Pike Place Market Foundation, which works to preserve the character of the market through public education and human service programs for the needy.

SAVORING AMERICA

Pacific Northwest

Grilled Asparagus with Toasted Hazelnuts

The rich volcanic soil and mild spring weather of eastern Washington prove ideal growing conditions for asparagus, making the state a top national grower of the hazelnuts in the United States. Oregon grows virtually all asparagus, making the state a top national grower (right behind California). Oregon grows virtually all of the hazelnuts in the United States. It seems natural to combine the vivid green stalks of asparagus with the nutty crunch of hazelnuts in this quintessential Pacific Northwest combination. Choose asparagus spears that are thick rather than thin; they are generally more flavorful and will hold up better on the grill.

1 lb (500 g) asparagus spears

2 teaspoons hazelnut (filbert) oil

2 teaspoons canola oil

salt and freshly ground pepper to taste

¼ cup (1½ oz / 45 g) chopped toasted and skinned hazelnuts (filberts)

☙ Prepare a fire in a grill.

☙ Trim off the tough ends of the asparagus spears, bending them near the end and allowing the stalks to break naturally where the tough portion ends.

☙ In a small bowl, combine the hazelnut oil and canola oil. Brush the asparagus spears with the oil blend. Season lightly with salt and pepper.

☙ When the fire is ready, lightly brush the grill rack with oil. Lay the asparagus on the grill, setting them perpendicular to the direction of the rack bars so that they do not fall onto the fire.

☙ Grill the asparagus, turning a few times to cook evenly, until tender and lightly browned, 2–3 minutes.

☙ Transfer the asparagus to a serving platter or individual plates, scatter the chopped hazelnuts over the spears, and serve at once.

serves 4

South

Vidalia Onion "Mums" with Pecans

Sweet Vidalia onions are one of the treasures of Georgia agriculture. This recipe can also be made with any of Vidalia's well-known rivals, including the Walla Walla, Maui, or Texas 1015 Supersweet. When cooked, these delicious baked onions open to resemble large chrysanthemum blossoms.

6 large Vidalia onions

½ cup (4 fl oz/125 ml) olive oil, plus extra for brushing

¼ cup (2 fl oz/60 ml) balsamic vinegar

½ cup (2 oz/60 g) chopped pecans

¼ cup (⅓ oz/10 g) chopped mixed fresh herbs such as flat-leaf (Italian) parsley, sage, rosemary, and thyme

salt and freshly ground pepper to taste

¾ cup (6 fl oz/180 ml) chicken stock

½ cup (2 oz/60 g) grated Parmesan cheese

❧ Preheat an oven to 425°F (220°C).

❧ Make a cut across the blossom end (top) of each onion and gently peel off the skin, leaving the root end intact. Using a sharp knife, make a cut through the center of the onion, going down to, but not through, the root end. Make a second cut perpendicular to the first, again stopping before the root end. The onion will now be quartered. Then make 2 more cuts, so the onion is in eighths but still attached at the root end.

❧ Place the onions side by side in a baking dish. Drizzle with the ½ cup (4 fl oz/125 ml) olive oil and the balsamic vinegar. Sprinkle with the pecans, herbs, salt, and pepper. Pour the chicken stock around the onions. Cover with aluminum foil.

❧ Bake the onions for 45 minutes. Remove the foil, brush the onions with olive oil, and top with the Parmesan cheese. Continue to bake until the onions are soft when pierced with a fork, about 15 minutes.

❧ Remove from the oven and allow to stand for at least 10 minutes. Serve the onions warm or at room temperature directly from the dish.

serves 6

Herbed Spaetzle

These tender noodlelike dumplings are traditionally all about technique, which inevitably depends on the type of equipment you have on hand. Spaetzle presses or slicers make the process much easier, but a colander with large holes or a steamer insert works fine with a little practice. In Germany where this dish originated, the dough is usually much stiffer. Cooks use a special "paddle" and a sharp knife to drop shards of dough expertly into boiling salted water.

For this version, the consistency should be that of drop biscuits, somewhere between a batter and a dough. The idea is to push or extrude the dough through the holes of the colander or steamer insert directly into boiling water. Choose one or more herbs that will complement the other dishes on the menu. Give spaetzle a home in soup, alongside roast meat, or under a stew rich with gravy.

1 cup (8 fl oz/250 ml) milk, or more if needed

2 eggs

1 tablespoon finely chopped fresh herbs (see note)

½ teaspoon kosher salt or coarse sea salt, plus salt to taste

⅛ teaspoon freshly grated nutmeg

2¼ cups (11½ oz/360 g) all-purpose (plain) flour, or more if needed

2 tablespoons unsalted butter

freshly ground white pepper to taste

❧ Fill a large pot three-fourths full of water, place over high heat, and bring to a boil. Ideally, the colander or steamer insert you use will sit above the water. If not, you might need a helper to hold it while you extrude the dough.

❧ In a bowl, beat together the 1 cup (8 fl oz/250 ml) milk, eggs, herbs, ½ teaspoon salt, and nutmeg until smooth. Add the 2¼ cups (11½ oz/360 g) flour and stir to combine. Let the dough rest for 10 minutes. It should be fairly wet, like the dough for drop biscuits or a thick pancake batter. If not, adjust accordingly with a little more milk or flour.

❧ When the water is boiling, begin making the spaetzle: Place the butter in the bottom of a pan set over very low heat and allow it to melt; keep warm. Salt the water lightly and reduce the heat so that it boils gently.

serves 4

❧ Put about one-third of the dough into the colander or steamer insert. Holding it over the boiling water and using a rubber spatula, potato masher, or plastic pastry scraper, push down on the dough. Dribbles of dough should emerge from the bottom and drop into the water. Do not stir. Free-form "noodles" will take shape and rise to the top when done. Between batches, scrape the bottom of the colander to finish forming the noodles. Try to keep the water at a steady gentle bubble. If it boils too hard, the delicate spaetzle will disintegrate.

❧ As the spaetzle rise to the top, lift out of the water with a slotted spoon or wire skimmer, draining off as much water as possible. Transfer to the pan with the butter and stir gently. Cover to keep the spaetzle warm, but do not allow them to cook further. Repeat the process until all the spaetzle are boiled and tossed in butter.

❧ Transfer the butter-coated spaetzle to a warmed bowl or individual plates and serve immediately.

California

Grilled Eggplant with Soy-Ginger Glaze

In some California farmers' markets and produce markets, the eggplant selection is as multicultural as the clientele. Shoppers may find slender, lavender-skinned types for Chinese recipes; the dark purple varieties, also elongated but shorter than the Chinese, that Japanese cooks prefer; small, round, green eggplants for Thai and Indian curries; an elongated purple variety sometimes labeled "Italian"; and the giant globe eggplant with its purple-black skin. In contrast to the familiar globe eggplant, the elongated varieties have more tender skin, fewer seeds, and a milder taste that many cooks have come to appreciate.

Halved lengthwise and grilled with a basting of teriyaki-style soy-ginger sauce, they become creamy inside and richly caramelized. Be sure the fire in your grill is not raging hot, or the eggplants will char before they cook through.

3 tablespoons soy sauce

2 tablespoons sake

2 tablespoons mirin

2 tablespoons sugar

1 tablespoon peeled and finely minced fresh ginger

2 teaspoons Asian sesame oil

1 lb (500 g) Asian eggplants (slender aubergines)

2 teaspoons sesame seed, toasted

2 green (spring) onions, including tender green tops, halved lengthwise and then very thinly sliced crosswise

☙ In a saucepan over medium heat, combine the soy sauce, sake, mirin, sugar, and ginger. Bring to a simmer, stirring to dissolve the sugar. Simmer for 1 minute to release the ginger flavor. Let cool, then stir in the sesame oil.

☙ Prepare a medium-hot fire in a grill.

☙ Cut the eggplants lengthwise into slices about ¼ inch (6 mm) thick. Brush the slices on one side with the soy mixture, then put the slices, brushed side down, on the grill. Cook, turning frequently and basting often with the sauce, until the slices are tender, about 5 minutes. Transfer the eggplant slices to a warmed platter. Garnish with the sesame seed and the green onions. Serve immediately.

serves 4

California

Thai-Style Long Beans

Available in California's many Asian markets and some supermarkets, long beans (also called Chinese long beans or yard-long beans) are more closely related to black-eyed peas than to green beans. Although "yard-long" is a bit of an exaggeration, they can be eighteen inches (45 cm) or more in length. These beans are sturdier and more deeply flavored than the familiar Western green beans and take well to stir-frying with pungent seasonings.

Nam prik pao, a Thai chile paste seasoned with fish sauce, shrimp paste, sugar, and roasted garlic, cloaks the beans with powerful sweet, salty, and roasted flavors. Look for it in Asian groceries and well-stocked supermarkets. If you have a choice of mild, medium, or hot styles, choose at least the medium strength. Thai fish sauce is a thin, pungent, salty liquid made from fermented anchovies. Serve these beans with steamed jasmine rice and roast duck, pork, or chicken.

1 lb (500 g) long beans, ends trimmed and cut into 3-inch (7.5-cm) lengths

1½ tablespoons peanut oil

4 cloves garlic, chopped

2½ tablespoons nam prik pao *(see note)* thinned with 2 tablespoons water

2 tablespoons Thai fish sauce *(see note)*

1 cup (1½ oz/45 g) coarsely chopped fresh cilantro (fresh coriander), plus sprigs for garnish

☙ Bring a large pot three-fourths full of salted water to a boil. Add the long beans and boil until they lose their raw crunch, 3–4 minutes. Drain well.

☙ Place a wok or a deep frying pan over high heat. When it is hot, add the peanut oil. When the oil is hot, add the garlic and stir-fry for a few seconds to release its flavor.

☙ Add the long beans and stir-fry until coated with oil, about 1 minute. Add the diluted *nam prik pao* and stir-fry until it coats the beans evenly, 1–2 minutes. Add the fish sauce and stir-fry for about 1 minute to distribute it well and evaporate any liquid in the pan. Remove the pan from the heat, add the chopped cilantro, and toss well.

☙ Transfer the beans to a warmed serving bowl. Garnish with cilantro sprigs and serve immediately.

serves 4

Southwest

Posole

Corn and beans are the two great staples of the Southwest. Eaten together, they provide the full complement of amino acids necessary for a healthful, though meatless, diet. Like beans, fresh corn originally needed to be dried to preserve it for year-round use. When slaked with lime, which helps remove the tough skins from the kernels, and then dried, corn becomes posole (pozole, as it is called in Mexico), a variation especially beloved by Native Americans of the region, as well as by descendants of the original Spanish settlers in northern New Mexico.

Canned hominy is the more familiar form of posole, but the dried version, soaked and simmered with a few simple seasonings, is far tastier and more authentic. Served thick or soupy, with a celebratory amount of meat or a more frugal one, posole functions as side dish or main and delivers a nostalgic hit of comfort similar to that of mashed potatoes. Make the posole a day or two ahead, for maximum flavor. If you cannot find dried posole in a well-stocked supermarket, look for it in a market specializing in Hispanic foods.

1 lb (500 g) dried posole or 2 lb (1 kg) presoaked dried posole

½–1 lb (250–500 g) boneless pork shoulder or boneless lamb shoulder

3 tablespoons lard, bacon drippings, or olive oil

2 yellow onions, finely chopped

8 cloves garlic, finely chopped

1 tablespoon dried Mexican oregano

1 teaspoon red pepper flakes

8 cups (64 fl oz) water

5 cups (40 fl oz / 1.25 l) chicken stock

2 teaspoons salt, plus salt to taste

1 teaspoon freshly ground black pepper, plus black pepper to taste

☘ If using dried posole, in a large bowl, combine the posole with water to cover and let stand overnight, stirring occasionally. Drain. If using pre-soaked posole, set it aside.

☘ Trim excess fat from the pork or lamb shoulder and cut the meat into ½-inch (12-mm) cubes. Set the meat aside.

serves 12

In a large, tall (rather than wide) 6-qt (6-l) or larger pot over medium heat, warm the lard or other fat. Add the onions, garlic, oregano, and red pepper flakes, cover, and cook, stirring once or twice to prevent browning, until the onions and garlic are almost tender and golden, about 10 minutes. Add the water, stock, and posole and bring to a simmer.

Meanwhile, place a large frying pan over medium-low heat. Scatter the meat over the bottom and cook, stirring occasionally, until the meat is firm, has lost its pink color, and has given up a generous amount of liquid, about 10 minutes. Raise the heat to medium-high and cook, stirring often, until the liquid evaporates and the meat is well browned in its rendered fat, 10–12 minutes.

Remove the frying pan from the heat and transfer the meat to the pot with the posole. Add 2 cups (16 fl oz/500 ml) of the posole cooking liquid to the frying pan off the heat and stir well to dissolve any browned bits on the pan bottom. Return the liquid to the pot.

Bring to a simmer, cover partially, and cook, stirring once or twice, for 1 hour. Add the 2 teaspoons salt and the 1 teaspoon black pepper and continue to simmer partially covered, stirring often, until the meat is tender and most of the posole kernels have burst, 1–1½ hours longer. Add more water to the pot if you plan to serve the posole soup style.

Serve immediately, if desired, or, for a better flavor, let cool to room temperature, cover, and refrigerate for up to 3 days. (The posole can also be frozen for up to 1 month.) Rewarm over medium heat until piping hot, stirring often. Taste and adjust the seasoning, then spoon into individual bowls or small, deep, wide plates. Serve at once.

The Southwest's earliest cultivated corn varieties came in a rainbow of colors~red, yellow, white, blue.

Native American Traditions

The original inhabitants of the Southwest were primarily gatherers or gardeners, a result of the region's arid climate. Lack of a steady water source in any one spot forced the gatherers to keep moving, while the gardeners settled in enormous adobe communes, or pueblos, near the reliable Rio Grande. The pueblos, flat-roofed, thick-walled adobe buildings sometimes rising several stories high, may seem to have offered a more civilized existence, but the gatherers were never aimless wanderers. They were industrious and disciplined, with a well-developed knowledge of botany and a keen sense of timing for when plants came into season.

These nomads and settlers alike had a deep respect for nature and invested their food with a sacredness that prevented them from ever taking it for granted, an attitude that persists today. Then as now, those lucky enough to bring down a deer always asked its forgiveness.

Among the indigenous ingredients that the first Americans introduced to the world are chiles, melons, squashes, beans, and, most important, corn, believed to be the ultimate source of life. Corn is prepared in as many as 250 different ways by Native Americans and continues to be celebrated in song and dance as one of nature's most important gifts.

New England

Old-Fashioned Macaroni and Cheese

Cheddar cheese originated in the small town of Cheddar, England, and early English settlers in New England introduced their ancestral "cheddaring" technique—allowing the curds to become firm so they do not break when the cheese is turned—as a way of preserving milk. The best cheddar is a creamy, ivory color and ranges in flavor from mellow to extra sharp, depending on how long it has been aged. At the time of the Civil War, Vermont produced more cheese than any other state. Today, although no longer number one in production, it remains an important manufacturer of high-quality cheddars and other cheeses.

3 cups (24 fl oz/750 ml) milk

½ small yellow onion, finely chopped

1 clove garlic, minced

4 fresh thyme sprigs

½ small bay leaf

1 tablespoon plus 1½ teaspoons kosher salt

10 oz (315 g) dried rotelli or other short pasta shape

¼ cup (2 oz/60 g) unsalted butter

3 tablespoons all-purpose (plain) flour

½ lb (250 g) sharp Vermont cheddar cheese, shredded

¼ cup (⅓ oz/10 g) minced fresh chives

2 tablespoons dry sherry

freshly ground pepper to taste

TOPPING (OPTIONAL)

⅓ cup (1½ oz/45 g) fine dried bread crumbs

2 tablespoons grated Parmesan cheese

1 tablespoon olive oil or melted unsalted butter

🍋 Preheat an oven to 350°F (180°C). Lightly butter a 1½-qt (1.5-l) shallow baking dish.

🍋 In a saucepan over medium-high heat, combine the milk, onion, garlic, thyme, and bay leaf. Bring to a boil, remove from the heat, and set aside.

🍋 Bring a large pot three-fourths full of water to a boil. Add the 1 tablespoon salt and the pasta and stir well. Boil until about 1 minute short of al dente, about 10 minutes or according to the package directions. Drain the pasta well, rinse with cold water, and drain well again.

🍋 In the same pot in which the pasta was cooked, melt the butter over medium-low heat. Add the flour and whisk until well blended. Continue to cook, whisking constantly, until the mixture is bubbly but not browned, about 1 minute. Whisking constantly, slowly add the infused milk mixture. Raise the heat to medium-high and whisk constantly until the mixture boils. Reduce the heat to low and simmer gently, whisking occasionally, until the mixture is smooth and thick, about 5 minutes.

🍋 Remove the pot from the heat. Remove the bay leaf and the thyme sprigs, pluck off any thyme leaves still clinging to the stems, and return them to the pot, discarding the stems and bay leaf. Add the cheddar cheese, chives, sherry, 1½ teaspoons salt, and pepper. Stir until the cheese is just melted and smooth. Add the drained pasta and toss gently to combine. Pour into the prepared baking dish.

🍋 If desired, make the topping: In a small bowl, combine the bread crumbs, Parmesan cheese, and olive oil or butter. Stir until well blended. Sprinkle the mixture evenly over the pasta.

🍋 Bake the pasta until the sauce is bubbly around the edges of the dish and the top is browned, about 40 minutes. Remove from the oven and serve at once directly from the baking dish.

serves 6–8

Great Plains

Turnip Flapjacks

Even people who turn up their noses at the mention of turnips will love these savory griddle cakes. Because this root vegetable has little sugar or starch, the shreds brown slowly on a hot surface, giving the flapjacks time to develop a creamy interior. The results deliver several distinct textures and levels of flavor.

2 large or 3 or 4 medium turnips, about 1 lb (500 g) total weight

2 tablespoons unsalted butter, melted, plus about ¼ cup (2 oz/60 g)

1 cup (8 fl oz/250 ml) half-and-half (half cream)

1 egg

½ teaspoon kosher salt or coarse sea salt

1 cup (5 oz/155 g) all-purpose (plain) flour

milk if needed for thinning

½ cup (4 oz/125 g) sour cream (optional)

¼ cup (⅓ oz/10 g) minced fresh chervil (optional)

Peel the turnips. Using the large holes on a box grater-shredder, shred the turnips into ribbons as long as possible. You should have 2 packed cups (10 oz/315 g). Toss with the 2 tablespoons melted butter. In a large bowl, beat together the half-and-half, egg, and salt. Stir in the flour and mix just to combine. Fold in the shredded turnips until evenly coated. Thin with a little milk if the turnip mixture seems too dry. It should just coat the turnips.

Heat a heavy, large frying pan over medium heat. Sprinkle with a few drops of water. If they dance around for a moment and then evaporate, the temperature is correct. If they vaporize immediately, the surface is too hot. Coat with just enough of the ¼ cup (2 oz/60 g) butter to prevent sticking.

For each flapjack, spread a heaping forkful of turnip batter on the frying pan to form thin, wispy 3-inch (7.5-cm) cakes. Fry, turning once, until both sides are deeply browned, about 5 minutes on each side. Transfer to a platter and keep warm in a low oven. Butter the pan as needed to prevent sticking. Serve immediately, either plain or garnished with sour cream and chervil, if desired.

makes about 12 flapjacks; serves 4

Southwest

Pot Beans

Once a necessary protein staple in a harsh land with limited domestic and wild animal life, beans continue to be essential in the southwestern kitchen—accessible, accommodating, and rib-sticking. In New Mexico, especially in the north, the beans on your combination plate are likely to be pot beans, pintos simmered to creamy tenderness with just a touch of subtle seasoning and served whole, in a bit of their naturally thickened broth. For frijoles negros, simply replace the pinto beans with an equal amount of dried black beans. Note that either way, the beans will be tastier if they are prepared at least a day in advance.

4½ cups (2 lb/1 kg) dried pinto beans

1 yellow onion, finely chopped

¼ lb (125 g) lean salt pork, rind removed and meat finely chopped

5 cloves garlic, chopped

2 teaspoons salt

❧ Pick over the beans and place in a large bowl. Cover with tepid water and let stand for 10 minutes. Drain and repeat twice more.

❧ Transfer the beans to a large, tall (rather than wide) 6-qt (6-l) or larger pot. Add fresh water to cover the beans by 4 inches (10 cm) and place over medium heat. Add the onion, salt pork, and garlic and bring to a simmer. Cover partially and cook the beans, stirring occasionally, for 1 hour. Stir in the salt, re-cover partially, and continue to simmer, stirring often and adding boiling water if the beans are becoming dry, until tender, 1–1½ hours longer. The finished beans should be tender but still hold their shape, and be surrounded by a rich, thick broth.

❧ Serve immediately, if desired, or, for better flavor, let cool to room temperature, cover, and refrigerate for up to 3 days. (The beans can also be frozen for up to 1 month.) Rewarm over high heat until piping hot, stirring often. Taste and adjust the seasoning. Transfer the beans and some of the broth to a warmed serving bowl and serve at once.

serves 12

Southwest

Green Rice

Rice came to Mexico from Spain, and few countries do more with it. Some of this expertise has crossed the border into the Southwest, mostly in the ubiquitous form of what is known as "Spanish rice." Red, mildly spiced and seasoned, it is usually mushy from a long sit in a restaurant steam table. As an alternative, try this verdant, cilantro-fragrant pilaf, which is worthy of its heritage. For the best results, use long-grain (or even extra-long-grain) rice and do not rinse it. The dish should be cooked just before serving, but the cilantro purée can be prepared up to four hours in advance. The recipe can be doubled to serve eight.

1 cup (8 fl oz/250 ml) chicken or beef stock

1 cup (8 fl oz/250 ml) water

3 tablespoons olive oil

1 cup (7 oz/220 g) long-grain white rice

¾ cup (1 oz/30 g) chopped fresh cilantro (fresh coriander)

1 small jalapeño chile, chopped

2 green (spring) onions, including tender green tops, chopped

1 clove garlic, chopped

pinch of salt

❧ In a small saucepan over low heat, combine the stock and the water and bring to a simmer. In a heavy saucepan over medium heat, warm 2 tablespoons of the olive oil. Add the rice and cook, stirring occasionally, until the grains are separate and opaque, 2–3 minutes. Gradually stir in the simmering stock (it will boil up vigorously), then reduce the heat, cover, and cook undisturbed until the rice has absorbed the liquid and is tender, about 20 minutes.

❧ While the rice cooks, in a food processor, combine the cilantro, jalapeño, green onions, garlic, remaining 1 tablespoon oil, and salt. Process, stopping to scrape down the sides of the work bowl as needed, until fairly smooth.

❧ Remove the rice from the heat. Dollop the cilantro purée evenly over the surface of the rice, cover, and let stand undisturbed for 5 minutes. Uncover and thoroughly stir the purée into the rice, then taste and adjust the seasoning. Transfer to a warmed serving dish and serve immediately.

serves 4

Mid-Atlantic

Maple-Glazed Brussels Sprouts

In the fall, these small members of the cabbage family sprout on long, curving stalks in the cool, coastal regions of the Mid-Atlantic. The natural sturdiness of the tightly bound heads ensures that they can tolerate autumn's chilly days up until the first heavy frost, at which point they are harvested and stowed for easy weekday side dishes such as this one. Brussels sprouts are grown around the United States, but northeasterners consider Long Island, New York, home to the country's best specimens.

4 slices thick-cut bacon

2 tablespoons unsalted butter

1 lb (500 g) brussels sprouts, trimmed and halved lengthwise

1 clove garlic, minced

2 teaspoons chopped fresh thyme

¼ cup (2 fl oz/60 ml) chicken stock

3 tablespoons maple syrup

3 tablespoons chopped fresh flat-leaf (Italian) parsley

kosher salt and freshly ground pepper to taste

In a large frying pan over medium heat, fry the bacon slices, turning occasionally, until browned, about 7 minutes. Transfer to paper towels to drain, then crumble and set aside.

Add the butter to the same pan and swirl to melt. Add the brussels sprouts, garlic, and thyme and stir to coat with the bacon drippings and butter. Pour in the stock. Cover and simmer over medium heat, stirring frequently to scrape up the browned bits on the pan bottom, until barely tender, 10–12 minutes.

Uncover, raise the heat to medium-high, and add the maple syrup to the pan. Cook uncovered, stirring constantly, until the brussels sprouts are tender and glazed, about 3 minutes. Add the reserved bacon and the chopped parsley and toss until combined. Season with salt and pepper. Transfer to a warmed serving bowl and serve at once.

serves 4–6

Maple Syrup

Maple trees of all sizes and shapes grow throughout the world, all of them arrestingly beautiful. But the precious sap that streams from New England sugar maples in late winter is unique to the region. People elsewhere have tried in vain to draw sap from their sugar maples only to discover that not just the species of the tree matters, but also the climate in which it grows. The long, cold New England winter that gives way to a period of warm days and freezing nights sets up the perfect conditions for the sap to flow.

Eager to supplement the income from their usual crops, farmers are the most typical sugar makers. Often housebound by winter's frigid temperatures, they are keen to burst outdoors at the first sign of lengthening days so that they can begin tapping the maples. On a drive through the New England countryside in late winter, you will see row after row of silver collecting pails attached to the trees, their appearance an early harbinger of spring. Native Americans were instrumental in creating this enduring New England tradition. They showed the new settlers how to gather the sap

and then reduce it to a syrup. In time, the colonists revised and improved the collecting technique. Rather than gashing the bark with a hatchet, a practice that often resulted in the death of the tree, they drilled a hole in the trunk and then plugged the opening with a wooden peg from the same tree.

While further improvements in the process have been made, sugaring, as the sap-gathering procedure is known, is still time-consuming and arduous. It takes approximately forty gallons (160 l) of sap to yield one gallon (4 l) of syrup or nine pounds (4.5 kg) of maple sugar. Family, friends, and neighbors often help with the formidable task of carrying bucket after bucket of sap to the sugar shack, where they pour the contents into the evaporator. There the sap boils for hours until it is reduced to sweet, luscious maple syrup.

New Englanders revel in the first warm days of late February or early March. Dunking buttermilk doughnuts into warm syrup, or drizzling the syrup over fresh snow for a bona fide snow cone, is a New England rite of spring and a much-anticipated reward for a job well done.

Angel-Light Buttermilk Biscuits

The secret to a good southern biscuit depends on three things: choosing the correct flour, making sure the shortening and buttermilk are ice cold, and handling the dough as little as possible. The uncooked biscuit must be very wet on the inside and must have just enough flour coating the outside to permit shaping without sticking. Serve the biscuits with melted butter, honey, and fruit preserves. To make a savory version, reduce the buttermilk to ⅔ cup (5 fl oz/160 ml) and add ½ cup (4 oz/125 g) sour cream and ⅓ cup (½ oz/15 g) minced fresh chives to the dough.

3½ cups (14½ oz/450 g) self-rising soft winter-wheat flour such as White Lily (page 248)

1 teaspoon salt

¼ cup (2 oz/60 g) solid vegetable shortening (vegetable lard), well chilled

1¼ cups (10 fl oz/310 ml) buttermilk, well chilled

❦ Preheat an oven to 475°F (245°C).

❦ In a large bowl, stir together 2½ cups (10 oz/315 g) of the flour and the salt. Add the shortening and, using a pastry blender, cut in the shortening. Shake the bowl occasionally so that the larger pieces come to the top of the mixture and you can work them to a consistent size. The pieces of shortening should be the size of peas. Add the buttermilk and stir only until the ingredients are well combined and the dough holds together. Do not overwork.

❦ Sprinkle about ⅓ cup (1½ oz/45 g) of the flour over the dough, turn the dough, and sprinkle another ⅓ cup (1½ oz/45 g) flour over the dough. Flour your hands, pinch off a piece of dough about the size of a small egg, dip the wet part into the remaining ⅓ cup (1½ oz/45 g) flour, and gently knead by rolling the dough in your hands to form a ball. The outside should not be sticky; the inside should be very wet. Flatten the biscuit slightly and place in an ungreased 9-inch (23-cm) round cake pan. Repeat with the remaining dough, placing the biscuits, touching, in the pan.

❦ Bake the biscuits until they are golden brown, 15–18 minutes. Transfer to a rack and let cool slightly.

makes about 12 biscuits

Calabacitas with Chiles, Corn, and Cheese

Just like the rest of the United States, the modern Southwest now has all the arugula, bok choy, and shiitake mushrooms it can handle. This was not always the case, however, and in a harsh, dry country, vegetables were naturally limited in variety and season. Fortunately, there were saving graces, among them squashes, both summer and winter types, which could even be dried, like chiles and corn, for year-round use.

The word calabacitas means "little squash," and today it is commonly applied to this dish as well, a survivor of those harder times. When the starchy comfort of beans or posole begins to tire, think of this colorful little vegetable stew as an accompaniment to enchiladas or even a plain roast chicken, or as the centerpiece of a meatless meal, with some tortillas or corn bread on the side. For visual variety, this recipe replaces some of the zucchini and yellow squashes with baby green or yellow pattypans and adds a red bell pepper for color.

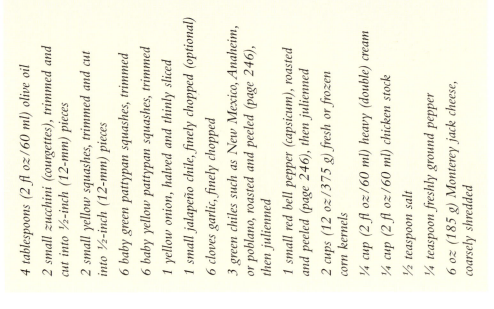

4 tablespoons (2 fl oz/60 ml) olive oil

2 small zucchini (courgettes), trimmed and cut into ½-inch (12-mm) pieces

2 small yellow squashes, trimmed and cut into ½-inch (12-mm) pieces

6 baby green pattypan squashes, trimmed

6 baby yellow pattypan squashes, trimmed

1 yellow onion, halved and thinly sliced

1 small jalapeño chile, finely chopped (optional)

6 cloves garlic, finely chopped

3 green chiles such as New Mexico, Anaheim, or poblano, roasted and peeled (page 246), then julienned

1 small red bell pepper (capsicum), roasted and peeled (page 246), then julienned

2 cups (12 oz/375 g) fresh or frozen corn kernels

¼ cup (2 fl oz/60 ml) heavy (double) cream

¼ cup (2 fl oz/60 ml) chicken stock

½ teaspoon salt

¼ teaspoon freshly ground pepper

6 oz (185 g) Monterey jack cheese, coarsely shredded

❦ In a large, deep frying pan over medium-high heat, warm 2 tablespoons of the olive oil. Add the zucchini, yellow squashes, and pattypan squashes and cook, turning once or twice, until browned, about 10 minutes. Using a slotted spoon, transfer to paper towels to drain. Discard the oil in the pan.

❦ Return the frying pan to medium heat and add the remaining 2 tablespoons oil. Add the onion, jalapeño chile (if using), and garlic, cover, and cook, stirring once or twice, until the vegetables begin to soften, about 8 minutes.

❦ Add the green chiles, bell pepper, corn, browned squashes, cream, stock, salt, and pepper to the pan. Bring to a simmer and cook uncovered, stirring occasionally, until the cream and stock have reduced and are coating the vegetables, 5–7 minutes. Remove from the heat, stir in the cheese, cover, and let stand until the cheese has melted, about 5 minutes.

❦ Taste and adjust the seasoning, then transfer to a warmed serving bowl. Serve at once.

serves 8

Pacific Northwest
Sautéed Wild Mushrooms

Days after the first big rains of early fall, mushroom foragers throughout the Pacific Northwest head to the foothills to see what mycological magic nature has provided. Wild mushrooms grow in abundance in the region, from yellow, white, and black chanterelles to hedgehogs, shaggy manes, porcini, and cauliflower mushrooms. This recipe can be made with any one of these, or a combination, or even with cultivated button mushrooms. Keep in mind that only trained mycologists should collect mushrooms from the wild. For most of us, it is best to stick with what the professional foragers bring to markets.

1½ lb (750 g) fresh wild mushrooms (see note), brushed clean and trimmed

3 tablespoons unsalted butter

½ cup (1½ oz/45 g) sliced green (spring) onion, including tender green tops

1 tablespoon minced garlic

¼ cup (2 fl oz/60 ml) dry white wine or dry vermouth

2 tablespoons minced fresh flat-leaf (Italian) parsley

2 teaspoons minced fresh thyme

½ teaspoon minced fresh rosemary

salt and freshly ground pepper to taste

❧ If using tender mushrooms, such as chanterelles, halve or quarter the larger ones and leave the small ones whole. For larger, denser mushrooms, such as porcini, cut into slices about ½ inch (12 mm) thick.

❧ In a large frying pan over medium-high heat, melt the butter. Add the green onion and garlic and sauté until aromatic, 1–2 minutes. Add the mushrooms and sauté, stirring, until tender, about 5 minutes.

❧ Add the white wine or vermouth, parsley, thyme, rosemary, salt, and pepper. Continue cooking, stirring often, until the liquid has reduced by about half and is slightly thickened, about 5 minutes longer. Transfer to a warmed serving dish and serve.

serves 4

South

Leek and Gruyère Spoon Bread

Spoon bread, a cornmeal-based classic with a custardy interior, is given a contemporary treatment with the addition of leeks and Gruyère cheese, turning it into a fine supper accompaniment.

2 tablespoons unsalted butter

3 leeks, including tender green tops, chopped (about 1 cup/4 oz/125 g)

2 cups (16 fl oz/500 ml) milk

½ cup (4 fl oz/125 ml) water

1 teaspoon salt

½ teaspoon freshly ground pepper

1 cup (5 oz/155 g) yellow cornmeal

⅔ cup (5 oz/160 g) sour cream

4 eggs

1½ cups (6 oz/185 g) shredded Gruyère cheese

2 green (spring) onions, chopped

✤ Preheat an oven to 350°F (180°C). Lightly butter a 1½-qt (1.5-l) soufflé dish.

✤ In a saucepan over medium-high heat, melt the butter. Add the leeks and sauté until soft and translucent, about 5 minutes. Add the milk, water, salt, and pepper and bring to a boil. Slowly whisk in the cornmeal. When the mixture returns to a boil, reduce the heat to medium and continue whisking until the mixture is thickened and pulls away from the sides of the pan, 2–3 minutes. Remove from the heat and whisk in the sour cream.

✤ In a bowl, using an electric mixer on high speed, beat the eggs until they are thick and pale lemon yellow, about 5 minutes. Gradually stir about one-fourth of the hot cornmeal mixture into the beaten eggs, then fold the eggs back into the remaining cornmeal, stirring constantly so as not to scramble the eggs. Fold in the Gruyère cheese and green onions.

✤ Pour into the prepared baking dish.

✤ Bake the spoon bread until a toothpick inserted into the center comes out clean, 35–40 minutes. Serve at once directly from the dish.

serves 6–8

California

Soft Polenta with Slow-Roasted Tomatoes

Baked slowly with herbs and olive oil, plum tomatoes become concentrated in flavor—like sun-dried tomatoes but moister. Serve them atop creamy polenta with nuggets of blue cheese to make a delicious side dish.

6 plum (Roma) tomatoes, about 1 lb (500 g)

1 teaspoon dried herbes de Provence

1½ tablespoons extra-virgin olive oil, plus more for drizzling

2 cloves garlic, finely minced

salt to taste

2½ qt (2.5 l) water

2 cups (10 oz/315 g) polenta

¼ cup (2 oz/60 g) unsalted butter

½ cup (2 oz/60 g) grated Parmesan cheese

⅓ lb (5 oz/155 g) blue cheese such as Maytag Blue or Gorgonzola

serves 6

☙ Preheat an oven to 275°F (135°C). Cut the tomatoes in half lengthwise and arrange, cut side up, in a baking dish just large enough to hold them in a single layer. Crumble the herbs over the tomatoes. In a small bowl, combine the 1½ tablespoons olive oil and the garlic and brush over the tomatoes. Season with salt. Bake the tomatoes until very soft and slightly wrinkled, about 4 hours. Baste once or twice during the final hour with any drippings in the dish.

☙ About 1 hour before serving the polenta, in a saucepan over high heat, bring the water to a boil. Add the polenta gradually, whisking constantly. When the mixture thickens, switch to a wooden spoon. Reduce the heat to maintain a gentle simmer and cook, stirring often, until the polenta is thick and creamy, about 45 minutes. Stir in the butter and the Parmesan cheese and season with salt.

☙ Divide the polenta among 6 warmed bowls. Cut the blue cheese into 6 pieces. Tuck a nugget of cheese into each bowl, then top with 2 tomato halves. Drizzle each portion with olive oil and serve.

Midwest

Wild Rice Pilaf with Pumpkin Seeds

Two foods traditional in the diet of midwestern Native Americans are featured in this dish. The origin of wild rice has been traced to the northern Great Lakes region, while pumpkin is native to Central and South America, where pumpkin is native to Central and of early inhabitants throughout the Americas. Add cherries, brought to the United States from Europe in the seventeenth century, and reconnect with a time when all food was earthy and unrefined.

½ cup (2½ oz/75 g) raw hulled green
pumpkin seeds

pinch of kosher salt or coarse sea salt

pinch of freshly ground pepper

2 tablespoons unsalted butter

2 tablespoons minced yellow onion

1 cup (6 oz/185 g) wild rice, rinsed

1¼ cups (10 fl oz/310 ml) water,
or more if needed

½ cup (3 oz/90 g) tart or sweet dried cherries

In a dry frying pan over medium–high heat, toast the pumpkin seeds, tossing constantly, until they start to pop, 3–4 minutes. Add the salt and pepper and continue to toss until the popping stops, about 1 minute longer. Remove from the heat and set aside.

In a saucepan over medium–high heat, melt the butter. Add the onion and cook until softened and golden, about 1 minute. Add the rice and stir to coat with the butter. Cook, stirring occasionally, until fragrant, 3–4 minutes.

Stir in the 1¼ cups (10 fl oz/310 ml) water and bring to a boil. Cover, reduce the heat to medium–low, and cook until the water is absorbed and the grains have begun to burst, 40–60 minutes. The cooking time will depend on whether the wild rice was cultivated or wild and where and how it was harvested. After 30 minutes, check to see if the pan is dry, and add a little water if it is. When the rice is ready, uncover and fold in the pumpkin seeds and dried cherries. Re-cover and remove from the heat. Let rest for 5 minutes, then taste and adjust the seasoning.

Transfer the rice to a serving bowl and serve hot or at room temperature.

serves 4–6

Native Grain

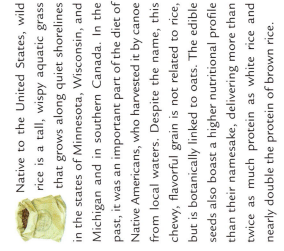

Native to the United States, wild rice is a tall, wispy aquatic grass that grows along quiet shorelines in the states of Minnesota, Wisconsin, and Michigan and in southern Canada. In the past, it was an important part of the diet of Native Americans, who harvested it by canoe from local waters. Despite the name, this chewy, flavorful grain is not related to rice, but is botanically linked to oats. The edible seeds also boast a higher nutritional profile than their namesake, delivering more than twice as much protein as white rice and nearly double the protein of brown rice.

True wild rice remains unique to the upper Midwest. When the needlelike seeds mature each autumn, two-man canoes slowly patrol the water's edge. The hand-harvest method has changed little over the millennia: one person carefully navigates the boat through the calm water, while the other gently bends the stalks and shakes the raw seeds free. Cultivated wild rice is no culinary match for its hand-gathered relative. It looks, tastes, and cooks differently, and has a nearly black hull that requires a longer cooking time to "burst" and become edible. The wild grain is parched dry over wood fires, which results in gray kernels that cook quickly and carry a more complex musky flavor.

SAVORING AMERICA

New England
Scalloped Potatoes

New England cooks like to "scallop" cod, vegetables such as potatoes, and even some fruits by drenching the ingredients with milk or cream, then baking them until they are meltingly tender.

5 cups (40 fl oz/ 1.25 ml) heavy (double) cream

3 cloves garlic, minced

2 teaspoons chopped fresh thyme

2 teaspoons kosher salt

⅛ teaspoon freshly ground black pepper

pinch of ground cayenne pepper

2 lb (1 kg) Yukon gold or white Kennebec potatoes (6 medium), peeled

1 lb (500 g) sweet potatoes (3 medium), peeled

½ cup (2 oz/60 g) grated Parmesan cheese

❧ Preheat an oven to 400°F (200°C). Butter a 15½-by-10½-inch (39-by-26.5-cm) baking dish.

❧ In a large saucepan over medium heat, combine the cream, garlic, thyme, salt, and black and cayenne peppers. Heat, stirring occasionally, until the cream reaches a boil. Remove from the heat and cover.

❧ Very thinly slice the potatoes, making them no more that ⅛ inch (3 mm) thick. Slice the sweet potatoes about ¼ inch (6 mm) thick. Combine the slices and then casually layer half of them in the prepared pan. Pour half of the cream mixture over the potatoes. Casually arrange the remaining slices in a layer on top. Pour the remaining cream over the potatoes to cover. Sprinkle the Parmesan cheese evenly over the top.

❧ Bake until the potatoes are very tender when pierced with the tip of a knife, the top is browned, and the cream is bubbling, about 45 minutes.

❧ Remove from the oven and let stand on a wire rack for 15 minutes. Serve directly from the dish.

serves 8–10

Midwest

Strudel with Cabbage, Apples, and Bacon

The nation's midsection is full of meat-and-potato fare, eating habits based on a tradition of German and Central European immigration. But real strudel, a product of the same settlers, has become hard to find. Fortunately, filo dough, widely available in the freezer section of well-stocked markets, makes versions of this dish easy for the home cook to prepare. Thinner than true strudel dough, filo leaves are brushed lightly with butter and layered, which enhances their flakiness.

1 lb (500 g) sliced bacon, preferably thick-cut

1 small yellow onion, minced

2 tablespoons minced fresh sage, or 1 tablespoon dried sage, plus 8 fresh sprigs for garnish (optional)

1 head green cabbage, coarsely shredded

3 green apples, peeled, cored, and coarsely shredded

kosher salt or coarse sea salt and freshly ground pepper to taste

12 filo sheets, each about 14 by 18 inches (35 by 45 cm), thawed overnight in the refrigerator if frozen

¼ cup (2 oz/60 g) unsalted butter, melted

To make the filling, in a large, deep frying pan over medium–low heat, cook the bacon slices, turning occasionally to render the fat, about 30 minutes. After the slices begin to brown, remove from the pan and drain on paper towels. Pour off the bacon fat and reserve. Coarsely chop the bacon and return to the pan. Continue to cook over medium heat, stirring constantly, until crisp, 3–5 minutes. You should have about 3 tablespoons bacon fat in the pan. If not, add a little of the reserved fat.

Add the onion to the same pan and cook, tossing constantly and scraping up the darkened bacon bits on the pan bottom, until the onion is golden and soft, 2–3 minutes. Add the minced or dried sage and stir until fragrant, about 1 minute. Add the cabbage and apples and continue to stir and scrape the pan bottom as they wilt and release liquid. Reduce the heat to medium and continue to cook, stirring occasionally, until the mixture is completely dry, 15–20 minutes. You should have about 3 cups (1½ lb/750 g) filling. Season with salt and pepper and set aside.

Preheat an oven to 350°F (180°C). Line a baking sheet with parchment (baking) paper. Carefully unwrap and unroll the filo sheets. Cover them with a lightly dampened kitchen towel to prevent them from becoming brittle. Put the melted butter in a bowl and have a pastry brush handy. Working on a large, flat surface, lay out 1 filo sheet with the long side toward you. Keep the remaining filo sheets covered. Brush the long edge farthest from you with a little butter and lay a long edge of a second sheet on top, then press the edges gently to seal. You should have 1 big rectangle about 18 by 26 inches (45 by 65 cm) with a short side close to you. Brush the big rectangle lightly with butter. Repeat the process twice more, topping the first large rectangle with 2 more large rectangles, using an additional 4 sheets.

Scatter half the cabbage mixture on top. Beginning with the short side closest to you, roll up the filo layers jelly-roll style. At about the halfway point, fold the 2 long sides inward about 1 inch (2.5 cm) to enclose the edges, then finish rolling. Brush the top and all visible sides with butter and place on the prepared baking sheet.

Repeat the process, using 6 more sheets and the remaining cabbage mixture, to make a second roll.

Bake the strudels until they are crisp and golden, 15–20 minutes. Remove from the oven and slice into pieces 2 inches (5 cm) thick. Arrange on a platter, garnish with the sage sprigs, and serve.

Makes 2 strudels; serves 8

Southern Barbecue

No matter where you go in the South, every cook has a barbecue secret. One cook might claim that success hinges on the firewood, while another will insist that it is the spice rub, and still others will point to the basting or the serving sauce. Ask a dozen southerners who makes the best barbecue below the Mason-Dixon line, and you will get a dozen different answers.

Do not confuse authentic southern barbecue with burgers quickly grilled on a hibachi. Barbecue demands slow, slow cooking so that the meat takes on a reddish hue and a smoky taste. The choice of fuel depends on state, county, town, or even household custom. While hickory, oak, and other hardwoods are used, so are dried corncobs, palmetto branches, fruit woods and pits, and pecan and peanut shells. Sometimes the fuel is given a preliminary soak in cider, beer, or even bourbon.

The choice of meat is likewise defined by tradition, with pork popular in the Southeast and coastal areas; beef in Texas, Arkansas, and Missouri; and lamb or mutton in Kentucky. Most barbecued meats begin with a dry spice rub, which is massaged into the meat and left to sit for at least several hours.

Next, the meat is doused with a sopping or basting sauce, usually a blend of tomatoes, vinegar, and spices along with other ingredients that give the sauce its local character. The meat is put over the fire, and the slow cooking begins. Then, a barbecue sauce is slathered on during the last several minutes of cooking or is simply passed at the table.

Not surprisingly, this crowning sauce is yet another source of serious debate and regional pride. For example, in eastern North Carolina, a thin table sauce based on vinegar and chiles is king, while in western North Carolina, folks prefer a tomatoey vinegar sauce. In southern Alabama and Georgia, a sweet sauce is standard; in northern Alabama and central North Carolina, a mustard sauce is favored; and in the western township of Owensboro, Kentucky, a so-called black dip, its rich color and flavor the product of a heavy dose of Worcestershire sauce, is served with the local mutton. Barbecued meats are sliced, shredded, pulled, or chopped, again according to where they are being served and who is serving them. Simply put, southern barbecue is as varied as its cooks are opinionated.

Skillet Corn Bread

The Algonquin Indians, who understood the versatility of corn, introduced the grain to the region's first colonists. The newcomers quickly saw the value of drying the corn kernels and then grinding them for baking. Soon they were using their newfound knowledge to make a rustic forerunner of this everyday bread of the southern table, which is traditionally cooked in a well-seasoned cast-iron skillet.

¼ cup (2 fl oz/60 ml) vegetable oil

2 cups (10 oz/315 g) yellow cornmeal

⅔ cup (3½ oz/105 g) all-purpose (plain) flour

1 tablespoon sugar

1 tablespoon baking powder

1 teaspoon salt

½ teaspoon baking soda (bicarbonate of soda)

2 cups (16 fl oz/500 ml) buttermilk

2 eggs, lightly beaten

3 tablespoons unsalted butter, melted

kernels from 2 large ears sweet yellow corn (about 1½ cups/9 oz/280 g) (optional)

☙ Preheat an oven to 450°F (230°C). Pour the vegetable oil into a large (about 10-inch/25-cm), well-seasoned cast-iron frying pan. Place in the oven and heat for 7–8 minutes.

☙ In a large bowl, sift together the cornmeal, flour, sugar, baking powder, salt, and baking soda. Stir in the buttermilk, eggs, and butter just until mixed; do not overmix. Add the corn kernels, if using, and stir just until blended. Again, do not overmix.

☙ Transfer the batter to the pan. Return the pan to the oven and reduce the temperature to 400°F (200°C). Bake until the corn bread is golden brown and a toothpick inserted into the center comes out clean, 30–35 minutes. Let cool in the pan on a rack for 5 minutes. To unmold the bread, invert the pan onto a cutting board. Cut the bread into 8 wedges.

makes 8 wedges

SAVORING AMERICA

Cranberry-Orange Relish with Walnuts

Long ago, wild cranberries flourished in dense bogs dotting picturesque Cape Cod. Today, these same sandy areas are planted with a highly productive commercial cranberry crop, most of which is harvested for processing into cranberry juice and cranberry sauce. The balance of the berries is sold fresh, during a season limited to just four months of the year.

3½ cups (12 oz/375 g) cranberries

1½ cups (12 fl oz/375 ml) fresh orange juice

1⅓ cups (9½ oz/295 g) firmly packed light brown sugar

½ cup (3 oz/90 g) golden raisins (sultanas)

1 teaspoon finely grated orange zest

pinch of ground cloves

pinch of salt

⅔ cup (2½ oz/75 g) chopped walnuts, toasted

❧ Pick over the cranberries; discard any damaged berries. In a large, heavy saucepan over medium-high heat, combine the cranberries, orange juice, and brown sugar. Bring to a boil, stirring occasionally. Once the juice is boiling and the berries are popping, reduce the heat to medium-low. Simmer until the cranberries burst and are tender, about 5 minutes. Uncover, add the raisins, and continue simmering, stirring occasionally, until the raisins are plump and tender and the relish is thick, 5–8 minutes.

❧ Remove from the heat and stir in the orange zest, cloves, and salt. Let cool to room temperature, cover tightly, and store in the refrigerator for up to 1 week. Just before serving, stir in the toasted walnuts.

makes about 3½ cups (28 oz/875 g); serves 12

Today's New England table is an echo of the cooking customs of colonial times.

Roasted Garlic Mashed Potatoes

The rich soil of the Northeast yields some of the tastiest potatoes in the country, including Yukon gold, Kennebec, Red La Soda, Katahdin, Norwis, and various russets. Over the centuries, the hardy tuber has also influenced countless immigrant food traditions. This recipe marries the Irish love for potatoes with the Mediterranean love for mellow roasted garlic.

1 head garlic

1 tablespoon olive oil

2 tablespoons kosher salt

3 lb (1.5 kg) Yukon gold or white Kennebec potatoes, peeled and cut into 3-inch (7.5-cm) chunks

1⅓ cups (11 fl oz/340 ml) half-and-half (half cream)

½ cup (4 oz/125 g) unsalted butter, cut into 4 equal pieces

freshly ground pepper to taste

❧ Preheat an oven to 375°F (190°C). Cut off enough of the pointed top of the garlic head to expose the cloves. Place the head, cut side up, on a piece of heavy aluminum foil. Drizzle with the olive oil and sprinkle with ½ teaspoon of the salt. Gather the foil around the garlic head to cover. Bake until the cloves are soft, about 1¼ hours. Unwrap and let cool.

❧ Bring a large pot three-fourths full of water to a boil. Add the potatoes and 1 tablespoon of the salt. Reduce the heat to medium-low and simmer the potatoes until tender, about 20 minutes. In a small saucepan over low heat, combine the half-and-half and butter. Heat until the butter melts and the cream is warm. Keep warm.

❧ When the potatoes are ready, drain and return to the pot. Separate the garlic cloves from the head and squeeze the pulp from 6–8 cloves into the potatoes. Reserve the remaining cloves for another use. Using a potato masher, mash the potatoes until almost smooth. Add the cream-butter mixture in 3 batches, stirring until well blended after each addition. Season with the remaining 2½ teaspoons salt and the pepper. Spoon into a warmed serving bowl.

serves 6–8

California

Grilled Radicchio with Anchovy Butter

When California chefs began using imported radicchio, the pleasantly bitter Italian chicory, in the 1980s, California farmers began to grow it. Today, it turns up regularly at farmers' markets, and a Monterey County grower is one of the largest in the world. When softened over a charcoal fire and slathered with peppery anchovy butter, radicchio is a superb complement to pork, rabbit, or duck. Be sure to leave a bit of the core attached to each wedge so it holds together.

The round heads of radicchio, Chiogga, are most common in markets, but the elongated variety, known as Treviso radicchio, is even better for this recipe. Simply halve or quarter it lengthwise before grilling.

¼ teaspoon peppercorns

1 clove garlic

pinch of sea salt, plus salt to taste

4 meaty anchovy fillets

3 tablespoons unsalted butter, at room temperature

2 heads radicchio, each cut into 8 wedges through the core

extra-virgin olive oil for brushing

☙ Prepare a medium-hot fire in a grill. In a mortar, grind the peppercorns until coarsely crushed. Add the garlic and a pinch of salt and pound well to crush the garlic. Then add the anchovies and pound to a purée. Add the butter and mix until smooth and well blended. Set aside.

☙ Brush the radicchio all over with olive oil, and season lightly with salt. Place on the grill rack and grill, turning once and brushing lightly with olive oil as needed to keep the wedges from drying out, until tender throughout. The timing will depend on the heat of your grill, but plan on about 3 minutes on each side.

☙ Transfer the grilled radicchio to a warmed platter and slather the wedges with the anchovy butter. Serve immediately.

serves 4

Buttermilk Sopaipillas with Honey Butter

Some southwestern specialties stubbornly refuse to travel. This is one of them. Visitors to the region who think they know a thing or two about enchiladas and tacos from chain restaurants back home are often puzzled by a basket of these hot, puffy breads and a pitcher of honey alongside their combination plates. Called sopaipillas or, affectionately, sofa pillows, the deep-fried breads, despite the honey, are not dessert. Instead, they are accompaniments to the meal, the breads assisting in the mopping up of every drop of chile sauce, and the honey helping to soothe spice-ravaged palates. Since sopaipillas are best straight from the pan, they are never better than when enjoyed at home. In this nontraditional version, buttermilk adds a welcome tang, while butter mixed with the honey raises the treat quotient.

½ cup (4 oz/125 g) unsalted butter, at room
   temperature

¼ cup (3 oz/90 g) honey

SOPAIPILLAS

2 cups (10 oz/315 g) unbleached all-purpose
   (plain) flour

2½ teaspoons baking powder

¼ teaspoon baking soda (bicarbonate of soda)

¼ teaspoon salt

2 tablespoons solid vegetable shortening
   (vegetable lard) or lard

¾ cup (6 fl oz/180 ml) plus 2 tablespoons
   buttermilk, at room temperature

about 4 lb (2 kg) solid vegetable shortening
   (vegetable lard) for deep-frying

☙ In a bowl, mix together the butter and honey. Cover and refrigerate until serving, returning it to room temperature before using. The honey butter can be prepared up to 3 days in advance.

☙ To make the sopaipillas, in a bowl, sift together the flour, baking powder, baking soda, and salt. Add the 2 tablespoons shortening or lard and, using a pastry blender or 2 knives, cut in the fat until it forms particles the size of small peas. Add the buttermilk, stir to moisten, and then briefly knead the dough in the bowl until it begins to come together. Turn the dough out onto a lightly floured work surface and knead until smooth, 10–12 times. Using a

floured rolling pin, roll out the dough to just less than ¼ inch (6 mm) thick. Using a pizza wheel or a long, sharp knife, cut out as many 4-inch (10-cm) triangles as the dough shape will allow. (Odd-shaped scraps can be deep-fried and nibbled, but excess dough cannot be rerolled to yield more sopaipillas.) Cover the triangles with a kitchen towel and let rest at room temperature for up to 30 minutes.

☙ Meanwhile, in a large, deep, heavy frying pan or large, wide, heavy saucepan, melt shortening to a depth of 3 inches (7.5 cm) and heat to 375°F (190°C). When the shortening is ready, lower 2 or 3 dough triangles into the hot fat. Using a metal spatula, immediately press the sopaipillas beneath the hot shortening, then pat them several times with the spatula to encourage them to puff. Cook, turning once, until golden, about 2 minutes total. Using a slotted spoon, transfer the sopaipillas to paper towels to drain. Repeat until all the sopaipillas are cooked.

☙ Arrange the hot sopaipillas in a napkin-lined basket. Serve immediately with the honey butter in a crock on the side. Diners spread the honey butter on and in the sopaipillas.

makes about 8 breads

South

Twice-Baked Stuffed Sweet Potatoes

Although the terms "sweet potato" and "yam" are often used interchangeably, they are not the same thing. True yams are tropical tubers popular in Central and South America, the Caribbean, and parts of Africa. How sweet potatoes became known as yams in the South is a mystery. Perhaps it was a marketing ploy, since canned sweet potatoes are often labeled "candied yams." But don't let the confusion baffle you. A true yam is simply not as sweet and is seldom available in the South except at specialty-produce markets. Most markets carry the two basic types of sweet potato: one with yellow-brown skin and pale yellow flesh, the other with dark reddish skin and dark orange flesh.

Any type of sturdy green, including spinach, turnip, kale, or mustard, may be substituted for the collards. A combination of sorrel and arugula (rocket), in equal quantities, would add a peppery bite to this side dish. Serve it alongside Pork Chops with Vidalia Onion Gravy (page 123) or Golden Cornmeal-Crusted Fried Chicken (page 131).

4 sweet potatoes, unpeeled

4 slices bacon, chopped

1 Vidalia or other sweet onion, chopped

2 cloves garlic, chopped

1 small bunch fresh collard greens, stems and ribs removed and leaves torn into bite-sized pieces (about 3 cups/6 oz/185 g)

⅔ cup (5 fl oz/160 ml) chicken stock

2 teaspoons chopped fresh rosemary

½ cup (4 oz/125 g) unsalted butter, at room temperature

⅓ cup (3 fl oz/80 ml) heavy (double) cream

½ cup (2 oz/60 g) grated Parmesan cheese

salt and freshly ground pepper to taste

½ cup (2 oz/60 g) shredded Swiss cheese

☙ Preheat an oven to 350°F (180°C). Using the tines of a fork, pierce the entire surface of each sweet potato several times. Place in the oven and bake until soft, 1–1¼ hours. Remove the sweet potatoes from the oven and let cool until they can be handled. Cut each potato in half lengthwise and, using a spoon, carefully scoop out the flesh from each half into a bowl, leaving about a ¼-inch (6-mm) lining of flesh in the skins to form shells with sturdy sides. Set the flesh and the shells aside separately.

❧ In a frying pan over medium-high heat, combine the bacon, onion, and garlic and fry until the bacon is crisp and brown and the onion is soft, 8–10 minutes.

❧ Add the collard greens and the chicken stock to the pan, cover, and cook, stirring occasionally, until the collards are tender, about 10 minutes. Uncover and continue to cook, stirring frequently, until the stock has evaporated, 5–7 minutes.

❧ Add the rosemary to the sweet potato flesh and, using an electric mixer on medium speed, beat until smooth. Add the butter, cream, and Parmesan cheese and continue to beat. Season with salt and pepper. Using a slotted spoon, transfer the contents of the frying pan to the mashed potatoes and fold until well combined.

❧ Divide the mixture evenly among the 8 potato shells, mounding it slightly in the center. Place the stuffed potatoes on an ungreased baking sheet and top evenly with the Swiss cheese.

❧ Bake the potatoes until the cheese is melted and the potatoes are heated through, about 30 minutes. Transfer to a platter and serve at once.

serves 8

Soul food is the well-spiced marriage of the South's native pantry with the foods and seasonings of Africa and the Caribbean.

Soul Food

"Soul food," though a relatively new term (circa 1960), describes a centuries-old kitchen tradition born when African American cooks were faced with creating nutritious meals from whatever was on hand. Tables were laid with simple dishes: stewed greens, boiled meat scraps, simmered beans, oven-roasted sweet potatoes, and sturdy corn bread.

After the Civil War, many African Americans went north to escape the devastation in the South. Faced with greater bounty than they had ever known, they experimented with fish from the Great Lakes, borrowed ingredients and techniques from the Pennsylvania Dutch, and began incorporating once-unattainable foods, such as pork chops and ham, into their culinary repertory. The African Americans who stayed behind taught a white community how to survive on what was available. Many observers credit these imaginative teachers with saving the South from starvation.

Today, the line between southern food and soul food is blurred. Yet one thing clearly separates them: the level of seasoning. Soul food, which still draws on inexpensive cuts of meat, greens, beans, and grains, is more highly flavored—sweeter, saltier, spicier, more pungent—than its subtler cousin. This piquant home cooking is sometimes called "southern food with an attitude."

Desserts

Americans are passionate for dessert, from chocolate layer cake to key lime pie to peach cobbler.

ON HOT SUMMER EVENINGS, just as many diners have finished their meal, a tinny musical jingle sounds in the street. An ice-cream truck is announcing its presence, in familiar notes that prompt every youngster within earshot to race for the door.

Coated with chocolate and served on a stick, melting alongside a warm wedge of pie, draped with an old-fashioned butterscotch sauce, or neatly scooped into an elegant coupe, ice cream is arguably one of America's most beloved desserts. On the Fourth of July, the supersized manually cranked machine comes down from the attic, and all present take their turn at hand-churning fresh peach or vanilla bean ice cream. Many home cooks now have small electric machines that turn a fruit purée into a silky sorbet, or an eggy custard into thick ice cream, with almost no effort.

Summer visits to the ice-cream parlor for a sundae or double-scoop cone remain cherished childhood memories for many. What to

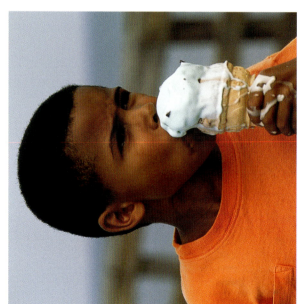

Preceding pages: Rides, livestock displays, and a rodeo are among the attractions at Washington's Puyallup Fair, held annually since 1900. **Top:** Truffles and other sweets make a tempting display at a California shop. **Above:** A boy indulges in one of America's favorite portable desserts. **Right:** In late winter, sap is collected from New England's sugar maples for processing into luscious, amber maple syrup.

choose? Bright green pistachio, lemon custard, toasted almond, chocolate chunk—the seemingly endless rows of canisters filled with tantalizing tastes are emblematic of a country whose people revel in choice.

Almost equal to the passion for ice cream is the American weakness for baked goods, from the simplest sugar cookie to the richest chocolate cake. In an age when many say they don't have time to cook, a surprising number of people still find time to bake. The deep-seated pleasure Americans derive from sharing something sweet underlies the continued popularity of such traditions as the Christmas cookie swap and such small-town fund-raising efforts as cakewalks and bake sales. Open a recipe box in any home and chances are that the dessert section will be the thickest by far, with handwritten, passed-down recipes for a grandmother's fruitcake and a great-aunt's chess pie. With those sweet creations, resurrected at Thanksgiving, for birthdays, or on other special occasions, cooks keep alive warm memories of family and hearth. America's desserts, more than any other part of her repertory, seem homegrown, owing more to native ingredients and abundance than to immigrant traditions. Working with the available fruits and nuts, with local butter and cream, with maple syrup, molasses, cranberries, cornmeal, and other ingredients unknown in their homeland, the nation's early cooks produced many desserts, like Indian pudding, that remain uniquely American.

Among the oldest is the beloved collection of colonial fruit-and-dough desserts with names like buckle, pandowdy, grunt, and slump. One can only speculate that their creators were plainspoken cooks who realized that their inventions tasted better than they looked. A buckle usually resembles a fruit-filled coffee cake with a crumb topping. Pandowdy is a one-crust pie, with the crust pushed down into the filling, or "dowdied," during the final moments of baking. Grunts, slumps, and cobblers have soft biscuit- or doughlike toppings that sink into the bubbling fruit. A brown Betty features fruit—typically apples—baked between layers of buttered bread crumbs. The origin of the name is

Left: In Miami's South Beach, hotels, restaurants, nightclubs, and boutiques occupy landmark art deco buildings from the 1920s and 1930s. **Top:** Blueberries, a favorite summertime fruit cultivated in more than thirty states, are a popular addition to muffins and pancakes and are the centerpiece of cobblers, shortcakes, and pies. **Above:** First brought to the United States from England in the 1900s, jersey cows are prized for their rich milk and thick cream, ideal for making ice cream.

shrouded in time, but it's not hard to imagine a connection to the French charlotte, a baked dessert of cooked apples and bread.

Today, New England and Mid-Atlantic chefs are finding inspiration for dessert in the region's superb artisanal cheeses. Vermont and New York have long been centers for cheddar production, but in recent years, many new producers have entered the industry, making a wide variety of top-notch cheeses. In Vermont, Shelburne Farms' magnificent cloth-wrapped farmhouse cheddar shows what that state's quality-oriented cheese makers can achieve. New York's Old Chatham Sheepherding Company makes sheep's milk cheeses to rival any in Europe, including its outstanding shepherd's wheel and ewe's blue. Increasingly, East Coast chefs are showcasing such cheeses on European-style cheese trays or pairing them with a sweet complement, such as a slice of mincemeat or apple pie with Vermont cheddar.

As for pie, it must be said that if America gave the world nothing else worth eating, its contributions to the pie repertory would

guarantee it a place in food history. Starting with the savory meat pies of their English forebears, Americans moved pie in a sweet direction and have never stopped inventing.

Is there a fruit or nut on the continent that Americans haven't figured out how to put in a crust? Even tart lemons make a luscious filling when sliced paper-thin and tossed with sugar and egg, the essence of Shaker lemon pie. Floridians turn their small, tangy key lime into a custard pie that has a national reputation, and Hawaii's macadamia nut pie—a memorable juxtaposition of creamy chiffon and salty nuts—leaves many visitors to the islands craving another taste.

Autumn's green tomatoes become pie in New England, typically mixed with sweet spices and raisins. Californians have been known to make avocado pie, and a sweet potato pie that the neighbors praise is the pride of any soul-food cook. Across the country, pie is the preferred vehicle for showing off the seasonal harvest: tart cherries in Michigan, blueberries in Maine, and pecans

in Georgia and Texas. Tellingly, the two most purely American holidays—Independence Day and Thanksgiving—elicit the most impressive evidence of the country's passion for pie. In some homes, Thanksgiving requires at least two types, and an appreciative audience determined to have some of each.

Dessert recipes travel easily and Americans move often, so it's surprising that regional differences persist. But they do, perhaps nowhere more so than in the South, which can claim some desserts that rarely leave its borders. Ambrosia would certainly be on that list, exotic in its use of tropical fruits such as orange, pineapple, coconut, and banana. Coconut layer cake, coconut cream pie, and coconut custard pie are similarly southern, bearing the mark of the Caribbean planters who first settled Charleston and made its port an entry point for tropical goods.

Another curiosity is the use of sesame seed in southern sweets. Africans brought it from home, where they knew it as *benne*. Believing that sesame seed had protective powers, they sprinkled it by their doors and

Left: A family-owned citrus farm in Southern California specializes in Meyer lemons, blood oranges, tangelos, and Oroblancos, a pomelo-grapefruit hybrid. **Top:** Nearly every block in San Francisco's North Beach neighborhood has a café, where locals and visitors take time for conversation and espresso. **Above:** Fruits such as angular starfruits (also known as carambolas), aromatic soursops, baby bananas, silken-textured mangoes, and juice-rich pineapples thrive in the Hawaiian subtropical climate.

grew it in their gardens, and it gradually worked its way onto the southern table. Southern cooks still use the seeds in savory crackers, in the thin, brown-sugar cookies known as *benne wafers*, and in pralinelike candies.

Visitors to New Orleans can count on a sugar rush from the town's legendary desserts, which may occasionally be reproduced elsewhere but never as well: specialties like bread pudding with bourbon sauce, pralines, pecan pie, and bananas Foster. The French influence is obvious in the city's famous beignets (deep-fried pastries), crepes, *gâteau des rois* (a sweet Mardi Gras bread with a charm inside), and café au lait.

Moving west from New Orleans, France's thumbprint quickly vanishes. But in New Mexico, another colonial influence emerges in the Spanish-style desserts that still infiltrate its kitchens. The New Mexican *capirotada*, or bread pudding, resembles its New Orleans cousin hardly at all. It is sweeter, spiced with cinnamon and clove, enriched with cheese instead of milk or cream, and made without eggs. Pine nuts, a native treasure, may nestle in its crevices.

The Spanish had almost 225 years to leave their mark on New Mexican sweets, from the founding of the first settlement in 1598 to Mexican independence in 1821. They left the region with a taste for flan, the silky caramel custard; *natillas*, or "floating islands" of poached meringue atop custard; and *cajeta*, the goat's milk caramel sauce that contemporary southwestern chefs use on everything from baked apples to ice cream.

On the West Coast, modern dessert making owes much to the streamlined, seasonal style advocated by the region's most influential pastry chefs. Preferring to put flavor first, many are known for desserts that highlight their superior ingredients rather than their technical legerdemain. At a California bakery whose proprietor shares this taste for simplicity, patrons might enjoy a changing parade of glistening fruit *galettes*, or rustic tarts, that celebrate the local harvest: peaches and raspberries in summer, heirloom apples in fall, quinces in winter, strawberries in spring. Biscotti flavored with anise and almonds would probably fill the

Left: Asian pears of many varieties and Fuji apples are just some of the fruits from the Asian continent that have been embraced by American growers. **Top:** A dramatic relief decorates one of the pylons supporting Chicago's Michigan Avenue Bridge, built in the 1920s across the Chicago River. **Above:** An evening stroll brings two women into a local bakery, where they choose pastries to enjoy at home with after-dinner coffee.

cookie jars, and the ice-cream selection would mirror the fruits at the nearby farmers' market, with vibrant flavors like nectarine, Meyer lemon, and apricot.

In the Pacific Northwest and Alaska, the summer berry bonanza sends cooks to the stoves to make preserves, jelly, and every conceivable berry-centered dessert. Although commercial farms send plenty of fresh, cultivated berries to market, purists seek the intense flavor of wild fruit. In woodsy areas, cars parked on the side of the road often signal foragers at work, hunting wild lingonberries in Alaska, wild strawberries in the Cascades, and wild blackberries just about anywhere. Thorny, scraggly blackberries threaten to overtake almost every vacant lot in the Pacific Northwest, but their profusion makes them no less tasty. A bucket filled with juicy wild blackberries handpicked on a hot summer day is the first step to a memorable cobbler.

Top: Charleston, South Carolina, with its hundreds of restored historic homes, is a showplace of Early American architecture. **Above:** Coffee plantations are found on all the major Hawaiian islands; the best-known variety is Kona, grown on the slopes of Hualalai and Mauna Loa volcanoes on the Big Island. **Right:** A shopkeeper in San Francisco's Chinatown stocks a window with baked goods.

California
Santa Rosa Plum Galette

California's magnificent summer fruits, either alone or in combination, make ravishing galettes. This version showcases the tangy Santa Rosa plum, the creation of renowned California plant breeder Luther Burbank, who named the plum for the town north of San Francisco where he pursued his horticultural research.

A galette is easy to make because the crust does not require crimping or fitting into a tart shell or pie pan. It bakes free-form on a baking stone, like a pizza. You can add some raspberries to this galette, if you like, or substitute peaches or nectarines for the plums.

DOUGH

2 cups (10 oz/315 g) unbleached all-purpose (plain) flour

¾ teaspoon salt

½ cup (4 oz/125 g) chilled unsalted butter, cut into small pieces

7 tablespoons (3½ oz/105 g) chilled solid vegetable shortening (vegetable lard), cut into small pieces

about ¼ cup (2 fl oz/60 ml) ice water

2 lb (1 kg) ripe, but firm Santa Rosa or other plums, pitted and cut into wedges ½ inch (12 mm) wide

¼ cup (2 oz/60 g) granulated sugar, or more to taste

1 egg yolk whisked with 1 teaspoon water

1½ tablespoons crystal sugar

🌿 To make the dough in a food processor, combine the flour and salt and pulse to blend. Add the butter and pulse a few times to coat the butter with the flour. Add the shortening and pulse until the fat particles are coated with flour and are about the size of large peas. Transfer to a large bowl.

🌿 To make the dough by hand, place the flour and the salt in a large bowl and stir to blend. Add the butter pieces and, using a pastry blender or 2 knives, cut the butter into the flour until the pieces are the size of large peas. Add the shortening and cut into the flour until the pieces are coated with flour and also the size of large peas.

🌿 Sprinkle the flour-butter mixture with enough of the ice water while tossing with a fork, just until the dough begins to come together. Then gather up the dough with your hands and shape it into a thick disk. You may have to knead the dough a little to get it to hold together, but that is preferable to adding more water. Enclose the dough in plastic wrap and refrigerate for at least 2 hours.

🌿 Put a baking stone or baking tiles on the center rack of an oven and preheat to 425°F (220°C) for 45 minutes.

🌿 Put a large sheet of parchment (baking) paper on a work surface. Unwrap the dough and place it on the parchment. Top with another sheet of parchment. Roll out the dough into a 15-inch (38-cm) round between the parchment sheets. Occasionally you may need to lift the top parchment sheet, flour the dough lightly, and then replace the parchment. Once or twice, flip the dough over so that the bottom sheet is on the top, lift the sheet, flour the dough, and replace the sheet. If the parchment sheets are not at least 15 inches (38 cm) square, you may need to use a second, overlapping sheet. When the dough is rolled out to the desired size, slide a rimless baking sheet or pizza peel under the bottom parchment sheet. Remove the top parchment sheet.

🌿 Place the plums in a bowl, sprinkle with the ¼ cup (2 oz/60 g) granulated sugar, and toss to coat evenly. Taste and add more sugar if desired. Scatter the plums over the surface of the dough, leaving a 2-inch (5-cm) rim uncovered. Slip an icing spatula or wide knife under the edge of the dough and gently fold it over the plums to make a wide border; make sure there are no cracks in the dough for juices to slip through. Brush the border with the yolk-water mixture, then sprinkle with the crystal sugar. Using scissors, cut away excess parchment.

🌿 Transfer the dough, still on the parchment sheet, onto the baking stone. Bake the *galette* until the crust is golden and the plums are tender, about 40 minutes. Using the rimless baking sheet or pizza peel, transfer the *galette* to a rack to cool briefly.

🌿 Transfer the *galette* to a flat serving plate. Cut into wedges and serve warm.

serves 10

Mid-Atlantic
Strawberry-Rhubarb Crisp

Rhubarb and strawberries grow in abundance in the fertile farmland of New York and New Jersey. Using strawberries in this crisp softens the rhubarb's sour edge, and the addition of nuts and oats to the topping delivers added crunch and flavor.

1½ lb (750 g) strawberries, halved or quartered

¾ lb (375 g) rhubarb, cut into ¾-inch (2-cm) pieces

1 teaspoon vanilla extract (essence)

1¼ cups (10 oz/315 g) granulated sugar

½ cup (2½ oz/80 g) all-purpose (plain) flour

1½ teaspoons finely grated lemon zest

2 pinches of salt

½ cup (1½ oz/45 g) old-fashioned rolled oats

½ cup (3½ oz/105 g) firmly packed light brown sugar

¼ cup (1½ oz/45 g) all-purpose (plain) flour

½ teaspoon ground cinnamon

6 tablespoons (3 oz/90 g) lightly chilled unsalted butter, cut into ½-inch (12-mm) pieces

⅔ cup (2½ oz/75 g) chopped walnuts or pecans

sweetened whipped cream (page 250) (optional)

🍴 Preheat an oven to 375°F (190°C). Butter a shallow 2-qt (2-l) baking dish. In a bowl, toss together the strawberries, rhubarb, and vanilla. Sprinkle the granulated sugar, ¼ cup (1¼ oz/40 g) of the flour, the lemon zest, and 1 pinch of the salt over the fruits and toss gently to coat. Spread evenly in the prepared dish.

🍴 In a bowl, combine the oats, brown sugar, remaining ¼ cup (1¼ oz/40 g) flour, the cinnamon, and the remaining pinch of salt. Add the butter and, using a pastry blender, cut in until the butter is in small pieces and the mixture begins to hold together. Add the nuts and mix just until combined. Scatter the topping over the rhubarb.

🍴 Bake the crisp until the filling is bubbling and the topping is browned, about 45 minutes. Remove from the oven and spoon the crisp onto individual plates. Top with whipped cream, if desired.

serves 6–8

South

Buttermilk Persimmon Pudding

The South, nearly destroyed by the Civil War, was slow to rebuild. One thing that gave a southerner hope for the future, however, was having a little something sweet served at the end of supper, even if it was only a biscuit with a spoonful of molasses. The small native persimmons that grew wild throughout the region were another source of sweetness, with their pulp used in simple desserts not unlike this one, which is a variation on crème brûlée. In this recipe, the pointy Hachiya persimmon is used. The fruit turns a bright orange long before it is actually ripe. To be at their best, Hachiyas must ripen to a mushy stage; if they appear too soft and ripe to eat, they are just right. This pudding can also be served without caramelizing the surface. Serve chilled, garnished with a dollop of sweetened whipped cream.

2 or 3 Hachiya persimmons

1 cup (8 oz/250 g) granulated sugar

⅓ cup (1½ oz/45 g) cornstarch (cornflour)

pinch of salt

2 cups (16 fl oz/500 ml) heavy (double) cream

1 cup (8 fl oz/250 ml) buttermilk

6 eggs, lightly beaten

finely grated zest of 1 orange

1 tablespoon dark rum

2 teaspoons vanilla extract (essence)

freshly grated nutmeg for dusting

8–16 tablespoons (3½–7 oz/105–220 g) firmly packed light brown sugar

crushed ice as needed

❧ Preheat an oven to 325°F (165°C).

❧ Peel 2 persimmons and pass them through a food mill fitted with the fine disk or a fine-mesh sieve to purée the flesh and remove the seeds. Measure the purée. You should have 1 cup (8 oz/250 ml). If there is less, purée the remaining persimmon.

❧ In a saucepan, stir together the granulated sugar, cornstarch, and salt. Whisk in the cream and the buttermilk. Bring the mixture to a boil over medium-high heat, whisking constantly.

❧ In a bowl, whisk together the eggs, persimmon purée, and orange zest. Gradually add the hot cream mixture to the eggs, whisking constantly. Return the mixture to the saucepan and bring back to a simmer. Remove from the heat and add the rum and the vanilla. Divide the mixture evenly among eight ⅔-cup (5-fl oz/160-ml) custard molds. Dust the tops with nutmeg. Set the molds in a baking dish and add hot water to the dish to reach about halfway up the sides of the molds.

❧ Bake the puddings until a knife inserted into the center of a pudding comes out clean, 28–32 minutes. The centers will still be slightly wobbly when the molds are gently shaken. Transfer the molds to a rack and let cool. Cover and refrigerate for at least 4 hours or for up to overnight.

❧ When ready to serve, preheat a broiler (grill). Evenly sprinkle each pudding with 1–2 tablespoons of the brown sugar. Place the puddings on a large rimmed baking sheet or jelly-roll pan and surround with crushed ice. Place under the preheated broiler about 5 inches (13 cm) from the heat source and broil (grill), rotating the molds as needed, until the sugar has caramelized, about 2 minutes. The caramelization is complete when the sugar melts and forms a dark golden surface. The surface will become brittle as it cools. Alternatively, melt the sugar with a small kitchen blow torch until it is caramelized and forms a hard glaze. (Do not caramelize the sugar more than 30 minutes before serving, as it will become soft.) Serve at once.

serves 8

Mid-Atlantic
New York Cheesecake

In 1921, Leo Lindemann opened Lindy's in Manhattan's theater district. Its big sandwiches and its appearance in the stories of Damon Runyon soon put the restaurant on the national map. But Lindy's owes its greatest fame to its creation of New York–style cheesecake, a now-legendary dessert known for its rich, dense taste and soaring calorie count. The original cake is made with a sweetened pastry crust, while the orange- or lemon-laced filling is loaded with sweetened cream cheese and heavy (double) cream.

This version of that Big Apple standard is enriched with sour cream and owes its bold flavor to vanilla beans. While the chocolate graham cracker crust definitely bucks tradition, it is easier to handle than the traditional pastry crust, and the chocolate makes the cheesecake even more irresistibly delicious.

CRUST

1½ cups (4½ oz/140 g) chocolate graham cracker cookie crumbs (about 14 cookies)

2 tablespoons sugar

¼ cup (2 oz/60 g) unsalted butter, melted

FILLING

2 lb (1 kg) cream cheese, at warm room temperature

2 tablespoons all-purpose (plain) flour

¼ teaspoon salt

2 large vanilla beans

1¼ cups (10 oz/315 g) sugar

½ cup (4 oz/125 g) sour cream

3 eggs, at room temperature

To make the cheesecake crust, preheat an oven to 400°F (200°C). Lightly butter a 9-inch (23-cm) springform pan.

In a bowl, combine the cookie crumbs, sugar, and melted butter. Stir until well blended and the crumbs are evenly moistened. Transfer the crumb mixture to the prepared springform pan and press evenly onto the bottom and about 1½ inches (4 cm) up the sides of the pan. (A straight-sided, flat-bottomed coffee mug or cup works well for this step.) Bake for 10 minutes. Transfer the baked crust to a rack and let cool completely. Reduce the oven temperature to 300°F (150°C).

To make the filling, in a large bowl, combine the cream cheese, flour, and salt. Using a sharp paring knife, split each vanilla bean in half lengthwise. Using the tip of the knife, scrape out the vanilla seeds from each half into the bowl. Using an electric mixer set on medium-high speed, beat until very smooth and fluffy, stopping frequently to scrape down the sides.

Add the sugar and sour cream to the cream cheese mixture and beat until well blended, again frequently scraping down the sides. Add the eggs one at a time, beating after each addition until blended before adding the next egg. Pour the cheese mixture into the baked crust.

Bake the cheesecake until the center jiggles slightly when the pan is nudged, 60–65 minutes. The edges will be slightly puffed and will have a few little cracks.

Transfer the cheesecake to a rack and let cool to room temperature. Cover and refrigerate until well chilled, preferably overnight.

To serve, unclasp and remove the pan sides, then run a long, thin flexible metal spatula under the bottom crust. Carefully slide the cake onto a flat serving plate. To slice, before each cut run a thin-bladed knife under hot water and wipe it dry.

serves 16

New York's Delmonico's, the city's first fine restaurant, was opened in 1831 by Swiss brothers.

California Citrus

The Santa Barbara farmers' market shines year-round, but in winter it glows with citrus. Platters of sliced oranges for sampling and mounds of lemons and limes beckon shoppers with their freshness and tangy promise. California citrus is shipped worldwide, but it's never more alluring than in its own sunny backyard. In addition to lemons and seedless navel oranges, the Golden State grows significant quantities of Valencia oranges, grapefruits, mandarin oranges, and pomelos. More adventurous farmers are planting blood oranges, Oroblancos (a pomelo-grapefruit hybrid), Meyer lemons, and kumquats. And thanks to California's trendsetting chefs, a growing demand exists for such exotic citrus as the Buddha's hand, limequat, citron, and Cara Cara orange, a pink-fleshed navel.

Citrus cultivation in the state can be traced to the 1840s, when William Wolfskill planted the first lemon and orange seedlings in what is now Los Angeles. Today, the San Joaquin Valley in Central California harbors most of the state's citrus groves. The orchards line the highway around Fresno, scenting the air at bloom time and providing a splendid sight when the fruit is mature. Home gardeners love tending citrus, and lemon and orange trees beautify many backyard gardens.

Meyer Lemon Ice Cream

Specialty citrus is a thriving niche in California agriculture, as farmers look for a high-value crop that will distinguish them from the crowd. Meyer lemons are one of the unusual citrus varieties that growers have planted in frost-free regions of the state, in Central and Southern California. The lemons are lower in acid than more common lemons and have an orange-blossom fragrance. Pair this ice cream with Blood Orange Sorbet (right), and accompany with tuiles or other crisp cookies.

¾ cup (6 oz/185 g) sugar

2 tablespoons finely grated Meyer lemon zest

6 egg yolks

1½ cups (12 fl oz/375 ml) half-and-half (half cream)

1½ cups (12 fl oz/375 ml) heavy (double) cream

pinch of salt

3 tablespoons fresh Meyer lemon juice, or to taste

❧ In a food processor, combine the sugar and the lemon zest and process until the sugar becomes very moist and the grated zest becomes even finer. In a bowl, whisk together the egg yolks and the processed sugar until the mixture is pale and thick and forms a ribbon when the whisk is lifted.

❧ In a saucepan over medium heat, combine the half-and-half and ½ cup (4 fl oz/125 ml) of the cream. Bring to a simmer. Pour the hot liquid into the beaten eggs, whisking constantly, then return the mixture to the saucepan. Add the salt and cook over medium-low heat, stirring with a wooden spoon, until the mixture thickens and coats the spoon, about 3 minutes. Do not allow it to simmer, or it will curdle. Remove from the heat and let cool for 15 minutes, stirring occasionally. Then stir in the remaining 1 cup (8 fl oz/250 ml) cream. Add the 3 tablespoons Meyer lemon juice, or enough to give the custard a tart edge.

❧ Pour the mixture through a sieve placed over a bowl, then cover and refrigerate to chill thoroughly. Transfer to an ice-cream maker and freeze according to the manufacturer's instructions.

❧ Serve the ice cream in a bowl or a parfait glass.

makes about 1½ qt (1.5 l) ice cream

California
Blood Orange Sorbet

Blood oranges are among the formerly exotic citrus fruits that have become more plentiful in California farmers' markets and produce stores.

Some blood orange varieties develop a blush on the rind; others look no different from navel oranges. The depth of color inside may also vary, depending on the variety, where the trees were grown, and how ripe the fruit was when picked. Trees raised in hot, dry climates with cold winters tend to have the deepest internal color. With their deep burgundy flesh, blood oranges yield dramatic-looking juice for this sorbet, a perfect complement to Meyer Lemon Ice Cream (left). The fruit's striking juice is sweet and tart, with hints of raspberry.

1½ cups (12 oz/375 g) sugar
½ cup (4 fl oz/125 ml) water
6 lb (3 kg) blood oranges

❦ In a saucepan over medium heat, combine the sugar and the water and bring to a simmer, swirling the pan to dissolve the sugar. Simmer the syrup for a few seconds, just until it becomes clear. Remove from the heat, then cover and refrigerate until cold.

❦ Halve and juice the blood oranges, then strain the juice. You should have about 5 cups (40 fl oz/1.25 l). Place in a bowl.

❦ Add enough of the syrup to the blood orange juice to sweeten it to your taste. You may not need all the syrup. Cover the bowl and refrigerate the sweetened juice to chill thoroughly.

❦ Transfer the chilled blood orange juice to an ice-cream maker and freeze according to the manufacturer's instructions.

❦ Serve the sorbet in a bowl or a parfait glass.

makes about 1½ qt (1.5 l) sorbet

Midwest

Cherry Pie with Vanilla Crumb Topping

Tart, or sour, cherries make the best pies. The fruit holds its shape better than sweet varieties, with the bright color and pucker-up flavor that define this classic pie. Michigan produces about 75 percent of the nation's tart cherries, with annual harvests averaging 200 to 250 million pounds (100 to 125 million kg). The shores of Lake Michigan provide the optimum microclimate for growing tart cherries because the large body of water tempers weather extremes. Montmorency is the region's most popular variety.

Buy fresh tart cherries when you see them, in the Midwest in July and in other regions off and on throughout the summer. Few are distributed for the fresh retail market, but are instead processed into frozen fruit, canned fruit, jellies, juice, and other products. This recipe uses individually quick-frozen (IQF) cherries, which are pitted and packed in bags without additives or syrups. Canned cherries packed in water are an acceptable substitute but must be drained thoroughly. If using fresh cherries, be aware that they release more juice during baking. Regardless of the fruit used, increase the tapioca if you prefer a firmer pie. A scoop of vanilla ice cream next to each wedge will effectively eliminate any extra juice.

pastry for a single-crust 9-inch (23-cm) pie (page 232)

CRUMB TOPPING

6 tablespoons (3 oz/90 g) unsalted butter, at room temperature

¼ cup (2 oz/60 g) firmly packed light brown sugar

1 egg white, lightly beaten

½ teaspoon vanilla extract (essence)

¾ cup (4 oz/125 g) all-purpose (plain) flour

⅛ teaspoon kosher salt or coarse sea salt

FILLING

5 cups (25 oz/780 g) frozen tart pitted cherries (see note)

1 cup (8 oz/250 g) granulated sugar

3–4 tablespoons instant tapioca

On a lightly floured work surface, roll out the pastry disk into a 14-inch (35-cm) round, dusting the rolling pin with flour as needed to prevent sticking. Drape the pastry around the pin and carefully ease it into a 9-inch (23-cm) pie dish, pressing it into the bottom and sides. Trim the overhang so that it extends ¾ inch (2 cm) beyond the edge of the dish. Roll this overhang under to shape a high edge that rests on top of the dish rim. Crimp attractively around the rim and refrigerate the pie shell.

Preheat an oven to 425°F (220°C).

To make the topping, combine the butter and brown sugar in a small bowl and, using a fork, blend until creamy. Mix in the egg white and vanilla until thoroughly incorporated. Sift the flour and salt into the butter mixture and stir until combined. Cover and refrigerate while preparing the filling.

To make the filling, in a large bowl, toss the cherries with the granulated sugar and the tapioca (use the smaller amount for a juicier pie), trying to break apart the fruit as it begins to thaw. Let stand for 20 minutes, stirring occasionally. The fruit should still be at least partially frozen.

Turn the filling into the pie shell, making sure to include all the sugar, syrup, and tapioca from the bowl. Mound the cherries slightly in the bottom of the bowl. Mound the cherries slightly in the middle. Crumble the topping over the cherries, keeping the topping at the center of the pie relatively thin. There should be fruit showing here and there so steam can escape from the filling while the pie bakes.

Bake for 10 minutes, then reduce the oven temperature to 400°F (200°C) and continue to bake, checking every 20 minutes or so to make sure the crust is browning evenly, until the edges of the crust and the topping are nicely browned and the cherries are bubbling, about 1 hour longer. If the edges darken before the pie is done, cover with 2 strips of aluminum foil for the final minutes of baking. Transfer to a rack and let cool completely before serving.

serves 8

Since 1926, Traverse City, Michigan, has held the National Cherry Festival to celebrate the local harvest.

Pacific Northwest
Coffee Pots-de-Crème

Many coffee-flavored desserts use instant espresso powder, but the very best flavor comes from infusing coffee beans, as in this recipe. Northwest coffee drinkers like their coffee with character, the product of a good dark roast, so choose whole French or espresso roast beans for the most flavor.

3 cups (24 fl oz/750 ml) half-and-half
(half cream)

½ cup (2 oz/60 g) dark roast coffee beans,
crushed

5 egg yolks

½ cup (4 oz/125 g) sugar

boiling water as needed

½ cup (4 fl oz/125 ml) heavy (double) cream

2 tablespoons coffee liqueur

6 chocolate-covered coffee beans (optional)

☙ Preheat an oven to 300°F (150°C). Set six ½-cup (4-fl oz/125-ml) *pot-de-crème* pots in a baking dish. In a saucepan over medium-high heat, combine the half-and-half and the coffee beans and bring just to a boil. Cover. Set aside for no more than 15 minutes.

☙ In a bowl, whisk together the egg yolks and the sugar. Line a sieve with dampened cheesecloth (muslin) and strain the coffee-infused half-and-half into a measuring pitcher. Slowly whisk the coffee mixture into the yolk mixture just until blended; do not allow it to become frothy. Pour back into the pitcher, then divide among the *pot-de-crème* pots.

☙ Add boiling water to the baking dish to reach halfway up the sides of the pots. Cover the baking dish loosely with aluminum foil. Bake until the custard is set, 30–40 minutes. Carefully transfer the pots to a rack to cool completely. Cover and re-frigerate if not serving right away. Just before serving, whip the cream until soft peaks begin to form, then whip in the coffee liqueur. Top each *pot-de-crème* with a dollop of the cream and finish with a chocolate-covered coffee bean, if desired.

serves 6

California

Bittersweet Chocolate Cake with Raspberry Sauce

Dense, moist, and intense, this flourless cake is pure chocolate bliss, especially for those who insist that chocolate is one of the four basic food groups. San Franciscans have had a long love affair with chocolate, thanks to Ghirardelli and Guittard, two top-quality manufacturers. The newest producer, Berkeley-based Scharffen Berger Chocolate Maker, promises to keep the Bay Area in the forefront of chocolate obsession. A raspberry sauce flavored with framboise (raspberry brandy) or kirsch makes the ideal complement.

1 cup (5 oz/155 g) plus 2 tablespoons hazelnuts (filberts)

3 tablespoons plus ¾ cup (6 oz/185 g) granulated sugar

6 eggs, separated

1 teaspoon vanilla extract (essence)

¾ cup (6 oz/185 g) unsalted butter

6 oz (185 g) bittersweet chocolate, coarsely chopped

SAUCE

1½ cups (6 oz/185 g) raspberries

3 tablespoons superfine (caster) sugar, or more to taste

1 teaspoon framboise or kirsch

❦ Preheat an oven to 350°F (180°C). Butter the bottom and sides of a 9-inch (23-cm) springform pan. Dust with flour, tapping out the excess.

❦ In a food processor, combine the hazelnuts and 1 tablespoon of the granulated sugar. Pulse until the nuts are very finely ground; do not grind to a paste.

❦ In a stand mixer fitted with the whip attachment, combine the egg yolks, the ¾ cup (6 oz/185 g) granulated sugar, and the vanilla and beat on high speed until pale and thick, 4–5 minutes, stopping to scrape down the sides of the bowl once or twice.

❦ In a small saucepan over low heat, melt the butter. Remove from the heat, add the chocolate, and let stand until the chocolate melts, 2–3 minutes. Stir until smooth. In a bowl, using a whisk or a handheld electric mixer on medium-high speed, whip the egg whites until soft peaks form, then gradually add the remaining 2 tablespoons granulated sugar. Whip until the whites are firm and glossy.

❦ With the stand mixer on low speed, add the chocolate mixture to the egg yolks. Beat until blended, stopping to scrape down the sides of the bowl once or twice. Add the ground nuts and beat just until incorporated; the batter will be stiff.

❦ Transfer the batter to a large bowl. Stir in one-third of the egg whites to lighten the batter, then gently fold in the remaining whites in 2 batches. Pour the batter into the prepared pan. Bake until the center is firm to the touch and the surface begins to crack, about 50 minutes. Transfer to a rack and let cool completely. Unclasp and remove the pan sides, then carefully slide the cake onto a flat serving plate.

❦ To make the sauce, in a food processor, purée the raspberries until smooth. Add the 3 tablespoons superfine sugar and process until fully incorporated. Taste and add more sugar if desired. When sweetened to taste, pass the purée through a fine-mesh sieve placed over a bowl to eliminate the seeds. Stir in the framboise or kirsch.

❦ To serve, cut the cake into 12 wedges. Accompany each wedge with 1 tablespoon raspberry sauce.

serves 12

Southwest

Bizcochitos

Spiced with toasted aniseed and cinnamon, bizcochitos are unique to the Southwest, where some natives form them in the shape of a fleur-de-lis. Dust the cookies with cinnamon sugar, if desired.

½ teaspoon aniseed

1½ cups (7½ oz/235 g) unbleached all-purpose (plain) flour

¾ teaspoon baking powder

½ teaspoon salt

½ cup (4 oz/125 g) lard

⅓ cup (3 oz/90 g) plus 2 tablespoons sugar

1 egg yolk

2 tablespoons brandy or fresh orange juice

1½ teaspoons ground cinnamon

pinch of freshly grated nutmeg

❧ Position racks in the upper and lower third of an oven and preheat to 325°F (165°C). In a small, heavy frying pan over low heat, toast the aniseed, stirring often, until lightly colored, 3–4 minutes. Let cool.

❧ Onto a piece of waxed paper, sift together the flour, baking powder, and salt. In a large bowl, using an electric mixer on high speed, beat together the lard, the ⅓ cup (3 oz/90 g) sugar, and the aniseed until light and fluffy. Reduce the speed to medium and beat in the egg yolk and then the brandy or orange juice. Add the flour mixture, stir to combine, and then beat by hand until well blended.

❧ Have ready 2 ungreased baking sheets. On a plate, combine the remaining 2 tablespoons sugar, the cinnamon, and the nutmeg. Divide the dough in half, shaping each half into a ball. On a floured work surface, roll out 1 dough ball ¼ inch (3 mm) thick. Dust a 2-inch (5-cm) round cookie cutter with flour and cut out cookies. Transfer to the baking sheets. Gather the scraps, reroll the dough, and cut out more cookies. Repeat with the second dough ball.

❧ Bake the cookies, exchanging the positions of the sheets on the racks and rotating them 180 degrees at the halfway point, until the bottoms are just golden, about 10 minutes. Let the cookies rest on the sheets for 2 minutes. Transfer to racks and let cool completely. Store, layered with waxed paper, in airtight tins at room temperature for up to 3 days.

makes about 24 cookies

Christmas in Santa Fe

Santa Fe sits on a high plateau amid a stunning landscape in the Sangre de Cristo Mountains of northern New Mexico. Founded by the Spanish more than four centuries ago, the city retains much of its original rustic charm and is never more beautiful than in winter. The skies are dazzlingly blue, and the sweet, piney essence of piñon-wood fires hangs in the air like a perfume.

As the seat of the Archdiocese of New Mexico, the city celebrates Christmas with reverence and style. The tan adobe houses are decorated with paper-bag lanterns, or *farolitos*, with flickering votive candles. At gates and on street corners, bonfires called *luminarias* blaze, symbolically lighting the way for the Christ child. Around the Plaza, the heart of Santa Fe, the ritual performance of *Las Posadas* (The Inns), the story of Mary and Joseph's search for shelter in an overcrowded Bethlehem, is annually enacted. When a place to spend the night is found, everyone heads off for assorted indoor comforts. Such festive spreads often feature bowls of chile-spiked posole, followed by plates of the holiday spice cookies called *bizcochitos* and steaming mugs of dark, fragrant coffee or rich hot chocolate.

South

Key Lime Pie

True key limes hail from the Florida Keys and the Caribbean Islands. These limes are the size of a golf ball or a bit smaller. They have yellowish (often blemished or two-toned) skin and lighter pulp and tarter juice than the more common Persian limes. If key limes are unavailable, you can use regular lime juice, but increase the amount to ¼ cup (2 fl oz/60 ml). The filling will be a pale lemon-yellow. A misguided baker will add a couple of drops of green food coloring, but true southerners find such cosmetics taboo.

CRUST

28 gingersnaps, about 1½ inches (4 cm) in diameter

½ cup (2 oz/60 g) chopped pecans

1 tablespoon chopped crystallized ginger

3 tablespoons granulated sugar

⅛ teaspoon ground cinnamon (optional)

¼ cup (2 oz/60 g) unsalted butter, melted and cooled

FILLING

4 eggs, separated

¼ cup (1 oz/30 g) cornstarch (cornflour)

½ cup (4 oz/125 g) granulated sugar

1 can (14 oz/440 g) sweetened condensed milk

½ cup (4 fl oz/125 ml) fresh key lime juice

2 tablespoons finely grated key lime zest

½ teaspoon cream of tartar

½ teaspoon vanilla extract (essence)

TOPPING

1 cup (8 fl oz/250 ml) heavy (double) cream

⅓ cup (1½ oz/45 g) confectioners' (icing) sugar

⅛ teaspoon almond extract (essence)

8 thin key lime slices

❧ Preheat an oven to 350°F (180°C). Lightly butter a 9-inch (23-cm) pie dish.

❧ To make the crust, in a food processor, combine the gingersnaps, pecans, ginger, and granulated sugar, and the cinnamon, if using. Pulse until the mixture resembles finely ground crumbs, 1½–2 minutes. Transfer the mixture to a bowl and add the melted butter. Mix until the crumbs are evenly dampened and the mixture resembles a coarse meal, about 1 minute.

Press the mixture in an even layer onto the bottom and up the sides of the prepared pie dish. (To make this step easy, place an empty pie dish of the same size on top of the crumbs and press down firmly, then lift off the dish.)

❧ Place the crust in the oven and bake until it is lightly browned, about 10 minutes. Transfer the crust to a rack to cool.

❧ To make the filling, in a large bowl, using an electric mixer on high speed, beat together the egg yolks and 2 of the egg whites with the cornstarch, granulated sugar, and condensed milk until light and fluffy, about 5 minutes. Add the lime juice and zest and beat until smooth.

❧ In a clean bowl, using clean beaters, whip the remaining 2 egg whites and the cream of tartar with an electric mixer on high speed for 1 minute. Continue beating until soft peaks form and the peaks hold their shape, 1–2 minutes. Whisk in the vanilla extract. Fold one-third of the egg whites into the key lime mixture to lighten it. Then fold the key lime mixture into the egg whites just until combined.

❧ Transfer the filling into the cooled pie crust and smooth the top with a rubber spatula. Bake the pie until just firm, about 20 minutes. Transfer to a wire rack to cool completely, then cover and refrigerate for at least 4 hours or for up to overnight.

❧ To make the topping, in a chilled bowl, using chilled beaters and the electric mixer on high speed, beat the cream until soft peaks form, about 2 minutes. Gradually add the confectioners' sugar and then the almond extract and beat until the peaks are thick and hold their shape, about 1 minute.

❧ Spoon the whipped cream into a piping bag that is fitted with a rosette or star tip. Pipe 5 straight lines across the surface of the chilled pie, spacing them evenly. Then pipe 4 lines diagonally over the first lines to form a lattice pattern. At each intersection of the lines, pipe a small rosette or star. Alternatively, pipe the whipped cream around the rim of the pie. Refrigerate for up to 2 hours.

❧ Remove the pie from the refrigerator. Cut the lime slices in half and arrange around the rim of the pie. Cut the pie into wedges and serve at once.

serves 8

New England

Indian Pudding with Dried-Fruit Compote

Hasty pudding, a slow-cooked, flour-and-water porridge that dates back to the Middle Ages, arrived in the Northeast with the early English settlers, who doled out the bland fare for breakfast. In time, they traded the flour for cornmeal and added molasses, a local and inexpensive sweetener, thus creating the tasty dessert now known as Indian pudding. Topped with simmered dried fruits, this modern version of the pudding is cooked more quickly and is sweetened with the region's maple syrup. Any leftover fruit compote is delicious spooned over ice cream.

PUDDING

1⅓ cups (11 fl oz/340 ml) heavy (double) cream

1⅓ cups (11 fl oz/340 ml) milk

½ cup (2½ oz/75 g) fine-grind cornmeal

⅓ cup (4 oz/125 g) maple syrup

⅓ cup (3 oz/90 g) firmly packed light brown sugar

2 tablespoons unsalted butter, cut into 2 equal pieces

2 eggs, lightly beaten

1 teaspoon vanilla extract (essence)

COMPOTE

1 cup (8 fl oz/250 ml) apple cider

⅔ cup (4 oz/125 g) loosely packed dried apricots, coarsely chopped

⅓ cup (1½ oz/45 g) dried tart cherries

⅓ cup (1½ oz/45 g) dried cranberries

⅓ cup (2 oz/60 g) golden raisins (sultanas)

¼ cup (1 oz/30 g) dried plums, coarsely chopped

¼ cup (2 oz/60 g) firmly packed light brown sugar

pinch of ground cinnamon

pinch of ground cloves

1 tablespoon unsalted butter

½ teaspoon vanilla extract (essence)

❧ To make the pudding, preheat an oven to 325°F (165°C). Set six ¾-cup (6–fl oz/180–ml) custard dishes in a baking pan.

❧ In a large saucepan over medium heat, combine the cream and milk. Gradually whisk in the cornmeal, then whisk in the maple syrup, brown sugar, and butter until well blended. Cook, whisking constantly, until thickened and boiling, about 4 minutes. Remove from the heat and, while whisking constantly, slowly add the eggs and vanilla.

❧ Ladle or pour the mixture into the prepared custard dishes, dividing it evenly. Pour enough hot tap water into the baking pan to reach halfway up the sides of the dishes. Bake the puddings until set and a knife inserted into the middle of a pudding comes out almost completely clean, about 55 minutes. Transfer the custard dishes to a rack and let cool. The puddings can be served warm or at room temperature.

❧ To make the compote, in a saucepan over medium-high heat, combine the apple cider, apricots, cherries, cranberries, raisins, plums, brown sugar, cinnamon, and cloves. Bring to a boil, stirring occasionally. Reduce the heat to medium-low and simmer, stirring occasionally, until the fruit is tender and the liquid is reduced and syrupy, about 10 minutes. Remove from the heat and add the butter and vanilla. Stir until the butter is melted.

❧ Serve the compote warm or at room temperature, spooned on top of the puddings.

serves 6

South

Peach-Molasses and Brown Sugar Cobbler

A true cobbler is a fruit-based dessert with a dense cakelike or biscuit topping that is either baked over the fruit or, as is the case here, baked around the fruit. This latter style is a direct descendant of the French clafouti and is not at all similar to the deep-dish pie that many diners expect when a cobbler is on the menu. Peaches, a big commercial crop in Georgia and South Carolina, are used here, but any ripe stone fruits or berries can be substituted.

¾ cup (6 oz/185 g) unsalted butter
1½ cups (7½ oz/235 g) all-purpose (plain) flour
1 cup (7 oz/220 g) firmly packed brown sugar
1 tablespoon baking powder
½ teaspoon salt
¼ teaspoon ground cinnamon
1½ cups (12 fl oz/375 ml) milk

⅓ cup (4 oz/125 g) dark molasses
2 eggs, beaten
2 teaspoons vanilla extract (essence)
1 cup (4 oz/125 g) chopped pecans
6–8 ripe peaches, peeled and sliced (about 4 cups/1½ lb/750 g)

❧ Preheat an oven to 350°F (180°C). Put the butter in an 8-by-12-inch (20-by-30-cm) baking dish and place in the oven to melt.

❧ In a large bowl, stir together the flour, brown sugar, baking powder, salt, and cinnamon. In a bowl, whisk together the milk, molasses, eggs, and vanilla. Stir the milk mixture into the flour mixture until well blended. Stir in the pecans. Remove the hot baking dish with the melted butter from the oven and pour the batter into it. Evenly spoon the sliced peaches with any juices over the batter.

❧ Return the dish to the oven and bake until the batter is browned and has risen around the fruit, 40–45 minutes. Transfer to a rack to cool for 30 minutes, then serve warm directly from the dish.

serves 8

California

Almond–Raisin Biscotti

When Californians discovered caffè latte in the 1980s, they also discovered these Tuscan cookies meant for dipping or, as here, paired with sorbet.

½ cup (3 oz/90 g) raisins

2 cups (10 oz/315 g) unbleached all-purpose (plain) flour

1½ teaspoons baking powder

½ teaspoon salt

½ cup (4 oz/125 g) unsalted butter

1 cup (8 oz/250 g) granulated sugar

2 eggs

1 tablespoon brandy

2 teaspoons vanilla extract (essence)

1 cup (5½ oz/170 g) almonds, toasted

½ cup (2½ oz/75 g) hazelnuts (filberts), toasted and skinned

¼ cup (2 oz/60 g) crystal sugar

❧ Preheat an oven to 325°F (165°C). Line a heavy baking sheet with parchment (baking) paper. In a bowl, combine the raisins with lukewarm water to cover. Let stand for 1 hour to soften, then drain.

❧ In a bowl, stir together the flour, baking powder, and salt. In a bowl, using an electric mixer on medium speed, beat the butter until smooth and creamy. Add the granulated sugar gradually and beat until light and creamy. Add the eggs one at a time, beating well after each addition. Scrape down the bowl, then beat in the brandy and the vanilla. Reduce the speed to low and add the flour mixture gradually, beating just until blended. Add the almonds, hazelnuts, and raisins and beat just until incorporated.

❧ Transfer the dough to the baking sheet and form into 3 logs each about 14 inches (35 cm) long and 1½ inches (4 cm) wide. Sprinkle with the crystal sugar, pressing it into place. Bake until lightly colored and firm, 30–35 minutes. Let rest for 10 minutes. Transfer to a cutting board. Using a serrated knife, cut the logs on the diagonal into slices ½ inch (12 mm) thick. Place, cut side down, on 2 unlined baking sheets and bake, 1 sheet at a time, until lightly colored, 12–15 minutes. Transfer the cookies to a rack to cool. Store them in an airtight container for up to 2 weeks.

makes about 6 dozen cookies

Hawaii

Mango Sorbet

Tropical Hawaii is the only state where such seemingly exotic crops as coffee beans, cacao beans, and a stunning variety of flavorful tropical fruits can all be grown. For this sorbet, be sure to use ripe mangoes (they should give gently when pressed) for maximum flavor and aroma.

1 cup (8 oz/250 g) sugar

1 cup (8 fl oz/250 ml) water

3 large, ripe mangoes

¼ cup (2 fl oz/60 ml) fresh lime juice

1 teaspoon grated lime zest

❧ In a small saucepan over medium heat, combine the sugar and the water. Heat the mixture, stirring occasionally, until the sugar has dissolved, 2–3 minutes. Raise the heat to high and bring just to a boil. Remove from the heat and set the sugar syrup aside to cool completely.

❧ Holding 1 of the mangoes on a narrow side on the cutting board, carefully cut away the flesh from each side of the flat pit. Peel away the skin from each mango half and coarsely chop the flesh. Repeat with a second mango.

❧ Place the mango pieces in a food processor and purée until smooth. Add the sugar syrup and the lime juice and zest and process another minute to blend thoroughly, stopping to scrape down the sides of the bowl as needed. Transfer the mango purée to an ice-cream maker and freeze according to the manufacturer's instructions. Transfer to a plastic container, cover, and place in the freezer until fully set, 2–3 hours longer.

❧ When ready to serve the sorbet, cut away the flesh from each side of the flat pit of the remaining mango and peel away the skin. Cut the flesh into ½-inch (12-mm) dice. Scoop the mango sorbet into individual dishes and garnish with diced mango, dividing it evenly. Serve immediately.

serves 6–8

Pacific Northwest
Mulled Wine Poached Pears

Oregon and Washington are top producers of pears, including yellow and red Bartlett (Williams'), Bosc, Comice, Anjou, and even beautiful little Seckels. Bosc pears, with their firm texture even when ripe, are the ideal choice for this recipe, although you could use other pears that are ripe but not soft. The recipe brings together two favorite late-fall, early-winter treats: sweet Northwest pears and aromatic mulled wine. The pears may also be halved and cored before poaching.

1 bottle (750 ml) Pinot Noir or other medium-bodied, fruity red wine

1 cup (8 fl oz/250 ml) water, or as needed

½ cup (4 oz/125 g) sugar

1 orange zest strip

2 cinnamon sticks

5 whole cloves

2 star anise

few gratings of nutmeg

4 ripe, but firm whole pears (see note), peeled

1 pt (500 ml) vanilla ice cream

In a large saucepan over medium-high heat, combine the wine, 1 cup (8 fl oz/250 ml) water, sugar, orange zest, cinnamon sticks, cloves, star anise, and nutmeg. Bring just to a boil, stirring occasionally until the sugar has dissolved, then reduce the heat to medium so the liquid simmers gently. Add the pears to the wine mixture along with enough water so that the pears are fully submerged in the liquid. Cover the pears with a round of parchment (baking) paper cut to fit just inside the pan and press directly onto the surface of the poaching liquid. Poach the pears gently until just tender when pierced with the tip of a knife, 20–30 minutes. Using a slotted spoon, transfer the pears to a bowl and let cool.

Raise the heat to medium-high and boil the poaching liquid until reduced by about two-thirds and slightly thickened, about 15 minutes. Scoop out and discard the orange zest and spices, and set the syrup aside to cool to room temperature.

For each serving, place a pear upright on a dessert plate and drizzle with the reduced syrup. Set a generous scoop of ice cream alongside and serve.

serves 4

Midwest
Chunky Apple Cake

For this fluffy and spicy apple cake, call on your favorite pie apples (page 232). The locally grown Mutsu, a Japanese hybrid, is a good choice.

2½ cups (12½ oz/390 g) all-purpose (plain) flour

1½ teaspoons baking powder

½ teaspoon each baking soda (bicarbonate of soda), kosher salt, and ground cinnamon

¼ teaspoon each ground cloves, ground allspice, and freshly grated nutmeg

about 2 lb (1 kg) baking apples (see note)

½ cup (4 oz/125 g) unsalted butter, at room temperature

1 cup (8 oz/250 g) granulated sugar

1 cup (7 oz/220 g) firmly packed brown sugar

2 eggs

¾ cup (6 fl oz/180 ml) buttermilk

¼ cup (1 oz/30 g) confectioners' (icing) sugar

❧ Preheat an oven to 350°F (180°C). Butter a 10-inch (25-cm) tube pan.

❧ In a bowl, sift together the flour, baking powder, baking soda, salt, cinnamon, cloves, allspice, and nutmeg. Peel and core the apples. Chop into coarse ½-inch (12-mm) dice. You should have 4 heaping cups (about 1¼ lb/625 g) diced apples.

❧ In a bowl, using an electric mixer on medium speed, beat the butter and granulated and brown sugars until soft and fluffy, about 3 minutes. Add the eggs one at time, beating well after each addition. Beat 1 minute longer until creamy. Reduce the speed to low and add the flour mixture in 3 batches alternately with the buttermilk, beginning and ending with the flour mixture. Gently fold in the apples, making sure the pieces are all coated with batter and are evenly distributed. Pour into the prepared pan.

❧ Bake the cake until a toothpick inserted into the center comes out clean, 50–60 minutes. Transfer to a rack to cool. Invert the cake onto a cake plate and lift off the pan. If desired, reposition the cake upright. Using a fine-mesh sieve, dust the top with the confectioners' sugar.

serves 12

America's Bread Basket

As the America of the early 1800s expanded westward, its hardworking pioneers discovered that the dry, harsh climate of the Great Plains was ideal for growing wheat, especially the hard-kerneled varieties from Russia. Small family plots quickly merged to form oceans of supple grass that turned first green, then gold, as the stalks dried before harvest. Within a hundred years, this undulating landscape grew to feed the entire nation and much of the world. As soon as the wheat fields were established, big flour mills and large commercial bakeries sprouted up alongside them.

Today, central and western Kansas specializes in hard red winter wheat, a type grown throughout the Great Plains that is planted in fall and harvested in early summer. Containing a relatively high protein level, this workhorse wheat is valued for its versatility and is milled into sturdy flours for making breads, rolls, buns, and a range of other baked foods, and for export. Hard white winter wheat, a related class grown in the same areas, has a slightly sweeter flavor and lighter color and is gaining favor among makers of artisanal breads and Asian noodles.

In North Dakota, most wheat farmers grow durum, a hard, high-protein class that is the source of the semolina used for making the best dried pasta. This state and others in the north also grow hard red spring varieties, which contain the most protein. Like durum, these wheat fields are harvested in the fall. Less versatile than hard red winter wheat, the flours milled from these grains go into making bread and rolls. A small part of the upper Midwest is also planted with soft white wheat, used for crackers, snack items, and pastries.

Wheat is typically brought to market as flour through a commodity supply chain that involves a series of grain elevators, mills, and specialty grains out of this mixed-wheat basket, has gained momentum. In much the same way that chefs have become involved with their ingredient producers, American bakers are working to identify and isolate the grains and blends that they prefer, and to establish relationships with the farmers who grow them. Harvests from many farms are weighed, graded, paid for, and then combined at the elevator. But a movement toward "identity preservation," which would keep organic and specialty grains out of this mixed-wheat basket, has gained momentum. In much the same way that chefs have become involved with their ingredient producers, American bakers are working to identify and isolate the grains and blends that they prefer, and to establish relationships with the farmers who grow them.

Yankee Pumpkin Pie

When most Americans think of pumpkins, it is the big Connecticut field pumpkin that comes to mind. In colonial times, settlers would slice off the top of a pumpkin, fill the hollow with milk and honey, and then bury the big gourd in a bed of hot ashes to bake. These same pumpkins have thin walls that are perfect for carving scary faces at Halloween. Sadly, jack-o'-lanterns make lousy pies, as their flesh is watery, stringy, and irretrievably bland. Sugar and New England pie pumpkins are just two varieties that are small enough to handle easily and have flesh that is creamy and flavorful, making them the perfect base for this beloved national pie.

1 pumpkin (see note), about 1 lb (500 g)

pastry for a single-crust 9-inch (23-cm) pie (page 232)

½ cup (3½ oz/105 g) firmly packed light brown sugar

4 teaspoons all-purpose (plain) flour

¾ teaspoon ground cinnamon

¼ teaspoon freshly grated nutmeg

pinch of ground cloves

pinch of salt

1 cup (8 fl oz/250 ml) heavy (double) cream

¼ cup (3 oz/90 g) maple syrup

3 eggs, at room temperature, lightly beaten

¾ teaspoon vanilla extract (essence)

MAPLE WHIPPED CREAM (OPTIONAL)

1 cup (8 fl oz/250 ml) heavy (double) cream

3 tablespoons maple syrup

serves 10

❧ Preheat an oven to 400°F (200°C). Line a jelly-roll pan or a baking sheet with aluminum foil and lightly grease. Cut the pumpkin in half through the stem end. Using a spoon, scrape out the seeds and fibers and discard. Place each half, cut side down, on the prepared pan. Bake until tender when pierced with a knife, about 1 hour. Set the pan on a wire rack to cool. When the pumpkin is cool enough to handle, scrape the flesh into a food processor and purée until smooth, about 3 minutes. Alternatively, scoop the flesh into a sieve set over a large bowl and, using a rubber spatula, press the pumpkin through the sieve. You will need 1¾ cups (12 oz/375 g) purée for the filling.

❧ Meanwhile, on a lightly floured work surface, roll out the pastry disk into a 14-inch (35-cm) round, dusting the rolling pin with flour as needed to prevent sticking. Drape the pastry around the pin and carefully ease it into a 9-inch (23-cm) pie dish, pressing it into the bottom and sides. Trim the overhang so that it extends ¾ inch (2 cm) beyond the edge of the pie dish rim. Roll the overhang under to shape a high edge that rests on top of the rim. Crimp attractively around the rim and freeze the pie shell for at least 30 minutes.

❧ Raise the oven temperature to 425°F (220°C). Line the frozen pie shell with a large piece of aluminum foil, fill with pie weights or a combination of uncooked rice and dried beans, and bake until set to the touch, about 15 minutes. Remove the weights and foil and continue to bake the shell until golden, 4–5 minutes longer. Transfer to a rack and let cool. Reduce the oven temperature to 325°F (165°C).

❧ In a large bowl, combine the reserved pumpkin purée, brown sugar, flour, cinnamon, nutmeg, cloves, and salt and whisk until smooth. Add the cream, maple syrup, eggs, and vanilla and whisk until just smooth. Pour into the cooled pie shell.

❧ Bake until the center jiggles slightly when the dish is nudged, about 50 minutes. Transfer to a rack and let cool. Cover and refrigerate until chilled.

❧ To make the whipped cream, in a chilled bowl, using an electric mixer set on medium–high speed, beat until soft peaks form, about 2 minutes. Add the maple syrup and continue to beat until well blended and the cream forms soft peaks, about 30 seconds longer. When you lift the beaters, the tips of the peaks should flop over gently.

❧ To serve, cut the pie into wedges and top each serving with a spoonful of cream, if desired.

Come, all, pumpkin patches are a knot of green vines and orange globes.

the pod. Bring to a simmer over medium heat. Cover and let stand for 15 minutes. In a bowl, whisk together the egg yolks and ¾ cup (6 oz/185 g) sugar until a ribbon forms when the whisk is lifted, about 1 minute. Whisk in the warm cream mixture, then return to the saucepan. Cook over medium-low heat, stirring constantly with a wooden spoon, until the mixture coats the spoon, about 2 minutes. Do not allow it to simmer, or it will curdle.

✿ Remove from the heat and let cool, stirring occasionally, for 15 minutes, then whisk in the crème fraîche. Pour through a sieve placed over a bowl to remove the vanilla pod. Cover and chill thoroughly. Transfer to an ice-cream maker and freeze according to the manufacturer's instructions. You should have about 1 qt (1 l).

✿ About 30 minutes before serving, place the apricot slices in a bowl. Add the 1 tablespoon sugar, or more if the fruit is underripe, and the lemon juice. Stir gently and set aside.

✿ Scoop the ice cream into dessert goblets or compote dishes. Arrange the apricot slices alongside and drizzle with some of the accumulated juices.

serves 6

California

Crème Fraîche Ice Cream with Apricots

This luscious ice cream has the flavor of cheesecake. Peaches, peeled and sliced, or 2 cups (8 oz/250 g) mixed berries may be used in place of the apricots.

1 cup (8 fl oz/250 ml) half-and-half (half cream)

1 cup (8 fl oz/250 ml) heavy (double) cream

½ vanilla bean, split lengthwise

6 egg yolks

¾ cup (6 oz/185 g) sugar

1 cup (8 fl oz/250 ml) crème fraîche

6 apricots, halved, pitted, and sliced

1 tablespoon sugar, or to taste

2 teaspoons fresh lemon juice

✿ In a saucepan, combine the half-and-half and the cream. Using the tip of a small knife, scrape the vanilla bean seeds into the cream mixture, then add

Gingerbread Squares with Jeweled Lemon Sauce

The original English colonists are credited with putting gingerbread on the southern table. This dense, dark cake, flavored with molasses and sweet spices, gets its appealing "warmth" from the addition of three types of ginger—ground, fresh, and crystallized—and freshly ground black pepper. It has a long shelf life, which makes it an ideal "snacking" cake to have on hand when neighbors show up unexpectedly. Store tightly wrapped in the refrigerator for up to a week and bring to room temperature before serving.

1 cup (11 oz/345 g) dark molasses

½ cup (3½ oz/105 g) firmly packed dark brown sugar

½ cup (4 oz/125 g) unsalted butter

1 cup (8 fl oz/250 ml) fresh orange juice finely grated zest of 2 oranges

2 tablespoons chopped crystallized ginger

1 tablespoon peeled and grated fresh ginger

2½ cups (12½ oz/390 g) all-purpose (plain) flour

2 teaspoons baking soda (bicarbonate of soda)

2 teaspoons ground ginger

2 teaspoons ground cinnamon

½ teaspoon freshly grated nutmeg

¼ teaspoon ground cloves

¼ teaspoon salt

¼ teaspoon freshly ground pepper

2 eggs, lightly beaten

1 tablespoon vanilla extract (essence)

SAUCE

⅔ cup (5 oz/155 g) granulated sugar

2 tablespoons cornstarch (cornflour)

1½ cups (12 fl oz/375 ml) water finely grated zest and juice of 3 lemons

1 tablespoon Grand Marnier (optional)

2 tablespoons unsalted butter

❧ Preheat an oven to 375°F (190°C). Butter an 8-by-12-inch (20-by-30-cm) baking dish. Dust with flour, tapping out the excess.

❧ In a large saucepan over medium heat, combine the molasses, brown sugar, and butter. Cook, stirring,

until the butter is melted and the mixture is bubbly, about 5 minutes. Stir in the orange juice, orange zest, crystallized ginger, and fresh ginger. Remove from the heat and let cool for 15 minutes.

❧ In a large bowl, stir together the flour, baking soda, ground ginger, cinnamon, nutmeg, cloves, salt, and pepper. When the molasses mixture is lukewarm, beat in the eggs and the vanilla. Pour into the bowl of flour and stir until well combined. Pour the batter into the prepared pan.

❧ Bake the cake until the top is springy and a toothpick inserted into the center of the cake comes out clean, 40–45 minutes. Let cool on a wire rack for 20 minutes.

❧ To make the sauce, in a saucepan, stir together the granulated sugar and cornstarch. Place over medium-high heat and pour in the water, whisking until the mixture just boils and is smooth and thickened, about 5 minutes. Remove from the heat and stir in the lemon zest and juice and the Grand Marnier, if using. Add the butter 1 tablespoon at a time, stirring until it melts and is well incorporated and the sauce is glossy. (The sauce can be cooled, covered, and refrigerated for up to 3 days. To serve, reheat gently over low heat, stirring to prevent scorching.)

❧ Cut the cake into squares. Serve it warm, drizzled with the warm sauce.

serves 8–10

New England

Cranberry-Apple Pie

Long before sweet apples and tart cranberries were paired together in pies, Native Americans looked to cranberries for their nutritional value. The Pequots, a Cape Cod tribe, mixed together cranberries, which they called ibimi, the "bitter berry"; animal fat; and dried deer meat to make pemmican, an early iron-rich snack that could be stored almost indefinitely due to the high acidity of the berries. European settlers, who saw in the beautiful blossoms of the berry's low-growing vines the head and bill of a crane, gave the berry its common name.

At harvesttime, a small part of the cranberry crop is dry-picked for the fresh market. After that, the planting areas are flooded and one of the most unusual—and lovely—sights of a New England fall is visible: brilliant, glistening red berries float on the surface of the bogs, ready for wet-harvesting and then processing into sauces and juices. For this pie, a northeasterner might pair cranberries with Northern Spy, Macoun, or Rhode Island Greening apples. The recipe yields pastry for a double-crust 9-inch (23-cm) pie; halve the recipe if you are making a single-crust pie.

PIE PASTRY FOR DOUBLE-CRUST PIE

2½ cups (12½ oz/390 g) all-purpose (plain) flour

2 tablespoons granulated sugar

1 teaspoon salt

½ cup (4 oz/125 g) chilled unsalted butter, cut into ¾-inch (2-cm) pieces

6 tablespoons (3 oz/90 g) chilled solid vegetable shortening (vegetable lard), cut into ¾-inch (2-cm) pieces

6 tablespoons (3 fl oz/90 ml) very cold water

FILLING

2½ lb (1.25 kg) apples (see note), peeled, cored, and cut into slices ¼ inch (6 mm) thick

¾ cup (3 oz/90 g) cranberries

1 cup (7oz/220 g) firmly packed dark brown sugar

¼ cup (1½ oz/45 g) all-purpose (plain) flour

1¼ teaspoons ground cinnamon

¼ teaspoon freshly grated nutmeg

1 teaspoon vanilla extract (essence)

pinch of salt

Apple Harvest

Autumn in the Northeast is known for chilly nights, Indian summer days, fiery-colored foliage, and, perhaps best of all, apple picking. Heading to the nearest orchard to gather a basket or two of the trees' best fruits is a fall tradition practiced by every true New Englander. A few orchard owners still allow folks to ramble among the trees and handpick the fruits.

Despite the New Englander's—and seemingly every American's—love of the apple, buying the fruits can be confusing. New England and Mid-Atlantic apple varieties are many, and a number of them are available year-round both in big grocery stores and in smaller specialty markets. The best thing to do is divide them into three categories, baking, eating, and juicing. The MacIntosh apple, a New England classic, is among the best of the eating category. Along with its cousins, Jerseymac, Paulared, and Jonamac, the Mac is known for its crisp texture and juicy, full-flavored taste, characteristics that also make these apples ideal for juicing.

Another New England favorite is the Macoun. Developed in New York in the early 1900s, the variety has a firm texture and a slightly tart taste that make it a wonderful choice for baking and eating. Other favorites for baking are the Jonathan, the Northern Spy, and the Baldwin. Finally, the all-purpose Roxbury Russet is an old but prized variety. It was first grown in New England in the mid-1600s, and the resurgence of interest in heirloom fruits has brought this wonderful old-timer back into farmers' markets.

To make the pastry in a food processor, combine the flour, granulated sugar, and salt and pulse to blend. Add the butter and shortening and pulse until the fats are in ½-inch (12-mm) pieces. Add the water and pulse until the dough just begins to come together in a rough mass.

To make the pastry by hand, stir together the flour, granulated sugar, and salt in a bowl. Add the butter and shortening pieces and toss to coat with flour. Using a pastry blender or 2 knives, cut the fats into the flour mixture until the pieces are no larger than small peas. Drizzle with the water and toss with a fork until the dough is evenly moist and begins to come together in a rough mass.

Turn the dough out onto a lightly floured work surface, divide in half, and shape each half into a 5-inch (13-cm) disk. Wrap the disks in plastic wrap and refrigerate until well chilled, at least 2 hours.

Preheat an oven to 425°F (220°C). Line a jelly-roll pan or baking sheet with aluminum foil. Have ready a 9-inch (23-cm) pie dish. On a lightly floured work surface, roll out 1 of the pastry disks into a 14-inch (35-cm) round, dusting the rolling pin with flour to prevent sticking. Drape the pastry around the pin and ease it into the pie dish, pressing it into the bottom

and sides. Cover the pastry-lined dish with plastic wrap. Roll out the other pastry disk and drape a sheet of plastic wrap over it.

In a large bowl, combine the apples, cranberries, brown sugar, flour, cinnamon, nutmeg, vanilla, and salt. Toss with a fork or spoon until well blended.

Uncover the pastry. Pile the apple mixture into the lined pie dish along with any accumulated juices. Brush the dough around the edge of the pie dish with water. Drape the second pastry circle around the pin, and then center the dough over the filling. Press the bottom and top pastry edges together. Using scissors, trim the overhang to ½ inch (12 mm) beyond the edge of the dish. Roll the overhang under to shape a high edge that rests on top of the dish rim. Crimp attractively around the rim to seal the edges together. With a paring knife, cut 3 vents in the top crust.

Set the pie plate on the foil-lined pan. Bake for 15 minutes. Reduce the heat to 350°F (180°C) and continue to bake until the apples are very tender when pierced with a knife through the vents, about 50 minutes. Transfer to a rack and let cool. Serve the pie warm or at room temperature.

serves 8–10

South

Coconut Layer Cake with Ambrosia Filling

In the late 1800s, coconuts, pineapples, and bananas arrived by ship at southern ports, then were sent by rail to local markets. The new and exotic tropical fruits were enjoyed on special occasions in cakes such as this one with ambrosia filling, named for the food of the Greek and Roman gods.

CAKE LAYERS

½ cup (4 oz/125 g) unsalted butter, at room temperature

1¼ cups (10 oz/310 g) sugar

3 eggs, separated

3 cups (12 oz/375 g) soft winter-wheat flour such as White Lily (page 248)

1 tablespoon baking powder

½ teaspoon salt

1⅓ cups (11 fl oz/340 ml) unsweetened coconut milk

2 teaspoons vanilla extract (essence)

½ teaspoon coconut extract (essence) (optional)

FILLING

1½ cups (12 fl oz/360 ml) heavy (double) cream

1¼ cups (10 oz/315 g) sugar

⅔ cup (5 oz/155 g) unsalted butter, at room temperature

4 egg yolks, lightly beaten

2 teaspoons vanilla extract (essence)

½ cup (2 oz/60 g) chopped pecans, lightly toasted

⅓ cup (1½ oz/45 g) sweetened flaked dried coconut, lightly toasted

1 can (8 oz/250 g) crushed pineapple in its own juice, drained and squeezed dry

1 navel orange, peeled, seeded, and chopped

¼ cup (1½ oz/45 g) chopped maraschino cherries

ICING

1⅓ cups (11 oz/345 g) sugar

⅛ teaspoon salt

4 egg whites

1 teaspoon vanilla extract (essence)

¼ teaspoon coconut extract (essence) (optional)

4 cups (1 lb/500 g) sweetened flaked dried coconut

❦ To make the cake layers, preheat an oven to 350°F (180°C). Butter two 9-inch (23-cm) round cake pans. Line the bottoms with parchment (baking) paper. Coat with butter and dust with flour. In a bowl, using an electric mixer on medium-high speed, beat the butter and 1 cup (8 oz/250 g) of the sugar for about 5 minutes. Add the egg yolks one at a time, beating for 20 seconds after each addition. On a piece of parchment paper, sift the flour, baking powder, and salt. Add to the butter mixture in 3 batches alternately with the coconut milk, beginning and ending with the flour mixture. Beat in the vanilla and the coconut extract, if using.

❦ In a clean bowl, using clean beaters, beat the egg whites until they form soft peaks. Add the remaining ¼ cup (2 oz/60 g) sugar 1 tablespoon at a time, beating until the whites hold their shape. Using a rubber spatula, stir one-third of the egg white mixture into the batter. Fold the batter into the remaining egg whites. Divide between the prepared pans. Bake until a toothpick inserted into the centers comes out clean, 28–32 minutes. Transfer to racks, let cool in the pans for 5 minutes, then invert onto the racks.

❦ To make the filling, in a saucepan over medium heat, combine ¾ cup (6 fl oz/180 ml) of the cream, the sugar, and the butter. Cook, stirring, until the butter melts. In a bowl, whisk together the remaining ¾ cup (6 fl oz/180 ml) cream and the egg yolks. Stir into the saucepan. Cook over medium heat, whisking, until thickened, about 10 minutes. Remove from the heat. Stir in the vanilla, pecans, and coconut. Let cool, stirring occasionally. Fold the pineapple, orange, and maraschino cherries into the filling.

❦ To make the icing, in a heavy saucepan over low heat, combine the sugar, salt, and ⅔ cup (5 fl/160 ml) water. Stir until the sugar is dissolved. Raise the temperature to medium-high and bring to a rolling boil. Cook until a syrup forms and registers 230°F (110°C) on a candy thermometer. In a bowl, using an electric mixer on medium-high speed, beat the egg whites until they form soft peaks. When the sugar syrup has reached 240°F (115°C), pour in a thin, steady stream into the egg whites while beating on high speed. Beat until the frosting is cooled, thick, and glossy, about 7 minutes. Beat in the vanilla and the coconut extract, if using.

❦ Place 1 cake layer, top side down, on a serving plate. Spread with half of the cooled filling. Top with the second layer, top side up. Spread the top and the sides with icing. Press the flaked coconut onto the cake. Cover and refrigerate until ready to serve Pass the remaining filling at the table.

serves 12

Pacific Northwest
Berry Gratin with Late-Harvest Wine Sabayon

Sabayon is typically made with Marsala, but here the frothy sauce calls for some of the Northwest's fruity, complex late-harvest wine. Naturally sweetened by the grapes' extended ripening time on the vine, these fragrant wines are made primarily from Riesling, Gewürztraminer, and Chenin Blanc grapes. Oregon and Washington are also top national producers of blackberries, loganberries, blueberries, boysenberries, and raspberries, making this gratin a regional classic.

¾–1 lb (375–500 g) mixed berries (see note)

3 egg yolks

¼ cup (2 oz/60 g) sugar

½ cup (4 fl oz/125 ml) late-harvest wine (see note)

¼ teaspoon grated lemon zest

❧ Stem the berries and halve or quarter any berries that are large. Arrange the berries attractively in 4 individual gratin dishes, and set the dishes on a baking sheet. Set aside.

❧ Preheat a broiler (grill).

❧ In the top pan of a double boiler or in a heat-proof bowl, whisk together the egg yolks and the sugar until well blended, then whisk in the wine. Set the bowl over (but not touching) gently simmering water in the lower pan or a saucepan. Continue whisking until the mixture is light in color and very frothy, about 5 minutes. Do not let the water boil or touch the bowl, or the egg yolks will curdle.

❧ Remove the pan or bowl from over the water and whisk in the lemon zest. Spoon the sabayon evenly over the berries. Slip the baking sheet under the broiler about 5 inches (13 cm) from the heat source and broil (grill) until the top is nicely browned, about 2 minutes.

❧ Transfer the gratin dishes to heatproof dessert plates and serve at once.

serves 4

Southwest

Orange Flan

Smooth, cool, and custardy, with an elegant burnt-sugar edge, flan made its way from Spain to Mexico to the American Southwest, where it stands first among a small handful of indigenous desserts, easily seducing even satisfied diners into ordering something sweet. (It is a plus that the sugar in the flan also has a cooling effect on palates still tingling from a chile-spiked main course.) This almost-classic formula contains a welcome and refreshing touch of orange zest, which lightens the rich treat slightly.

1⅓ cups (11 oz/345 g) plus ½ cup (4 oz/125 g) sugar

⅓ cup (3 fl oz/80 ml) water

4 teaspoons minced orange zest

3 whole eggs, plus 5 egg yolks

3½ cups (28 fl oz/875 ml) heavy (double) cream

2 teaspoons vanilla extract (essence)

¼ teaspoon salt

✤ Preheat an oven to 325°F (165°C).

✤ In a heavy saucepan, stir together the 1⅓ cups (11 oz/345 g) sugar and the water. Set over medium-high heat and bring to a boil, stirring occasionally and brushing down the pan sides with a pastry brush dipped in cold water to remove any sugar crystals. Once the sugar has melted, simmer briskly, swirling the pan but not stirring the sugar mixture, to promote even cooking, until the mixture turns a rich brown and is highly fragrant, about 8 minutes.

✤ Working quickly, spoon about 2 tablespoons of the caramel into a ¾-cup (6–fl oz/180–ml) custard dish or ramekin. Immediately tilt the dish, which will be hot from the caramel, to coat as much of the inside as possible. Work quickly but carefully, as the caramel will be very hot. Repeat with the remaining caramel and 7 more custard dishes. Let stand until cool. Set the dishes in a shallow roasting pan that will just hold them comfortably.

✤ In a large bowl, using the back of a spoon, mash together the remaining ½ cup (4 oz/125 g) sugar and the orange zest. Add the eggs and egg yolks and whisk until thick and smooth.

✤ In a saucepan over medium heat, bring the cream to a simmer. Gradually whisk the hot cream into the egg-sugar mixture. Whisk in the vanilla and salt. Strain the egg mixture into a pitcher or a measuring cup with a pouring lip, then divide the mixture evenly among the custard dishes. Add hot tap water to the roasting pan to come halfway up the sides of the custard dishes.

✤ Bake until the custards are evenly but not firmly set and the tops are golden, 35–45 minutes. (The flans will firm further when they are refrigerated.) Carefully remove the custard dishes from the water bath and let cool to room temperature. Cover with plastic wrap and refrigerate overnight.

✤ Remove the flans from the refrigerator and let stand at room temperature for 15 minutes. One at a time, run the tip of a thin knife around the inside edge of each custard dish. Invert a small plate over the custard dish and, holding the dish and plate together, invert them. Lift off the custard dish and drizzle the unmolded flan with any excess liquid in the bottom of the dish. Repeat with the remaining flans. Serve immediately.

serves 8

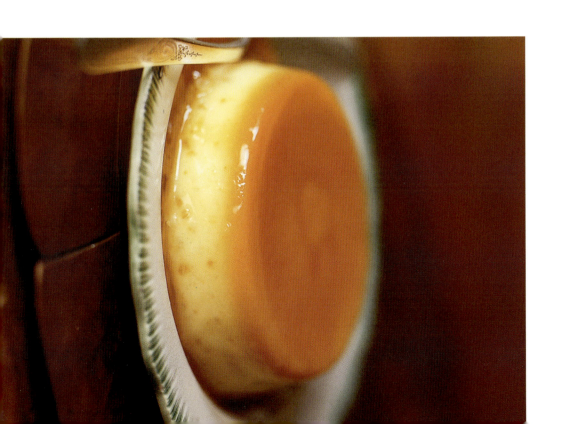

New England

Blueberry Shortcakes

During the summer months, New England farm stands are loaded with ripe berries nearly bursting with juice. The New England cook's credo is to use the freshest and ripest fruits available.

3 pt (1½ lb/750 g) blueberries

⅓ cup (3 oz/90 g) plus 3 tablespoons sugar

2 teaspoons fresh lemon juice

½ teaspoon finely grated lemon zest

¼ cup (¼ oz/7 g) fresh mint leaves, cut into narrow strips

1⅔ cups (8 oz/250 g) all-purpose (plain) flour

1 tablespoon baking powder

¾ teaspoon salt

½ cup (4 oz/125 g) chilled unsalted butter, cut into ½-inch (12-mm) pieces

¾ cup (6 fl oz/180 ml) buttermilk

½ teaspoon vanilla extract (essence)

sweetened whipped cream (page 250)

❧ In a bowl, using a fork, toss together the blueberries, ⅓ cup (3 oz/90 g) sugar, and lemon juice and zest, lightly crushing about one-third of the berries. Stir in the mint. Cover and refrigerate, stirring occasionally, until well chilled or for up to 4 hours.

❧ Preheat an oven to 400°F (200°C). In a bowl, whisk together the flour, 3 tablespoons sugar, baking powder, and salt. Scatter the butter over the flour mixture and, using a pastry blender or 2 knives, cut in the butter until the pieces are no larger than peas. Add the buttermilk and vanilla and toss with a fork until the dry ingredients are just moistened and blended. Turn the dough out onto a work surface and press into a thick rectangle about 6 by 4 inches (15 by 10 cm). Using a knife, trim the edges even and cut the dough into 6 equal squares. Place on an ungreased baking sheet. Bake until puffed and brown, 15–18 minutes. Transfer to a wire rack.

❧ Split the shortcakes in half horizontally. Place the bottom halves, cut sides up, on dessert plates. Spoon half of the blueberry compote, including the juices, over the halves, dividing it evenly. Top with whipped cream, dividing it evenly. Spoon on the remaining blueberries and top with the remaining halves.

serves 6

Coffee Culture

Not too long ago in the United States, coffee was coffee. It didn't matter much where it came from or what brand it was. But, since the early 1990s, as coffee trends in the country have seen a major shift in coffee consciousness, consumers are able to choose from various styles of roasting and types of beans for their daily cup. Nowhere has good coffee become so much a part of daily routine as it has in the Pacific Northwest.

Seattle alone boasts hundreds of coffee outlets, ranging from branches of international chains to small independent carts wheeled daily onto downtown street corners. Between the chain and the cart, a slew of inviting coffeehouse options prevail in the larger Northwest cities, from sleek cafés that look as if they were imported lock, stock, and espresso machine from Rome to no-frills neighborhood hangouts. Patronage tends to be split between the grab-and-go types and those who bring the newspaper so they can linger over their cappuccinos. Coffee loyalties are so strong in these parts that regulars show up with their own thermal cups, prompting the experienced barista to ask simply, "Same as usual?"

California
Orange and Walnut Cake with Honey Whipped Cream

California's famed navel oranges and the state's walnuts flavor this large, dense cake. It slices neatly like a pound cake, making it a good choice for a buffet, and it is even better when made a day ahead. Serve the cake with hot tea in the afternoon or with a dessert wine after dinner.

Historians suspect that walnuts came to the state with the Franciscan friars who established the missions in California in the late 1700s. Today, California's Central Valley produces 95 percent of the nation's walnut crop, and most of the state's growers belong to a cooperative that markets the nuts worldwide. California walnuts are shipped to more than forty-five countries around the world.

3 cups (12 oz/375 g) sifted unbleached all-purpose (plain) flour

½ teaspoon baking soda (bicarbonate of soda)

½ teaspoon salt

1 cup (8 oz/250 g) unsalted butter, at room temperature

2½ cups (1¼ lb/625 g) granulated sugar

8 egg yolks

1 tablespoon finely grated orange zest

2 teaspoons vanilla extract (essence)

¾ cup (6 fl oz/180 ml) buttermilk

¼ cup (2 fl oz/60 ml) fresh orange juice

1 cup (4 oz/125 g) chopped walnuts, toasted

6 egg whites

confectioners' (icing) sugar for dusting

1½ cups (12 fl oz/375 ml) heavy (double) cream

6 tablespoons (4 oz/125 g) honey

1 tablespoon bourbon, or to taste

✿ Preheat an oven to 350°F (180°). Lightly butter a 10-inch (25-cm) tube pan. Dust with flour, tapping out the excess.

✿ In a bowl, sift together the flour, baking soda, and salt. In another bowl, using an electric mixer on medium speed, beat the butter until smooth and creamy. Gradually add the granulated sugar and beat until light and creamy, stopping to scrape down the bowl sides once or twice. Add the egg yolks one at a time, beating well after each addition and stopping to scrape down the bowl sides once or twice. Beat in the orange zest and the vanilla. Add the sifted ingredients in 3 batches alternately with the buttermilk and the orange juice, beginning and ending with the sifted ingredients, and beating just enough to blend. Add the walnuts and mix briefly.

✿ In a clean bowl, using clean beaters, beat the egg whites until they form firm and glossy peaks. Using a rubber spatula, gently fold them into the batter in 3 batches. Pour the batter into the prepared pan and smooth the surface with the spatula.

✿ Bake the cake until golden brown and beginning to pull away from the sides of the pan, about 1 hour and 10 minutes.

✿ Remove from the oven and let the cake cool in the pan for 10 minutes, then invert onto a rack, lift off the pan, and invert again onto another rack. Let the cake cool completely.

✿ Just before serving, using a shaker, a sieve, or a sifter, dust the top of the cake with the confectioners' sugar. In a chilled bowl, whisk the cream until soft peaks form. Beat in the honey, and then the 1 tablespoon bourbon just until combined. Taste and add more bourbon if desired.

✿ To serve, slice the cake and accompany each slice with a dollop of the honey whipped cream.

serves 16

In the 1870s, a Southern California couple planted two Brazilian orange trees, "parents" of the state's now-giant navel industry.

The Southern Sweet Tooth

Southerners love their sweets. In fact, they are so central to the supper table that many southern cafeterias display the dessert offerings before the main dishes. That way, customers know they had better leave enough room for a big wedge of cake or pie. For a southerner, sweets make a meal complete.

What is responsible for this elaborate menu of sweets? The first reason is a practical one: sugarcane initially arrived in what is now St. Augustine, Florida, with the Spanish in 1565 (having been brought to Santo Domingo from the Canary Islands by Christopher Columbus during his voyage in 1492), and by the mid-1800s, the region's sugar refineries were so large and efficient that the sweetener was priced to fit into everyone's budget.

The second reason looks to the roots of the southern sweet tooth. The English contributed various puddings and pies to the local dessert table, but the majority of southern desserts seem to be based on French technique and tradition, a legacy due in large part to Thomas Jefferson, America's third president and the country's first serious food aficionado. Jefferson, who also served as the American minister to France, was a great champion of

French cuisine and regularly served French pastries, meringues, ice creams, pralines, cakes, and cookies at Monticello, his Virginia estate. It did not take long for the region's cooks to copy Jefferson's lead.

Today, the southern sweet tooth is kept sated with a full schedule of bake sales. Every community group from the children's theater to the neighborhood softball team, the local church to the high school band, holds these traditional southern fund-raisers. The town's home bakers display their cakes, pies, cobblers, and cookies, each labeled with a price, on long tables, and the most prized sweets are purchased quickly by savvy buyers who know which neighbor makes the best banana cream pie or Mississippi mud cake.

Come holiday time or a special occasion, elegant baked goods—a mile-high layer cake cloaked in buttercream frosting, a lemon meringue pie with a billowy, gold-tipped crown—are first set out on the sideboard for family and friends to admire. This is when a home baker gets to show off, and when the lucky guests, happy to sing the praises of the host, get to sit down and indulge in the baker's finest efforts.

South

Fig and Pecan Pie

Many southerners have a pecan tree or two growing on their property. Most cooks will use some of the nuts for the region's iconic pecan pie. In this version, fig preserves added to the pie filling make it less sweet than its traditional counterpart.

southern pie pastry (page 250)

⅓ cup (3 oz/90 g) sugar

3 tablespoons cornstarch (cornflour)

¼ teaspoon salt

½ cup (5 oz/155 g) light corn syrup

½ cup (6 oz/185 g) cane syrup or dark molasses

2 tablespoons vanilla extract (essence)

4 eggs, lightly beaten

1½ cups (6 oz/185 g) chopped pecans

¼ teaspoon ground cinnamon

freshly grated nutmeg to taste

1 cup (8 fl oz/250 ml) fig preserves (page 248)

❧ On a lightly floured work surface, roll out the pastry disk into a round about 11 inches (28 cm) in diameter. Drape the pastry around the rolling pin with flour to prevent sticking. Drape the pastry around the pin and ease it into a 9-inch (23-cm) pie pan, pressing it into the bottom and sides. Trim the overhang so that it extends about ¾ inch (2 cm) beyond the edge of pan. Roll the overhang under to shape a high edge that rests on top of the pan rim. Crimp attractively around the rim. Freeze for 30 minutes.

❧ In a large bowl, stir together the sugar, cornstarch, and salt. Add the corn syrup, cane syrup or molasses, vanilla, and eggs. Whisk briefly to combine. Do not overmix. Stir in the pecans, cinnamon, nutmeg, and fig preserves. Pour into the chilled pie crust.

❧ Bake the pie until the crust is golden brown and the center yields to slight pressure, 50–55 minutes. The filling will become firmer as the pie cools. Transfer to a wire rack to cool for at least 1 hour before serving.

serves 8

Great Plains
Cinnamon Honey Rolls

Sit down to a meal in a home-style regional restaurant, and the breadbasket will probably include cinnamon rolls. At first, the idea of mopping up pan gravy with a sweet bread may make you long for plain sliced white bread, but you will get used to the custom quick. This recipe is timed for the more common ritual of serving fresh-baked morning treats.

DOUGH

1 teaspoon plus ¼ cup (2 oz/60 g) granulated sugar

¼ cup (2 fl oz/60 ml) warm water (105°–115°F/41°–46°C)

2 teaspoons active dry yeast

½ cup (4 fl oz/125 ml) half-and-half (half cream)

5 egg yolks, at room temperature

2 tablespoons honey, at room temperature

½ teaspoon kosher salt

¼ cup (2 oz/60 g) unsalted butter, melted and cooled to room temperature

3–3½ cups (15–17½ oz/470–545 g) all-purpose (plain) flour

FILLING

½ cup (3 oz/90 g) raisins

¼ cup (2 oz/60 g) firmly packed brown sugar

2 teaspoons ground cinnamon

GLAZE

1 cup (4 oz/125 g) confectioners' (icing) sugar

2 tablespoons honey

1 tablespoon water, or more as needed

※ To make the dough, in a small bowl, dissolve the 1 teaspoon granulated sugar in the warm water. Sprinkle the yeast over the mixture and let stand until quite foamy, about 5 minutes.

※ To make the dough by machine, in a stand mixer fitted with a whisk attachment, beat together the ¼ cup (2 oz/60 g) sugar, half-and-half, egg yolks, honey, and salt until foamy, about 2 minutes. Add the melted butter and beat until thickened, about 2 minutes longer. Beat in the yeast mixture. Switch to the dough hook and mix in 3 cups (15 oz/470 g) of the flour. Add more flour, a little at a time, until the mixture just pulls away from the sides of the bowl. Do not allow the dough to become too dry. Continue to knead with the dough hook for about 5 minutes,

then turn the dough out onto a lightly floured work surface and knead by hand, working in only enough flour to keep the dough from sticking, until soft, elastic, smooth, and somewhat tacky, about 3 minutes.

※ To make the dough by hand, in a large bowl, whisk together the ¼ cup (2 oz/60 g) sugar, half-and-half, egg yolks, honey, and salt until foamy, about 2 minutes. Add the melted butter to the bowl and continue to whisk until thickened, about 2 minutes longer. Whisk in the yeast mixture. Switching to a wooden spoon, beat in 3 cups (15 oz/470 g) of the flour. Beat in more flour, a little at a time, until the dough just pulls away from the sides of the bowl. Turn the dough out onto a lightly floured work surface and knead, working in only enough flour to keep the dough from sticking, until soft, elastic, smooth, and somewhat tacky, 10–15 minutes.

※ Gather the dough into a ball. Butter a large bowl, place the dough in the bowl, and turn the dough to coat the surface with butter. Cover the bowl tightly with plastic wrap and let the dough rise in a warm place (80°F/27°C is ideal) until doubled, about 1 hour.

※ Meanwhile, make the filling: In a small bowl, combine the raisins, brown sugar, and cinnamon and toss to coat the raisins evenly.

※ Line a large baking sheet with parchment (baking) paper. Turn the dough out onto a lightly floured surface and knead a couple of times. Pat down and roll into a rectangle about 10 inches (25 cm) wide by 15 inches (37.5 cm) long, with the long side closest to you. If necessary, trim the edges to straighten them. Sprinkle the filling evenly across the surface. Beginning with the side closest to you, roll up the dough tightly to encase the filling in a log about 15 inches (37.5 cm) long. Using a sharp knife, mark 12 uniform sections, then cut through to create the rolls. Place the rolls on the prepared baking sheet, cut side down and spacing them about 2 inches (5 cm) apart. Tuck the seam end of each roll under a bit to prevent it from popping out during baking. Completely cover with plastic wrap and place in the refrigerator for 8–14 hours.

※ Preheat an oven to 350°F (180°C). To make the glaze, in a small bowl, combine the confectioners' sugar and the honey and stir until smooth. Add 1 tablespoon water or more if needed to achieve a spreadable consistency.

※ Remove the rolls from the refrigerator, uncover, and bake until puffed and golden, 15–20 minutes. Transfer the rolls immediately to a rack and spread with the glaze while the rolls are still slightly warm.

makes 12 rolls

GLOSSARY

The following glossary entries cover key ingredients and basic techniques called for throughout the book. For information on items not found below, please refer to the index.

BELL PEPPERS, RED

Also called capsicums and sweet peppers, large and meaty green bell peppers turn red and become sweeter when fully ripened. As attractive as they are versatile, red bell peppers add crunch when used raw in appetizers; take on a silky sweetness when cooked slowly in soups, stews, or sauces; and contribute a distinctive smokiness when roasted over an open flame.

TO ROAST BELL PEPPERS, using tongs or a large fork, hold a whole pepper over the flame of a gas burner for 10–15 minutes, turning it to char and blister the skin evenly. Place in a bowl, cover, and leave for 10 minutes. The steam will loosen the skin and allow for easier peeling. When the pepper is cool, peel off the blackened skin, then slit the pepper lengthwise and remove the stem, seeds, and membranes. If you have a large number of peppers to roast or if you have an electric range, broil (grill) the peppers, turning as needed, until charred on all sides. Cut as directed in individual recipes.

BOURBON, AGED KENTUCKY

In 1791, the federal government levied an excise tax on whiskey, and Pennsylvania rye farmers, who transformed most of their crop into the more easily portable spirit, launched the Whiskey Rebellion. When peace was restored, many of the Pennsylvania distillers headed south to escape the revenuers, settling in Bourbon County, Kentucky. There they began making a corn whiskey, and the distinctly American spirit, bourbon, was born. Kentucky still produces much of the country's high-quality bourbon. The slightly sweet whiskey is made primarily from fermented corn and must be aged for at least two years in new, charred white-oak barrels. Straight bourbon is distilled from a grain mash that includes at least 51 percent corn, though most bourbons are made from 60 to 70 percent corn. By law, blended bourbon contains at least 51 percent straight bourbon.

BUTTERMILK

After churning butter from fresh milk, Early American cooks used the tangy liquid leftover to make biscuits, cakes, and other baked treats. Today, buttermilk is made commercially by adding a bacterial culture to skim or nonfat milk. Still valued for its slightly tart flavor, buttermilk is also available in a dehydrated form. To make a quick substitute for buttermilk, stir 1 tablespoon fresh lemon juice into 1 cup (8 fl oz/250 ml) milk and let stand for 10 minutes until thickened.

CANE SYRUP

Workers from the sugarcane plantations of the Caribbean introduced this very sweet, thick, amber-colored syrup to southern cooks. Also known as golden syrup or light treacle, cane syrup is available in tins at shops that specialize in Caribbean or British ingredients. If unavailable, substitute a mixture of 2 parts light corn syrup and 1 part molasses, or stir together equal parts corn syrup and honey.

CHILES

One of the earliest plants to be domesticated in the Americas, the chile is an indispensable item in the Southwest kitchen, where local cooks still draw on long-ago Inca, Aztec, and Mayan culinary traditions. As versatile as they are varied in size and heat, chiles are added fresh to stews and salsas, are roasted and peeled for stuffing or for cutting into strips for garnishing, or are dried and puréed for using as a sauce or ground for using as a seasoning.

TO ROAST AND PEEL CHILES, arrange whole chiles on an aluminum foil-lined pan. Place in a pre-heated broiler (grill) 6 inches (15 cm) from the heat source and broil (grill), turning as needed, until the skins are evenly blackened and blistered, 10–15 minutes. Take care not to burn the flesh. Transfer the chiles to a bowl, cover, and let stand until cool enough to handle. Wearing kitchen gloves if your hands are sensitive, remove the skin with your fingers or a small paring knife. Resist the temptation to rinse the chiles under water, or you will wash away much of their flavor. Make a lengthwise slit in each chile, cut out the stem, and, taking care not to tear the chile, scrape out the seeds and membranes. Roasted chiles can be refrigerated in a covered container for up to 3 days.

TO MAKE RED CHILE PURÉE, use ½ lb (250 g) dried red New Mexico hot chiles and ½ lb (250 g) dried red New Mexico mild chiles. Slip on kitchen gloves if your hands are sensitive and then stem the chiles and shake out and discard the seeds. Using scissors, cut the chiles into 1-inch (2.5-cm) pieces. Place in a large, heat-proof bowl and add 2½ qt (2.5 l) boiling water. Cover and let stand at room temperature, stirring occasionally, for at least 4 hours or as long as overnight. Drain the chiles, reserving 1½ cups (12 fl oz/375 ml) of the soaking liquid. Working in batches, purée the chiles in a food processor, using the reserved liquid to help free the blades and stopping to scrape down the sides of the work bowl. Transfer the purée to a coarse-mesh sieve set over a bowl and, using a rubber spatula, force it through the sieve. Discard the tough chile pieces in the sieve. You will have 3 cups (24 fl oz/750 ml) purée. Use the purée immediately, or cover tightly and refrigerate for up to 3 days or freeze for up to 1 month.

CORNMEAL

Once dried, corn kernels can be ground to a fine, medium, or coarse texture by steel rollers or stone mills. You can use the grinds interchangeably in most recipes, depending on your preference for texture. Although white cornmeal is regularly found in the pantries of southern and midwestern kitchens, yellow cornmeal is generally more popular and more readily found on store shelves. Some cooks prefer stone-ground cornmeal for its nutty flavor, softer texture, and modestly higher nutrient content. Milled with the germ intact, stone-ground cornmeal has a shorter shelf life. Store stone-ground cornmeal for up to 4 months in the refrigerator. More common steel-cut cornmeal can be kept in a cool, dark place for up to 1 year.

CORN SYRUP

Derived from the sucrose in cornstarch, this thick, liquid sweetener is used primary in desserts. Baked goods made with corn syrup retain their moisture longer than those containing granulated sugar. Because it does not crystallize or become grainy when cold, corn syrup is an essential ingredient in fudges and other confections and in frostings and dessert sauces. Light corn syrup is almost clear and has a more delicate flavor than dark corn syrup. Difficult to find outside the United States, it can be substituted with an equal amount of golden syrup or honey.

CHEESE

English colonists brought their cheese-making skills with them to New England, while German and Scandinavian settlers helped establish cheese operations throughout the northern Midwest. Cheddar quickly became as much an American classic as an English tradition, and today, the United States is the world's largest producer of cheese.

GOAT CHEESE, FRESH During the 1970s, small-scale cheese makers in California revived artisanal techniques for making goat cheeses that mimicked the style of French goat cheeses, or chèvres. American goat cheese has since become a staple on trendy restaurant menus and cheese-tasting platters. It is available as logs, disks, or pyramids in the popular fresh form, when the cheese is still soft, creamy, snowy white, and only slightly pungent. You can also choose versions flavored with black pepper or herbs.

HOOP CHEESE This moist, fresh curd cheese is pressed from skim cow's milk. Although it is sometimes dry enough to slice, its consistency is usually closer to that of farmer cheese or ricotta, which can be used as an adequate, though richer substitute. Highly perishable, hoop cheese should be used within 3 days of purchase. Look for it in specialty-cheese shops or health-food stores.

MONTEREY JACK A mild cheese that was first made near Monterey Bay in Northern California. Similar to the cheese created in the Spanish missions along the Pacific Coast, it is now popular as a topping and filling in the Mexican-inspired dishes of California and the Southwest. A version with bits of chile pepper mixed into the cheese provides extra heat for those who like their food spicy.

MOZZARELLA BALLS, FRESH Also known as *bocconcini*, Italian for "little mouthfuls," these small, egg-shaped balls are stored in their whey or a light brine. The soft, smooth mozzarella is perfect for composed salads and appetizers or briefly heated pizzas and pasta dishes.

MOZZARELLA, LOW-MOISTURE Mozzarella is an Italian pulled-curd cheese originally made from water buffalo's milk in an area near Naples, but excellent quality cow's milk mozzarella is now being produced in the United States. Appreciated for its mild, slightly sweet flavor and its moist, silky texture, mozzarella is the classic pizza cheese in America. For superior smoothness after heating and melting, look for mozzarella labeled "low moisture."

QUESO AÑEJO This Mexican cheese is an aged version of *queso fresco*, a grainy and acidic cheese made from a combination of cow's and goat's milk. California versions are made from cow's milk. As it dries, *queso añejo* becomes firmer and saltier. Traditionally, Mexican and southwestern cooks crumble it as a garnish over a variety of dishes. Romano cheese approximates its taste though not its texture or white color.

VERMONT CHEDDAR From the famed dairy farms of Vermont come cheddar cheeses that range from mild to extra sharp, are pale in color, and have a smooth texture. Although smoked and herbed versions are available, purists insist that the best cheddars are the ones that are made without flavorings; have natural, not waxed, rinds; and have been aged for at least a year.

CRAYFISH

Known variously as crawfish, crawdad, or *écrevisse*, this freshwater crustacean is the centerpiece of Creole and Cajun cooking in Louisiana, the self-proclaimed Crawfish Capital of the World. Harvested from the lakes and streams of the Mississippi basin, the sweet, tender tail meat of crayfish is highly prized throughout the South. The shellfish range in size from 3 to 6 inches (7.5 to 15 cm) long and look somewhat like miniature lobsters. Live crayfish and frozen crayfish tails are found at well-stocked seafood markets.

TO PREPARE LIVE CRAYFISH, immerse them in a large pot of boiling water for 30 seconds, drain, and rinse under running cold water. Then, to peel and devein the crayfish tails, one at a time, twist and pull the tail off the whole crayfish. Pinch the small fin beneath the tail flipper and pull it gently to remove the vein. Squeeze the tail firmly along its length, holding it between your thumbs and forefingers, until you hear a cracking sound. Press the shell open, splitting it along the underside, and carefully pull the tail meat away. You can also snip the shell along the bottom of each tail with kitchen shears to remove the meat. Most frozen tails come with the vein already removed.

FLOUR, WINTER-WHEAT

Southern cooks depend on flour finely milled from pure, soft winter wheat to give their biscuits extra flakiness and their cakes a distinctive lightness. Extra grinding, sifting, and refinement create flour, such as the much-loved White Lily brand, with a finer texture particularly suited for baking. Many cake recipes handed down in southern families assume the cook is using soft winter-wheat flour. Self-rising soft-wheat flours incorporate salt and leavening for more convenient cooking.

MIRIN

A staple in Japanese kitchens, this pale straw-colored cooking wine is stocked by many California and Pacific Northwest cooks. Made from glutinous rice and distilled spirits, it has a low alcohol content, more body than drinking wine, and a pronounced sweetness. The latter two characteristics make it ideal for use in sauces and glazes.

JELLIES AND PRESERVES

In colonial American homes, shelves laden with jars of brightly colored fruit and vegetables reassured families that they could enjoy summer's bounty throughout the year. Jars of apple butter, strawberry jam, and hot-pepper jelly are still "put up" using old-fashioned techniques developed generations ago. Both thick, chunky preserves and clear, shimmering jellies call for boiling fruit with sugar and then sealing the reduced mixture in glass jars. Hot-pepper jelly is the southern cook's best-kept secret. The sweet-spicy blend is delicious as a glaze on pork, poultry, or lamb; spread on bagels or biscuits; or spooned over cream cheese or goat cheese on crackers or baguette slices. Fig preserves, another southern favorite, are excellent served with biscuits, spread on sandwich bread, or used in pies and cookies.

HOT-PEPPER JELLY

3 red jalapeño chiles, seeded and coarsely chopped

3 green jalapeño chiles, seeded and coarsely chopped

½ Vidalia onion, chopped

1½ teaspoons celery seed

¾ cup (6 fl oz/180 ml) cider vinegar

2½ cups (1¼ lb/625 g) sugar

2 pouches (½ cup/4 fl oz/125 ml each) liquid pectin

In a food processor, combine the jalapeño chiles, onion, celery seed, and ¼ cup (2 fl oz/60 ml) of the vinegar and process until finely chopped. Transfer to a heavy 3½-qt (3.5-l) nonaluminum saucepan or dutch oven and add the remaining ½ cup (4 fl oz/120 ml) vinegar and the sugar. Bring to a boil over medium-high heat and cook for 1 minute. Remove from the heat and stir in the liquid pectin. Return to medium-high heat and boil for 1 minute longer. Remove from the heat again and let the jelly sit for 5 minutes. Skim off any foam or scum that accumulates on the top.

Carefully ladle the hot jelly into hot, sterilized jars to within ¼ inch (6 mm) of the tops. Wipe the rims clean with a hot, damp kitchen towel, top with metal canning lids, and seal tightly with screw bands. Invert the jars on a kitchen towel on the counter to cool, well spaced to allow for air to circulate. While the jelly cools and sets, invert the jars occasionally to distribute the peppers evenly. Store the jars in a cool, dark place for up to 6 months. Refrigerate any jar whose lid is not concave or makes a clicking sound when pressed, and use within 1 month.

makes three ½-pt (8-fl oz/250-ml) jars

FIG PRESERVES

6 cups (2½ lb/1.25 kg) sliced fresh Calimyrna or Kadota figs

1 cup (5½ oz/170 g) chopped dried figs

3 cups (1½ lb/750 g) sugar

1 cup (8 fl oz/250 ml) fresh orange juice

1 orange, peeled, seeded, and finely chopped

2 cinnamon sticks

⅓ cup (3 fl oz/80 ml) brandy

In a heavy saucepan, combine the fresh figs and 4 cups (32 fl oz/1 l) water. Bring to a boil and cook uncovered, stirring occasionally, for 15 minutes. Drain the fruit, then pass it through a food mill fitted with the medium disk, or through a sieve, discarding the skins. Place the pulp, dried figs, sugar, orange juice, chopped orange, and cinnamon sticks in the same saucepan over low heat. Bring to a simmer and cook, stirring, until the preserves are rich and thick and cling easily to a spoon, about 1 hour. Remove the cinnamon sticks and discard, then stir in the brandy.

Immediately spoon the hot preserves into hot, sterilized jars to within ¼ inch (6 mm) of the tops. Wipe the rims clean with a hot, damp kitchen towel, top with metal canning lids, and seal tightly with screw bands. Process in a boiling-water bath for 15 minutes. Using tongs, transfer the jars to a kitchen towel, well spaced to allow air to circulate, and let cool. Store the jars in a cool, dark place, letting them age for 3 weeks. The preserves will keep for up to 6 months. Refrigerate any jar whose lid is not concave or makes a clicking sound when pressed, and use within 1 month.

makes four ½-pt (8-fl oz/250-ml) jars

MOLASSES

Like many ingredients used during America's colonial era, molasses arrived on ships traveling north from the Caribbean Islands. In New England, large amounts of it was used for making rum, but everywhere in the new land it was the most common sweetener, as it was more affordable than white sugar. Molasses is a full-flavored liquid derived from the syrupy residue left after sugar crystals have been extracted from fresh cane juice. A light, mild molasses is obtained from the first boiling of the sugar, while the second boiling yields a deep, smoky dark molasses. Less sweet than light molasses, dark molasses lends its distinctive flavor to countless southern sauces and desserts. Blackstrap molasses, too strong and bitter for most palates, remains after the third and final boiling. Unsulfured molasses is milder and sweeter than sulfured, which contains sulfur dioxide as a preservative. Dark corn syrup and maple syrup are adequate substitutions for dark molasses.

MUSHROOMS

During the cool mornings of spring and autumn, mushroom foragers head out to forests and fields around the country, from New England to California. Many consider the Pacific Northwest the nation's wild fungi hotbed, however, and strict regulations govern commercial foraging practices there. More and more of the exotic mushrooms once found only in the wild are now being cultivated, although some species continue to resist domestication. Despite advances in growing various types, the flavor of mushrooms harvested in the wild is superior to that of their cultivated counterparts, an opinion reflected in their higher prices. Only trained foragers and knowledgeable mycologists should harvest mushrooms in the wild. A good selection of fresh mushrooms, both wild and domesticated, can be found in well-stocked grocery stores and farmers' markets.

CHANTERELLE Found only in the wild, delicately flared and frilled chanterelles have a distinctive nutty flavor. The best-known varieties include golden-hued yellow chanterelle, mild but chewy white chanterelle, and the flavorful black trumpet of death. They are all most plentiful from late summer to late autumn.

CREMINI Although closely related to common button mushrooms, these widely cultivated, small mushrooms have light brown, rather than white, caps. Also known as Italian brown and common brown mushrooms, cremini have a firmer texture and slightly fuller flavor than buttons, making them increasingly popular with cooks. Available year-round, they can be used interchangeably with their white-capped kin.

HEDGEHOG Also known as the sweet tooth and the *pied de mouton*, this flavorful mushroom was named for the small, teethlike projections on the underside of its cap. Hedgehogs grow on the forest floor, and most have caps that are creamy to buff in color. At their best when young, they have a flavor reminiscent of mild chanterelles, but they quickly become bitter as they grow larger. Late bloomers, these wild mushrooms appear in January along the Pacific Coast and from July to November in the East.

OYSTER MUSHROOM Creamy to pale gray, this fan-shaped mushroom, available both wild and cultivated, has a delicate texture and a flavor that evokes seafood. Choose smaller ones, as oyster mushrooms become bitter and tough as they grow larger.

SHIITAKE Widely cultivated, this tasty mushroom is now available far beyond the Asian communities that first brought it to the United States. Light to dark brown, with a smooth texture, the shiitake appears in a broad variety of soups, salads, stir-fries, and pasta dishes.

NUTS

Some of America's grandest trees provided early settlers with rich, nutritious nuts. Today, California is the world's leading producer of walnuts and almonds, Oregon harvests most of the country's hazelnuts (filberts), and native pecans, which are grown throughout the South, add their distinctively sweet flavor to countless savory dishes as well as pies, cakes, and candies. Toasting nuts before use improves their taste and texture. Some nuts, such as hazelnuts, have a dark skin that can taste bitter and is often removed.

TO TOAST NUTS, for large amounts of nuts, spread them on a baking sheet and toast in a 325°F (165°C) oven until they are fragrant and take on a golden color, 10–20 minutes; the timing depends on the type of nut and the size of the nut or nut pieces. Stir once or twice to ensure even cooking. Remove from the oven and immediately pour onto a plate, as they will continue to darken if left on the hot pan. Toast small amounts of nuts in a frying pan over medium-low heat, stirring frequently, until fragrant and golden.

TO REMOVE THE SKIN FROM HAZELNUTS, while they are still warm from toasting, transfer the nuts to a thick, clean kitchen towel. Wrap the towel around them and rub them briskly to remove their skin. Gather the hazelnuts up carefully with your hands, leaving behind as much of the loose skin as you can.

ONIONS, SWEET

In 1898, a packet of onion seeds made its way from the Canary Islands to Texas. The surprisingly sweet and juicy onions that grew were instantly popular, and to this day, the more delicate cousins of the common onion remain summer stars. Other states champion their sweet onions as well. Known by the names of places where they are cultivated, sweet onions grow in the fertile, low-sulfur soils of Walla Walla in Washington, Vidalia in Georgia, and Maui in Hawaii. Farmers' markets and specialty grocers carry sweet onions during their peak seasons: the Maui and the Vidalia in spring and the Walla Walla in late summer. With their higher water and sugar content, sweet onions are more perishable than common onions. Store in a cool, dark, well-ventilated place, and use within 1 week of purchasing.

OREGANO, MEXICAN

Although similar in flavor to the more familiar Mediterranean oregano, Mexican oregano is closely related to lemon verbena. It is more pungent and less sweet than its Mediterranean kin, making it a perfect match for the spicy, cumin-laden dishes of the Southwest. Add it at the beginning of cooking to allow time for its complex flavor to emerge and meld with others. Purchase small packets of the dried herb in Latin American markets.

PUMPKIN SEEDS

For centuries, Mexican cooks have ground pumpkin seeds with spices and aromatics to make rich, festive stews and sauces. The large, green seeds add color and crunch to many dishes in the Southwest. Toasting pumpkin seeds before using them will bring out their rich, nutty flavor.

PIE PASTRY, SOUTHERN

Southern cooks take pride in their pie crusts, turning out the tender, flaky pastry shells that have made their pies famous around the country. Using soft-winter wheat and a higher proportion of shortening will ensure a properly light, thoroughly southern crust. Make sure the shortening and butter are cold, handle the dough as little as possible, and chill the dough for the allotted time when the recipe calls for it.

TO MAKE THE PASTRY BY HAND, in a bowl, stir together 1¼ cups (5 oz/155 g) soft winter-wheat flour (page 248), 1 teaspoon sugar, and ½ teaspoon salt. Add ¼ cup (2 oz/60 g) chilled solid vegetable shortening (vegetable lard) and, using a pastry blender or fork, cut in until the mixture resembles cornmeal. Cut ¼ cup (2 oz/60 g) chilled unsalted butter into small cubes, add to the flour mixture, and cut in until the size of small peas. Add 3–6 tablespoons ice water a little at a time, tossing the mixture with the pastry blender or fork until it is moist and holds together. **TO MAKE THE PASTRY IN A FOOD PROCESSOR,** combine 1¼ cups (5 oz/155 g) soft winter-wheat flour, 1 teaspoon sugar, and ½ teaspoon salt and process briefly to mix. Add ¼ cup (2 oz/60 g) chilled solid vegetable shortening (vegetable lard) and pulse only a few times. Add ¼ cup (2 oz/60 g) chilled unsalted butter, cut into small cubes, and pulse briefly. Add 3–6 tablespoons ice water a little at a time, pulsing just until the mixture begins to form a ball. **FOR BOTH METHODS,** gather the dough into a ball and flatten into a disk. Enclose the dough in plastic wrap and let rest in the refrigerator for 30–60 minutes before rolling out. The pastry makes one 9-inch (23-cm) pie crust.

SALT

For such a basic and humble ingredient, salt can raise strong opinions among cooks. Some contend that the iodine added to common table salt clouds stocks and clear sauces, and that the salt's fine grains lack the texture and depth of flavor of sea salt or kosher salt. Sea salt, gathered from evaporated seawater, retains small amounts of naturally occurring minerals, and it often carries a slight tint of gray or pink from these minerals. Available as coarse crystals and finely ground, sea salt is excellent used in cooking and is best sprinkled over dishes just before serving, to appreciate its complex flavor. Kosher salt was originally developed for the preparation of kosher meats, but its flat, coarse grains dissolve quickly, an often-desirable quality.

SUGAR, CRYSTAL

Bakers sprinkle crystal sugar on cookies, cakes, and other baked goods for an attractive sparkle and a pleasant crunch. Also known as sanding sugar or coarse sugar, it is white granulated sugar processed into large, oblong grains. Look for it in baking-supply stores.

TEQUILA

Made near the town of the same name, tequila is a spirit distilled from the sap of the blue agave, a large succulent indigenous to the arid highlands of central Mexico. A young, clear *blanco* tequila has a distinct agave flavor and a less refined edge than more aged tequilas. Sharper, peppery *reposado* tequila is aged in wood for 2 to 12 months, while a smooth, subtle *añejo* tequila may have been aged for up to 5 years. For high-quality tequila, check that the label indicates the spirit is 100 percent blue agave or *agave azul* and was bottled in Mexico. Less expensive *mixto* versions may be fermented with sugar and mixed with up to 40 percent grain alcohol and other additives.

TORTILLAS

Spanish for "little round cakes," tortillas are the staple bread throughout much of Mexico. They can be rolled around savory fillings, cut into thin strips for garnish, topped with a variety of ingredients, or eaten as an accompaniment to a meal. Cut up and fried, they become one of America's favorite snacks—tortilla chips. The thin, flat rounds were originally made of yellow corn, but the introduction of wheat from Europe led to flour tortillas. In recent years, blue corn tortillas have become popular for their unique color and nutty flavor.

WHIPPED CREAM

One of the most popular ways to serve this luscious, thick dairy product is as a whipped topping for pies, ice cream sundaes, and fruit desserts.

TO MAKE SWEETENED WHIPPED CREAM, in a chilled bowl, combine 1½ cups (12 fl oz/375 ml) chilled heavy (double) cream, 3 tablespoons sugar, and ½ teaspoon vanilla extract (essence). Using an electric mixer set on medium-high speed, beat until medium-firm peaks form, about 3 minutes. Cover and refrigerate until ready to serve or for up to 2 hours. Makes 1½ cups (12 fl oz/375 ml) whipped cream.

Recipes for homemade stock are simple, and the preparation minimal. By adding a variety of herbs or spices, you can infuse stocks with layers of flavor for specific recipes. Always store stocks in tightly covered containers. Beef and chicken stock will keep in the refrigerator for up to 5 days, while vegetable stock is best used within 3 days. Make large batches of a stock and freeze it in convenient amounts for up to 2 months. The vegetable stock may be prepared using additional vegetables as desired, such as tomatoes, rutabagas, parsnips, turnips, or celery root (celeriac).

CHICKEN STOCK

4 fresh flat-leaf (Italian) parsley sprigs

1 fresh thyme sprig

1 bay leaf

6 lb (3 kg) chicken necks and backs

3 celery stalks with leaves, cut into 2-inch (5-cm lengths)

3 carrots, cut into 2-inch (5-cm lengths)

2 large yellow onions, quartered

2 leeks, white and tender light green parts only, sliced

❧ Wrap the parsley, thyme, and bay leaf in a piece of cheesecloth (muslin) and secure the bundle with kitchen string to make a bouquet garni.

❧ In a large stockpot, combine the bouquet garni, chicken parts, celery, carrots, onions, and leeks. Add enough cold water just to cover the ingredients (about 3.5 qt/3.5 l). Slowly bring to a boil over medium heat. Reduce the heat to the lowest setting and simmer, uncovered, for 3 hours, regularly skimming off the foam that rises to the surface.

❧ Remove from the heat and let cool slightly. Strain through a fine-mesh sieve lined with cheesecloth into a large bowl. Let cool at room temperature for about 1 hour, then cover and refrigerate for at least 30 minutes or for up to overnight. With a large spoon, remove the hardened fat from the surface and discard it.

makes about 3 qt (3 l)

BEEF STOCK

4 lb (2 kg) beef bones with some meat attached

4 fresh flat-leaf (Italian) parsley sprigs

1 fresh thyme sprig

1 bay leaf

3 cups (24 fl oz/750 ml) water, or as needed

2 carrots, cut into 2-inch (5-cm) lengths

1 large yellow onion, quartered

2 leeks, light green and dark green parts only, sliced

❧ Preheat an oven to 425°F (220°C). Place the beef bones in a large roasting pan and roast until browned, about 1½ hours, stirring a few times to ensure an even color.

❧ Meanwhile, wrap the parsley, thyme, and bay leaf in a piece of cheesecloth (muslin) and secure the bundle with kitchen string to make a bouquet garni. Set the bouquet garni aside.

❧ Remove the pan from the oven and transfer the bones to a large stockpot. Add the 3 cups (24 fl oz/750 ml) water to the roasting pan and place it over medium-high heat. Bring to a boil and deglaze the pan, stirring to scrape up the browned bits. The water will turn a rich brown. Pour the deglazed juices into the stockpot and add enough cold water just to cover the bones (about 3.5 qt/3.5 l). Add the carrots, onion, leeks, and bouquet garni and bring to a boil over medium heat. Reduce the heat to the lowest setting and simmer, uncovered, for 4 hours, regularly skimming off the foam that rises to the surface.

❧ Remove from the heat and let cool. Remove the bones from the stock and strain it through a fine-mesh sieve lined with cheesecloth into a large bowl. Let cool to room temperature, then cover and refrigerate for 2 hours. With a large spoon, remove the hardened fat from the surface and discard it. Line the sieve again with cheesecloth, and pour the stock through it to remove any remaining fat. The stock should be clear.

makes about 3 qt (3 l)

VEGETABLE STOCK

2 large yellow onions, quartered

2 leeks, white and tender light green parts only, sliced

4 celery stalks with leaves, cut into 2-inch (5-cm lengths)

4 carrots, cut into 2-inch (5-cm lengths)

1 red potato, diced

¼ lb (125 g) fresh mushrooms, brushed clean and quartered

6 cloves garlic

8 fresh flat-leaf (Italian) parsley sprigs

2 bay leaves

8 peppercorns

❧ In a large stockpot, combine all the ingredients and add enough cold water just to cover the ingredients (about 2.5 qt/2.5 l). Bring to a boil, then reduce the heat to medium-low and simmer, uncovered, for 1½ hours, regularly skimming off the foam that rises to the surface.

❧ Remove from the heat and let cool. Strain through a fine-mesh sieve lined with cheesecloth (muslin) into a large bowl. Press on the vegetables with the back of a spoon to extract as much of the flavor as possible. Cool to room temperature, cover, and refrigerate.

makes about 2 qt (2 l)

ACKNOWLEDGMENTS

Noel Barnhurst wishes to thank his assistant Noriko Akiyama for her invaluable help. George Dolese thanks Elisabet der Nederlanden, food stylist, for her extraordinary work in preparing the recipes for photography, and Mixed Pickles in Berkeley, California, for generously providing props.

Weldon Owen thanks all of the authors who contributed to the book: Janet Fletcher, for writing the chapter text and for providing the California recipes and sidebars; Kerri Conan, for the Midwest and Great Plains recipes and sidebars; Abigail Johnson Dodge, for the New England and Mid-Atlantic recipes and sidebars; Michael McLaughlin, for the Southwest and Mountain States recipes and sidebars; Cynthia Nims, for the Northwest, Hawaii, and Alaska recipes and Northwest sidebars; and Ray Overton, for the South recipes and sidebars. Weldon Owen also thanks Anna Mantzaris for writing the captions; Thy Tran for contributing her culinary expertise to the writing of the glossary; Linda Bouchard for her invaluable production assistance; Lauren Burke for her digital work; Desne Ahlers for proofreading; Ken DellaPenta for indexing; and Teri Bell for her color work.

The following photographers and organizations generously gave permission for their copyrighted photographs to be reproduced in this book (b=bottom, t=top): © Cedric Angeles, 14, 16t, 79t, 152; © Quentin Bacon, 154b; © Charles Beisch, 151t, 197b; © Leigh Beisch, 197t; © Per Breiehagen, 148–49; © Brown W. Cannon III, 16b, 30b; © Maren Caruso, 27, 150; © Daniel Clark, 72b; © DaveCurranImages.com, 12–13; © Robin Bachtler Cushman, 21b, 156t; © Bob Firth, 1, 30t, 32t, 33, 78–79, 153b, 154t; © Lois Ellen Frank, 17, 79b, 80b; © Dana Gallagher, 202t; © Fran Gealer, 77b; © Sheri Giblin, 29b, 73; © Thayer Allyson Gowdy, 29t; © Meredith Heuer, 200; © Cheryl Himmelstein, 18–19; © Leisa Johnson, 153t; © Guy Kloppenburg, endpapers; © James Lemass, Index Stock, 81, 196; © Michael Melford, 4–5, 20, 21t, 22–23, 72t, 75t, 75b, 157b; © Jeff Morgan, MIDWESTOCK, 19b; © National Geographic Society (NGS) Image Collection, William Albert Allard, 8–9, 80t; © NGS, Ira Block, 30–31; © NGS, Raymond K. Gehman, 15t; © NGS, Richard T. Nowitz, 194b; © Madeline Polss, 76, 77t; © 1993 Eric Rank, 26t; © 1995 Erik Rank, 195; © Lisa Romerein, 28, 151b, 155; 201b, 202b, 203; © Zubin Shroff, 75t; © 1988 Paul Slaughter, 23b; © Brad Swonetz, 201t; © Rachel Weill, 6–7, 15b, 26b, 32b, 70–71, 156b, 157t, 194t, 198, 199t, 199b; © George White Jr., www.gwlocphoto.com, 24–25, 74, 192–93.

OXMOOR HOUSE INC.

Oxmoor House books are distributed by Sunset Books
80 Willow Road, Menlo Park, CA 94025
Telephone: 650-321-3600 Fax: 650-324-1532

Vice President/General Manager: Rich Smeby
New Accounts Manager/Special Sales: Brad Moses

Oxmoor House and Sunset Books are divisions of Southern Progress Corporation

WILLIAMS-SONOMA INC.

Founder and Vice-Chairman: Chuck Williams
Book Buyer: Cecilia Michaelis

WELDON OWEN INC.

Chief Executive Officer: John Owen
President: Terry Newell
Chief Operating Officer: Larry Partington
Vice President International Sales: Stuart Laurence
Associate Publisher: Hannah Rahill
Consulting Editors: Sharon Silva, Norman Kolpas
Design: Kari Ontko, India Ink
Photo Editor: Sandra Eisert
Production Director: Stephanie Sherman
Production Manager: Chris Hemesath
Editorial Assistant: Dana Goldberg
Prop and Style Director: George Dolese
Calligraphy: Jane Dill

pp 4–5: Fall is harvesttime for New England cranberries. After the cranberry bogs are flooded, the fruits are loosened from their vines by a small combine and then swept into trucks. **pp 6–7:** Many of the scores of wineries in California offer tours and tastings, and some invite visitors to sample food and wine pairings. **pp 8–9:** As cowboys did a century ago, today's ranchers in Montana, Wyoming, and other western states often herd their cattle to new pasturage every season. **pp 12–13:** Seen from a butte-top viewpoint in eastern Washington, fields of wheat spread as far as the eye can see. Thanks to an ideal mix of climate and fertile soil, the state is the fifth largest grower of wheat in the United States, 90 percent of which is exported.

THE SAVORING SERIES

conceived and produced by Weldon Owen Inc.
814 Montgomery Street, San Francisco, CA 94133
Telephone: 415-291-0100   Fax: 415-291-8841

In collaboration with Williams-Sonoma Inc.
3250 Van Ness Avenue, San Francisco, CA 94109

Separations by Colourscan Overseas Co. Pte. Ltd.
Printed in Singapore by Tien Wah Press (Pte.) Ltd.